CROSS AND COMMISSAR

CROSS AND COMMISSAR

The Politics of Religion
in Eastern Europe
and the USSR

PEDRO RAMET

INDIANA UNIVERSITY PRESS
Bloomington and Indianapolis

Manufactured in the United States of America

Library of Congress Cataloging-in-Publication Data

Ramet, Pedro, 1949–
Cross and commissar.

Bibliography: p.
Includes index.
1. Church and state—Communist countries—History.
2. Church and state—Soviet Union—History—20th century.
3. Communism and Christianity—Europe, Eastern—History—
20th century.   4. Communism and Christianity—Soviet
Union—History—20th century.   5. Europe, Eastern—
Church history.   6. Soviet Union—Church history—
1917–   I. Title.
BR738.6.R26   1987   322'.1'0947   86-46165
ISBN 0-253-31575-1

1 2 3 4 5 91 90 89 88 87

*For Andrzej Korbonski,
my friend and mentor*

Contents

Preface

Recent years have seen an explosion of scholarly writing on church-state interaction in the communist world. Much of it is, however, purely factual or apologetic in nature, and very little of it has any substantial theoretical underpinning, even though students of comparative politics have been otherwise very active in developing theories of different kinds.

This book is not intended to provide a country-by-country analysis of religious conditions in Eastern Europe and the Soviet Union. Trevor Beeson's *Discretion and Valour* (2d ed., 1982) already does an excellent job with this task. What this book offers is, rather, the first systematic attempt at theorizing about church-state interaction in Eastern Europe and the Soviet Union, grounding these theories in extensive substantive research. Two of the chapters (2 and 4) focus on the relationship of religion and nationalism in the region, outlining the relationship between historical patterns of religio-national symbiosis and contemporary dynamics in church-state interaction. Other chapters (1 and 6) probe the importance of factionalism in church-state relations, pointing out that both church and state are factionalized and that their relations are therefore highly complex, as factions on each side have particularized dealings with factions on the other side. Still other chapters (8 and 9) bring the story up to the present.

From a theoretical point of view, chapters 8 and 9 operate at the level of lower-range theory (simple hypotheses), chapters 2 to 7 operate at the level of middle-range theory (specific to a particular aspect of this field), and chapter 11 endeavors to integrate the several theories into a general theory. Both chapters 10 and 11 are also concerned with metatheoretical considerations.

All the communist countries of the Soviet/East European area are discussed in this book, with individual chapters devoted to the religious situation in the Soviet Union, East Germany, Yugoslavia, Bulgaria/Serbia, and—in triad—Poland, Czechoslovakia, and Hungary.

I wish to thank the following scholars for their generous and most helpful comments on drafts of individual chapters: Peter F. Sugar, Donald W. Treadgold, and Michael A. Williams for comments on the introduction and conclusion; Paul Mojzes for comments on chapter 2; Zachary T. Irwin for comments on chapters 2 and 3; Leslie Laszlo for comments on chapter 4; Stella Alexander for comments on chapter 6; and Dennis J. Dunn for comments on the entire manuscript. I am also grateful to Marija Jankowska for translating the Polish material cited in chapter 4 and to Marjorie Behrens for gathering material used for chapter 8. Finally, I am deeply indebted to Janet Rabinowitch of Indiana University Press for her meticulous attention to detail and for her invaluable feedback.

Chapter 2 appeared originally in Pedro Ramet (ed.), *Religion and Nationalism in Soviet and East European Politics* (Duke University Press, 1984), chapter 5 in *Problems of Communism* (July–August 1984), chapter 6 in *Slavic Review* (Summer 1985), and chapter 8 in *Survey* (Winter 1984). I wish to thank Duke University Press and the respective journals for permission to reprint these articles.

PART I

Introduction

ONE

How Church and State Coexist under Communism

Western scholarship on church-state interaction in Eastern Europe and the Soviet Union has tended to be relatively untheoretical and often to downplay, if not ignore altogether, the considerable complexity underlying this relationship. Influenced perhaps by communism's claim to operate on the basis of democratic centralism (which bans factional activity) and long constrained by the ostensible paucity of evidence of the impact of factional activity in policy spheres, scholars have, more often than not, portrayed church-state interaction as a relationship between monoliths.[1]

I shall argue that, on the contrary, the study of church-state interaction in communist countries—and in Eastern Europe and the Soviet Union, in specific—must be sensitive to complexity in several dimensions. First, both the political elites and the sundry church bodies themselves are often factionalized, so that it becomes impossible to speak of church-state relations in a simple sense. Second, in the Yugoslav case, at any rate, the federalization of the religious policy apparatus and the legal structure produces a federalization of religious policy, with the result that church-state relations may be cordial in Slovenia even while they are strained in, for instance, Croatia and Bosnia.[2] Third, differences in the availability of institutional links with ecclesiastical bodies abroad may contribute to a differentiation within the same regime's policy toward different religious groups. Fourth, the emergence and spread of neo-Protestant groups, weaning away adherents from the older established churches, becomes in itself a factor in the calculation of the regime's policies toward the established churches. And fifth—where the Catholic Church is concerned—the autonomy from the Vatican enjoyed by the national ecclesiastical organization varies from country to country as a factor of several variables, including regularity of contacts between local hierarchs and the Vatican, local regime policy, and the personalities of the hierarchs; and this autonomy affects both the strategy and tactics of the regime in question.

It should be emphasized at the outset that the distinction between *religion* and *church* has not merely theoretical but also practical significance. Thus, a religious revival is not necessarily tantamount to a church revival, for example, just as a policy that erodes church presence is not necessarily, ipso facto, corrosive of religious faith or of spirituality. In Counter-Reformation Bohemia, for example, church revival went hand in hand with a decline in religiosity. Conversely, in contemporary Hungary, elements of a religious revival may be found precisely among sectors of the population that are dissolving their traditional bonds with the churches.

The chief difference between communist regimes and most noncommunist regimes in the sphere of religion is that the former, viewing all religious organizations as potential political rivals and some religious organizations as also potential policy tools, adopt a policy that strives simultaneously to control and manipulate existing religious organizations and to erode the bases of their grass-roots loyalty. It is this operational "ambivalence" in communist religious policy that sets it apart from the religious policy of other systems.

Hence, communist regimes take an active stance vis-à-vis religion, proceeding from the assumption that it is in their interest to frame religious policies with an eye to broader political objectives. Communist religious policies tend to be geared to producing concrete benefits for the regime rather than merely to assuring a particular behavioral formation. This tendency can be seen quite clearly in the organization of the Russian Orthodox Church. If this church were able to organize its affairs according to its own priorities, one might expect the department for the training of clergy, or perhaps the department for the religious education of the laity, to be its largest administrative department. Instead, the Department of External Church Affairs, founded in 1946, has more employees than all the other administrative departments of the Moscow patriarchate combined. Interestingly, employees of this department pay a much lower rate of income tax than most members of the clergy, the rationale being that their work is useful to the state.[3] The secret statute of the USSR's Council of Religious Affairs makes it clear that this department is to be viewed as an ancillary of the foreign policy apparatus, and stresses the council's responsibility to "work with religious organizations in the realization of international relations, participating in the struggle for peace, for strengthening friendship among nations."[4] Not surprisingly, in view of close KGB supervision, the Moscow patriarchate "condemned the Hungarian uprising of 1956, approved the Warsaw Pact invasion of Czechoslovakia in 1968, and approved the Soviet invasion of Afghanistan, thus taking a view diametrically opposed to that of the Christian world at large."[5] The patriarchate also criticized the trial of members of the Sanctuary Movement in the United States in 1985.[6]

Other interchurch organizations (e.g., the Prague-based Christian Peace Conference and the Berlin Conference of Catholics) and churches (especially the Bulgarian Orthodox Church and the larger churches in Hungary) have played a similar role, and the bloc press regularly highlights reports of Christian support for communist policies.[7] Regime-sponsored priests' associations, such as the Pacem in Terris organization in Czechoslovakia, also figure in this "ambivalent" policy, undercutting the independent authority of the hierarchy and promoting regime objectives.[8]

If one were to "blend" the church-state relationships of the eight East European communist states and the Soviet Union, the resulting composite picture would look roughly like this: As a general rule, believers are guaranteed the right to believe and to worship, and are assured that religion is the "private affair" of the individual.[9] But insofar as religion is a "private affair," it is not accorded any legitimate public role in the discussion of social and political concerns. Believers are treated as second-class citizens—excluded from membership in the party, from the officer corps in the military, and from upper-level positions in the government, industrial management, sociopolitical organizations, and the media. Schools include mandatory courses in atheism, even at the university level, and in Bulgaria and Czechoslovakia, also in the seminaries; regime-sponsored youth organizations are likewise decidedly atheist in orientation. The average believer, as portrayed in the party-controlled press, has only primary or at most secondary education, and is rural, old, politically apathetic, and ill informed about current developments in general. Religion per se is consistently treated as a remnant of the past and is rarely conceded to have exercised any positive role in moral development. On the contrary, the Czech news organ, *Rude pravo,* wrote in 1984:

> All religions inhibit man's moral development, which molds his best characteristics. To be sure, religion necessarily causes dichotomy in moral consciousness and creates two rival authorities—the authority of God and the authority of the society in which man lives. Morality that is derived, as it were, from God's demands inevitably clashes with the moral demands which flow out of the needs of societal life.[10]

A Romanian source likewise dismissed the notion that religion could play a positive role in society:

Differing or even contradictory opinions circulate about the social role of religion. Some maintain that certain religions characteristic of stages of historical development have been conservative and have obstructed social programs while others, on the contrary, have been factors for the rising evolution of society. Still others claim that the same religion is progressive in one stage and reactionary in another. And there are quite a few who, whether they are believers or unbelievers, categorically support the idea that religion has always been and still is a major force for humanity's development. These equally erroneous views overlook the fact that religions limit the effectiveness of any human action by their nature and by belief in the supernatural.[11]

And in Poland, sociologists of religion have often tried to portray Roman Catholicism as "an alien anti-Polish force." Antoni Nowicki, for instance, claimed that church leaders felt "contempt" for the Polish language and wanted to obstruct the progress of the Polish nation.[12]

Our composite picture should also mention that while church and state are technically separated, in practice the state often pays subsidies toward priests' salaries, censors or controls church publications, controls church construction and renovation by requiring building permits and by providing subsidies, issues state licenses for the practice of priestly functions, monitors sermons in the churches, approves and rejects prospective church appointees for ecclesiastical leadership positions, and uses the churches as agents for the promotion of foreign policy objectives—practices which, in the West at least, would normally be seen as incompatible with the concept of the separation of church and state. Typically, there is also a proregime priests' association, whose members receive pensions, health care, and other benefits. These associations usually figure, in one way or another, as "Trojan horses" within the church.

The state also determines which religious organizations shall be legal and which illegal; accordingly, the Greek-Rite Catholic Church, the Jehovah's Witnesses, and certain Baptists are, among others, typically illegal in the Soviet bloc.

When a church oversteps the bounds of what the regime considers acceptable by criticizing regime policy in one area or another, it is apt to be lambasted for "clericalism"—routinely defined as the misuse of religion for political purposes. Usually, however, the regime endeavors to depict church-state relations as positive, except for the negative activity of a few extremists. This characterization undoubtedly reflects a more general strategy of trying to isolate outspoken clergy and lure the churches into more acquiescent relations with the regime. The Polish newspaper *Gazeta wspolczesna*, for instance, writes:

A considerable proportion of the hierarchy and the clergy is perfectly loyal to the state. There is also, of course, an extreme wing of clergymen who actively fight the system and the state. In that group we can point to about 100 priests who can be described as inexorable enemies.[13]

This "salami tactic," which recurs whenever the regime confronts an outspoken church, is related to a final but nonetheless important aspect of the church-state relationship: the vulnerability of the clergy to defamation in the press, administrative harassment, and incarceration on fabricated charges. The use of this dual tactic is characteristic of Poland, Czechoslovakia, Yugoslavia, Romania, Bulgaria, and the Soviet Union. To enter the priesthood in these countries entails acceptance of the risk of being ridiculed in the press (perhaps even by name, especially where bishops are concerned), placed under surveillance, and jailed for periods ranging from a month to five years or more.[14]

Although broad policy parameters are set by the central authorities, one may encounter regional or local differences in religious policy in several of these countries. Yugoslavia is the most extreme example, with primary responsibility for almost all facets of internal policy lying within the purview of the eight constituent federal units. In the USSR, as Pospielovsky observed, central control is tight, but local authorities enjoy the prerogative of being more antireligious than the central authorities—and sometimes they are.[15]

RELIGION AND MODERNIZATION

The term *modernization* has been defined in diverse ways, and the body of excellent literature on this subject is now vast. Most readers will no doubt consider the meaning to be clear enough. And so it is. Yet, because I wish to highlight a particular aspect of modernization, I shall spell out my own definition. In the pages that follow, *modernization* means the displacement of a system of values based on divine law, honor, and custom by a system of values based on civil law, self-interest, fashion, and monetary terms of exchange. Thus, the more modern a society, the fewer customs and the more fashions it has, the less respect it has for notions of inherent (divine or natural) law, and the greater the tendency it has to measure individual accomplishment and esteem in terms of acquired or inherited wealth.

The term *religious modernization* as used in these pages means the adaptation of a religious organization, including its doctrine, rites, mores, attitude toward authority, and activities, to "modernizing" society. So understood, religious modernization is clearly a dependent variable linked to a more general social modernization. Indeed, social modernization may exert pressure on religious organizations to "modernize." The modernization of churches is a component of the general secularization of society, in which religious and political unity has been shattered and churches have been driven from a position of privileged access to the holders of power to a position of having to build their power on the basis of their ability to command influence among a large or mobilized congregation.[16] Modernization shatters communal consensus on values and mores [17] and throws up alternative behavioral prescriptions, producing culture crisis and role confusion among individuals, especially among youth. As one sociologist has pointed out, "The appearance of exotic new religions led by Asian prophets, the upsurge of pentecostal sects, and the development of quasi-religious psychotherapies in the late 1960s [in the US may be] seen as responses to the fragmentation of cultural symbol systems that before that time had served to integrate institutions and give meaning to personal experience."[18] The inextinguishability in the Soviet Union and East Europe of such smaller sects as Jehovah's Witnesses, Seventh-Day Adventists,[19] Hare Krishnas (who appeared in the Soviet Union in 1971 and numbered 3,000 adherents there by early 1986),[20] and others is an early adumbration of this trend. Lithuanians have recently become interested in mysticism, extrasensory perception, and Eastern religions, and in 1985 the Lithuanian journal *Svyturys* published a two-part article about Lithuanians traveling to the Karakalpak ASSR in Central Asia to visit a guru named Mirza.[21] The spread of Asian prophets and quasi-religious psychotherapies in the region may not be far off.

Because modernization impinges on and potentially draws from the ranks of established religions, it exerts, ipso facto, internal pressure on them as well. Members begin to develop doubts about specific dogmas or injunctions, and they respond either by becoming less devout or by joining a different church. Ironically, as Soviet sociologists of religion have found,[22] religiosity is apt to be more intense among adherents of "modern" religious organizations than among adherents of the more traditional Russian Orthodox Church.

This lessened religiosity has been a problem not merely for the Russian Orthodox Church. The Roman Catholic Church has had to face the same dilemma, as the French Catholic writer F. Roulot has pointed out. "The contemporary person," he writes,

> has no way of believing in a substantial number of dogmas, especially that of the resurrection of the dead. . . . The Catholic language as a whole, its symbolic system, and the attendant rituals have lost their meaning for people who were born into a social and cultural world which differs fundamentally from that which gave rise to these symbols.[23]

The result is the incremental decay of personal belief systems.

Institutional responses to this challenge differ. But in general, religious organizations—aside from the more traditional religions—have, under the pressure of modernization, tended to shift emphasis, from obedience and respect for institutional authority to fidelity to one's own conscience (Protestantization), or to obedience to a charismatic leader (e.g., an Asian prophet in a cult religion). The modification of religious rites, typically in the direction of greater popular participation, is another possible response to modernization. Beyond such modification, the nature of participation also changes, and that may be one reason for the recent success of the Baptist Church in Romania.

Modernization also shatters the high value placed on stability and conservation. "Modernity" instead prizes progress and innovation— sometimes without regard to the damage done to long-standing institutions and practices. In communist systems, where traditional institutions are frequently viewed as obstacles to party programs, this consequence of "modernization" may be positively welcomed.

For their part, religious organizations may assimilate ideas of progress, displacing earlier ideas of stability.[24] But that can be only part of the answer, because it relates to "modernization" in general rather than to regime-promoted social change in its specifically communist versions. Hence, to the extent that a communist regime cuts the church off from society (by limiting it to liturgical ceremonies) and retards currents of embourgeoisement (the ultimate source of "modernization") of society generally, it may in fact retard or discourage religious modernization. As William Fletcher notes,

> at first glance, it would appear that Russian Orthodoxy's answer to the modernization of society has been a conscious attempt to go the opposite direction. So far from attempting the modifications and innovations normally associated with modernization, the Russian Orthodox Church has moved further and further away from innovation and experimentation. In 1917 Russian Orthodoxy was one of the world's more reactionary Churches: it reacted against change, innovation and modernization in society. Today, however, the Church is not even reactionary: it does not react at all to change in society, much less attempt to adapt its practice, doctrine or mission to the modernizing society.[25]

The same could probably be said of the other Orthodox churches of Eastern Europe. Yet while this strategy has served the Romanian Orthodox Church rather poorly, it may well account for such vigor as the Russian Orthodox Church has been able to retain.[26]

"Modern" religious organizations are inherently (whether overtly or covertly) hostile to tradition; in this respect, "cult" religions are the most "modern" religions. The repudiation of materialism by certain cult religions is the obverse of an underlying absorption with material goods. Similarly, the adoption of specific antifocal garb betrays a conviction that modes of attire are of central cultural importance—from which cult adherents conclude (or accept) that attire should be dictated by cult leaders. According to recent sociological studies, cult religions attract persons who are most confused by the focal society;[27] to the extent that social change in Eastern Europe is apt to heighten uncertainty and increase the frequency of role and norm confusion, one may predict the spread of cult religions into Eastern Europe.

THE DIVERSITY OF CONTEXTS

Although I have outlined a composite or idealized picture of church-state relations in the region, important differences are found from country to country, in terms of confessional heterogeneity, general religious climate, prerogatives allowed the churches, and penetration of "modernizing" religious forms. East Germany is, in many ways, the most liberal of the nine societies in religious matters. Yugoslavia, unlike East Germany, regularly slanders its clergy in the secular press but would probably rank in second place, ahead of either Poland or Hungary. Albania, where all religions were declared illegal in 1967, is the harshest terrain for religious organizations, followed by the USSR, Czechoslovakia, and Romania.

This book is organized into four parts, each serving different substantive as well as different theoretical purposes. In chapter 2, I set forth the basic elements of religious policy in the area in the postwar period, with emphasis on the relationship of this policy to considerations of nationalities policy. In part II, I explore individual country contexts, harnessing distinct theoretical tools in each case. Chapter 3 applies functional analysis to the Soviet context. Chapter 4 uses a specific form of historical analysis that I call geneticism-monism to come to grips with differences in religio-national symbiosis in Polish, Czech, Slovak, and Hungarian Catholicism. Chapter 5, which deals with East Germany, is inspired by the political culture school. Chapter 6 investigates factionalism in Croatian church-state relations, and chapter 7 uses organization theory to probe differences between Yugoslav and Bulgarian religious policies. Part III outlines regionwide religious developments since 1978, with chapter 8 embracing all countries in the area and chapter 9 focusing on East Germany, Poland, Czechoslovakia, Hungary, and Romania. Part IV draws together some of the theoretical conclusions that I hope emerge from this study.

TWO

The Interplay of Religious
Policy and Nationalities Policy

Religion is a set of beliefs not merely about a world beyond but also, and perhaps more importantly, about how the present world—its law, its authority, its hierarchical relations—should be organized. Liturgy and ritual, valued by participants for the feelings of rapture and spirituality they impart, serve another function, clearly more important from the organizational point of view: communal reaffirmation of the authority of ecclesiastical leaders. The breadth of this authority may be narrow, limited essentially to social behavior (morality), or it may extend to prescriptions about attire, culture (as in proscription of certain kinds of music), civil codes, and political behavior. Religion, as Talcott Parsons recognized, "is the point of articulation between the cultural system and the social system, where values from the former are embodied in the latter."[1]

The claims of the great monotheistic religions (Christianity, Islam, Judaism) were traditionally absolute. The appearance in recent decades of "nondenominational" churches is one sign of an attenuation of this absoluteness. But even now, the moral injunctions of most, if not all, religions are certainly intended to have absolute and universal validity, and they are backed by the authority of a putative being said to be omnipotent and omnibenevolent. More generally, no religion has ever allowed that its doctrines might be only relatively true—not even the polytheist Olympian religion of ancient Greece and Rome. Moreover, the relative toleration found in many modern societies probably has less to do with the content of any one religion than with a compromise born in the mix of religions and with the diminishing ability of many religions to compel conformity

11

among their own members (as seen in the widespread acceptance of contraceptives among American Catholics). At the same time, religion has always looked back to its sources and read into them a particular meaning. This meaning constitutes a claim upon the loyalty of a community as a community: Poles, for example, are expected to be Catholic, Russians and Bulgarians to be Orthodox. The Orthodox Pole and the Baptist Russian are, in a very real sense, viewed as nationally disloyal.

Theocracy was one of the earliest forms of government, and perhaps the first form of government to become institutionally developed. The Papal States, the Caliphate, and the Orthodox churches under the Ottoman *millet* system all exemplify this principle in different forms. Regardless of what religious organizations may profess to be today, their incunabula were quintessentially political, and churches may accordingly be regarded as vestigial political organizations par excellence. Shorn of their governing function and, more and more in recent centuries, of their monopoly in spheres of socialization (education, historiography, literature, music, and the arts), the churches have retained their political character by adopting new countenances as the guardians of discrete interests, even as interest groups. When we say, then, that religion's claims are absolute, we perceive that religion has always played a powerful role in cementing the loyalty of citizens toward their national collectivities.[2]

That is only half the picture, however. To describe religion as merely an epiphenomenon of political development obscures the organic nexus between religion and nation (*Volk* in German, *narod* in Russian). Religion was, in its origin, tribal and then national, and its gods were the gods of tribe and nation. Wars waged between ancient peoples were assumed to have a supernatural dimension; the divine protectors of warring peoples were presumed to contest among themselves. And even when, in Greece, a polytheist universe became generally accepted, the individual city-states retained their favorite deities (Athena for Athens, for example). Religion, thus, was national before it was universal.

An early attempt by the Egyptian Pharoah Ikhnaton to establish universalist ethics based on a monotheist creed fell through for lack of support. And, as Freud noted, when his follower Moses organized the escape of Jewish captives and brought the universalist creed to them,[3] it soon became, in their hands, a national religion, and Adonai (Jehovah) reverted to the traditional role of protector of his "chosen people."

Christianity was the first religion to make the transition from national to universal. But the transition was incomplete, for two chief reasons. First, in the eastern Mediterranean basin, where Christianity first established roots, it evolved a network of national patriarchs who, as spiritual leaders of their nations, were inevitably cast also in the role of actual or potential national political leaders. Second, in the West, where the bishop of Rome established unchallenged primacy even before the demise of the West Roman Empire, the fragmentation later produced by the Protestant Reformation allowed the religion to become once more a source and exacerbant of international discord. The principle of *cuius regio eius religio* codified an outlook that only increased the likelihood that Poles should think of themselves as Catholics and Genevans, for example, should think of themselves as Calvinists.

This identification of religious affiliation with ethnic and national identity has made more difficult the self-appointed task (to erode religious affiliation) of the communist authorities everywhere. On the one hand, religious organizations can less easily be tamed, suppressed, or destroyed outright when they are widely viewed as national institutions. And on the other hand, among regimes that either deny ethnic heterogeneity (Bulgaria) or seek to assimilate and denationalize the ethnic minorities (the Soviet Union and Romania), the religious element infuses national survival with spiritual values, making assimilation—perhaps especially where Muslims are concerned—a threat to the religious community itself. Even in countries that have abandoned earlier assimilation programs (Czechoslovakia and Yugoslavia), the churches (in these cases, chiefly the Catholic Church) are identified in the popular memory with truncated national states and are viewed by some as hotbeds of ethnic secessionism.

Military conquerors and separatists alike have recognized the political potency of national churches and their utility in weaning populations from earlier allegiances. Thus, the Germans allowed believers in occupied Belorussia to organize a Belorussian Autocephalous Orthodox Church in 1941, with Metropolitan Panteleimon at its head,[4] and the Ukrainian Autocephalous Orthodox Church, revived the following year, was to play an active role in fomenting anti-Russian Ukrainian nationalism in German-occupied Ukraine during World War Two.[5] Similarly, Ante Pavelić, *Poglavnik* of the wartime Independent State of Croatia, established an autocephalous Croatian Orthodox Church in April 1942, placing the old Russian bishop, Germogen, at its head, in hopes of convincing some Orthodox believers that they were Croats.[6]

If the endeavor to break a people's link with its own past can take the form of the establishment of new and "autocephalous" churches, it can also manifest itself in the suppression of native liturgies. The Russian tsars wanted to sap Polish and Lithuanian nationalism and thus demanded that the Roman Catholic Church in Polish and Lithuanian districts substitute Russian for Latin as the official church language and language of the liturgy; a Russianized Catholic Church was supposed to serve as the vehicle of the Russification of these non-Russian lands.[7] The Austrian

Emperor Franz Josef adopted the opposite tactic for the same end, persuading the pope to withhold approval for the introduction of a Slavic-language liturgy in Croatia in the belief that the Latin rite was a most effective obstacle to Croatian-Serbian rapprochement. Contemporary Bulgaria affords a more radical example of the same tendency. Here, however, instead of merely suppressing a liturgy, the regime set out to efface cultural heterogeneity at a blow. Muslims in Bulgaria were ordered to adopt Christian names and to "adapt" to Bulgarian culture. In 1980, Turkish sources claimed that tens of thousands of recalcitrant Bulgarian Muslims, including many of Turkish ethnicity, had been drugged and tortured at mental institutions for resisting Bulgarianization.[8] The Bulgarian ruling party, like most communist parties, places a premium on homogenization; it views religious culture in this context.

Thus, if "national" churches can tangibly buttress the position of a government, they can also undermine its stability when they advocate the rights of ethnic minorities in multiethnic states. The examples of the Catholic Churches in Slovakia, Lithuania, Ukraine, Croatia, and Romania, of the Lutheran Church in Estonia, and of the Orthodox Churches of Serbia and Georgia all illustrate oppositionist politics in defense of national minorities. By contrast, the Orthodox Churches of Russia, Bulgaria, and Romania and the Catholic Church of Hungary have all managed to accommodate themselves to the political status quo, and church-state relations in these four instances are uniformly described by the authorities as good. It is worth noting that three of these countries—Bulgaria, Romania, and Hungary—are ethnically essentially homogeneous, with no large national minorities.[9]

This chapter outlines the differences in the policies of European communist regimes toward, respectively, the Orthodox Churches, the Greek Catholic (Uniate) Churches, the Roman Catholic Church, and the Muslim community. It argues that these differences are, at least in part, explicable in terms of considerations of nationalism. It also highlights the interplay of religious policy and nationalities policy in multiethnic states and suggests ways in which nationalities policy, conversely, is affected by considerations of religious policy.

CHURCHES AND NATIONALISM

A religion may be understood as an interrelated set of assumptions about the nature and meaning of human existence, assumptions that are thought to have absolute validity and are actively propagated by an institution or organized sect. Accordingly, the defense of national culture by religious organizations implies some superordinate value or right enjoyed by the nation. And because the validity of religious assumptions is usually taken as a given—beyond scrutiny—religion, like national culture, contains within itself the possibility of intolerance. At least until recently, persons holding other assumptions have been generally viewed as errant and mistaken at best, as cursed and reprehensible at worst.

The definition of *nationalism* used here follows that of Dimitry Pospielovsky: a collective affectivity focused on the cultural-linguistic group and manifested in the attribution of central importance to the group's culture—including its religion—and in the aspiration to promote the culture.[10] Thus, when a religious organization becomes involved in nationalism, there is a strong tendency to "spiritualize" the concept of national destiny and to infuse the preservation of ethnic culture with intrinsic value.

At its most extreme, this tendency is manifested in the neotribal revival—consciously or unconsciously—of the primeval myth of the "chosen people," a myth inextricably bound up with the concept of a historical task entrusted to the "chosen people." Sarajevo Archbishop Ivan Šarić, for instance, told Croatian nationalists and *Ustaše* sympathizers in 1936 that "God sides with the Croats,"[11] later adding, in defense of the *Ustaše* program, that it was "stupid and unworthy of Christ's disciples to think that the struggle against evil could be waged in a noble way and with gloves on."[12] More recently, in a widely advertised book published by the Serbian Orthodox Church in the early 1970s, Orthodox priest Dr. Lazar Milin claimed this special place for the Serbs, associating it, however, with prolonged suffering. "The Serbian people is Christ's people," Milin wrote, adding that "the Serbian people as a whole has suffered more for the faith of Christ than many, many other peoples."[13] Among the Poles, Stanislaw Staszic (1775–1826), a Catholic priest, claimed for Poland a special civilizing mission and argued for the unification of Europe in a federation under Russia's political leadership and Polish cultural guidance. Similarly, the sixteenth-century Russian monk Filofei (Philotheus) linked the fate of Christianity to the fate of Russia, which he called the Third, and last, Rome.[14] This conviction of Russia's unique religiosity and special destiny would later inspire nineteenth-century Russian Slavophiles, for whom the purity of Russian Orthodoxy constituted evidence of Russian chosenness. And the pattern repeated itself in fifteenth-century (Hussite) Czechoslovakia, where, as Joseph Zacek noted:

> Catholic Europe's characterization of the Czechs as "a nation of heretics" provoked a feeling of defensive solidarity permeated with a national religious messianism, a mystical conviction that the Czech nation was the most Christian of all and had been elected by God to revive the fallen Church.[15]

National-religious messianism, which links religious "orthodoxy" to a God-given national mission, appears to arise in contexts of confrontation with external foes of rival religious affiliation. The consequences of national-religious messianism are to reinforce the linkage of national identity and a particular religion and to compel state authorities to deal with certain religious organizations as ethnic spokesmen.

SUPPRESSED GROUPS: UNIATES

Communist religious policy is adjusted to specific churches. Hence, within any given communist country one can expect to find differences in policy, depending on which religious group is being examined. Since some uniformities are confined to specific confessional groups, it becomes possible to identify patterns in communist religious policy across the region. Accordingly, I shall organize my discussion by religious group rather than on a country-by-country basis.

Communist religious policy is determined by at least six important factors: (1) the size of the religious organization in question; (2) the organization's disposition to subordinate itself to political authority and its amenability to infiltration and control by the secret police; (3) the question of allegiance to a foreign authority; (4) the loyalty or disloyalty of the particular body during World War Two; (5) the ethnic configuration of the respective country; and (6) the dominant political culture of the country.

What is clear from this list is that, although I will argue that general patterns differentiate communist policies toward the Orthodox from those toward Uniates, Roman Catholics, or Muslims, some variation will be evident from country to country, as determined chiefly by factors 1, 4, 5, and 6. The Catholic Church in Poland, thus, with more than thirty million adherents, is understandably less vulnerable than the Catholic Church proved to be in Bulgaria, where it numbers only 60,000 believers (less than "one" percent of the population). Again, while the Catholic Church in Slovakia and the Uniate (Greek Catholic) Church in Ukraine are susceptible to the charge of collaboration with the Nazis in World War Two, the Catholic Church in Poland was active in anti-Nazi resistance, as were many churches in Germany. Again, while the ethnic heterogeneity of the USSR and Yugoslavia and to a lesser extent of Czechoslovakia and Romania increase the likelihood that ethnically based confessional groups will prove to be destabilizing factors, the relative ethnic homogeneity of Poland and Bulgaria permits the Catholic Church in Poland and the Bulgarian Orthodox Church to play integrative roles—even if the former has been associated with opposition to the regime, while the latter has been coopted into a kind of "partnership." And where the political culture is both more quiescent and more anticlerical (as in the Czech lands), the church will be more vulnerable than in countries with a culture of defiance and religiosity (e.g., Poland).

In the USSR, this differentiated policy is facilitated by the presence within the Council of Religious Affairs of different departments for Orthodox, Catholic, and Islamic affairs.[16] In Yugoslavia, the existence of individual offices for religious affairs in each federal unit means that certain republican offices (Slovenia and Croatia) will be dealing almost exclusively with the Catholic Church, while others (Serbia, Macedonia, and Montenegro) will be dealing chiefly with Orthodoxy.[17]

To refer to Uniates and Jews as "suppressed groups" is not to deny that other religious groups in the Soviet-East European area are oppressed; but it will be argued that Uniates and Jews are more oppressed than others. Indeed, they are virtually unique in having been targeted as early as the late 1940s for suppression and institutional extirpation. Only the Catholic Church in Bulgaria, the short-lived autocephalous Orthodox Churches of Ukraine and Belorussia (which functioned during the 1920s and again during World War Two), and all religious organizations in Albania have been as completely suppressed as the Uniates and Jews in communist Europe.

At the end of World War Two, the Uniate or Greek-rite Catholic Church numbered about four million adherents in western Ukraine, 1.57 million in Romania, 320,000 in eastern Slovakia, and smaller numbers in Yugoslavia, Bulgaria, Poland, and Hungary.[18] The larger churches (Ukraine, Romania, Slovakia) were targeted for suppression and forced into the Orthodox fold. Hungary's Uniate Church was allowed to continue to function, however, since it presented no political threat, and Miklos Dudas, the Hungarian Uniate Bishop of Hajdudorog, was even allowed to attend the Vatican II Council.[19] Bulgaria's 15,000 Eastern-rite Catholics (1975) and Yugoslavia's 60,000 (1980), most of whom are Ruthenes or Ukrainians, continue to enjoy toleration, though the situation of Poland's 150,000 Uniates may be fairly described as difficult. The essential feature that distinguished the Uniate Churches of Ukraine, Romania, and Slovakia from other churches in communist lands—including the Hungarian and Yugoslav Uniate Churches, though not the Roman Catholic Church in Slovakia or, arguably, in Croatia—was their strong identification with the nationalism of their respective peoples and, in the case of Ukraine and Slovakia, with separatist projects feasible only in the framework of cooperation with the Nazis.

Created in 1596 by the Union of Brest, which drew a number of hitherto Ukrainian Orthodox into union with Rome, the Uniate Church had acquired standing as a national Ukrainian church by the end of the nineteenth century and came to play a significant role in the cultural and social development of Ukraine. The Soviets have always been especially hostile toward the Uniate Church, which they have accused of promoting "the denationalization of the Ukrainian people [through] their separation from the fraternal Russian people."[20] Even before the war, the Soviets drew up plans for the liquidation of the Ukrainian Uniate Church;[21] these plans were quickened by the addition to the Soviet Union in 1939 of Galicia and White Ruthenia, which had large congregations of Uniates. As the Nazis rolled into the Soviet Union in June 1941, Soviet secret police rounded up a large number of Uniate priests, murdering them or deporting them to the Soviet Far East. The Nazi occupation did not end the arrests of Uniate clergy, and the Ukrainian Church hoped ultimately to establish a state independent of both the USSR and Germany. Soviet repression of the Uniates resumed immediately with reoccupation in 1944, and, in March 1946, an orchestrated pseudo-synod of the Ukrainian Uniate Church, attended by 214 clergy, abrogated the Union of Brest and subordinated the Uniate Church to the Russian Orthodox Church.[22] Since then, Uniate clergy who have refused to be coerced into submission to a Russian Orthodox Church heavily infiltrated by the KGB[23] have had to operate clandestinely, outside the law. Remarkably, under the circumstances, the Uniates managed to hold an illegal congress in Lvov in 1965, drawing delegates from all over Ukraine, as well as from Belorussia and Moldavia.

Romania was next to ban the Uniates. Although a decree issued in September 1948 expressly recognized the Greek-rite Catholic Church and accorded it the right to organize two eparchies, a decree issued less than three months later, on December 1, placed the church under ban.[24] Its clergy were imprisoned, along with recalcitrant believers. Following the Soviet model, the authorities endeavored to replace Uniate personnel with party loyalists and soon convoked a pseudo-congress in Cluj that, predictably, voted "unanimously and with great enthusiasm . . . the reentry into the bosom of the Romanian Orthodox Church," as one communist party paper put it.[25] Although the regime used pay incentives to attempt to bribe the Uniate clergy into cooperation, some two thirds of Uniate priests, together with three quarters of the Uniate believers, resisted implementation of this decision.[26] The authorities responded with force, and, by the end of November, even before the Uniate Church was formally banned, some 600 Uniate clergy were in Romanian jails, including Bishop Ion Suciu, vicar of the Blaj Metropolitan See, and Bishop Valeriu Traian Frentziu of Oradea.

As in the case of the Ukrainian Uniates, the determination and brutality with which the regime suppressed the Romanian Uniates was a reflection of the obstacle posed by that church to the Russificatory or Slavicizing dimension of Stalinization. The Romanian Greek Catholic Church, which had come into being in 1698 on the strength of promises of concessions in education and elsewhere on the part of Austrian Emperor Leopold II, evolved into a cultural leader in Transylvania. The Uniate clergy, remarking on the profound similarity of Romanian and Latin, began to urge that Romanian was a Latin language and traced Romanian lineage to the Roman colonization of Dacia in A.D. 106.[27] In the early postwar period, however, this "Latinist" theory was distinctly out of favor, as Stalin wanted the Romanian party to stress the Slavic content and origin of Romanians and to portray Romanian as a Slavic language. Anything that drew attention to differences separating Romanians and Russians was branded "reactionary bourgeois nationalism."

Although the Roman Catholic Church is still tolerated in Romania, its adherents are mostly Hungarians and Swabians (Germans); it was the Uniate Church that catered to ethnic Romanians (mostly of Transylvanian extraction). The suppression of the Uniates was thus aimed specifically at cutting the links between ethnic Romanians and the Vatican, between Romanian national identity and Catholicism. The Romanian communist party chief Gheorghiu-Dej's subsequent defiance of the Soviets in economic planning and the independent stance adopted by his successor, Nicolae Ceauşescu, encouraged underground Uniates to hope for change. More particularly, Ceauşescu's exuberant nationalism and his rehabilitation of the Latinist thoery of Romanian ethnogenesis encouraged Uniates to press for relegalization. An early such petition was one submitted by Rev. V. Vorobchievici to Ceauşescu in 1968,[28] and similar petitions have continued to be presented (thirty-two by August 1977). The regime has refused to budge, however.

The Uniate Church met a similar fate in Czechoslovakia, where its union with Rome was abolished by order of the state on April 28, 1950, and its adherents were pronounced Orthodox. The more than 300,000 Uniate believers of Slovakia's Prešov diocese far outnumbered the 35,000 Orthodox believers scattered across three dioceses. When the Dubček government began to discuss various liberal reforms in 1968, some 135 Uniate clergymen organized a committee that sought and obtained the annulment of the pseudo-council of Prešov (which had abrogated the union with Rome) and the rehabilitation of the Uniate Church. Even though the revival of this church excited Uniate currents in neighboring Ukraine, stimulated a renewal of Ukrainian nationalism, and contributed to the Soviet decision to invade Czechoslovakia,[29] the return to the Uniate Church was so overwhelming and the symbiosis of religion and nationalism so potent that the authorities have been loathe to attempt a second suppression.[30] Despite this formal legality, the Czechoslovak Uniates have had to endure severe pressure at the hands of the authorities since 1970. In the early 1980s, Prague targeted the Slovak villages for atheization campaigns.

Communists in several East European countries, including Czechoslovakia, Yugoslavia, and Bulgaria, assumed in the late 1940s that they would very shortly be absorbed into an expanded Soviet Union. In a typical expression of this anticipation, Gustav Husak, later to become president of Czechoslovakia, wrote in *Nove Slovo* (October 15, 1944):

> Six years of the existence of the Slovak state have weakened the will of the Slovak nation to live in one state with the Czech nation. . . . The Slovak working masses have in recent years moved politically and nationally in the direction of the Soviet Union and the call for the incorporation of Slovakia into the Soviet Union has frequently been heard.[31]

It is conceivable that the coercion of the Uniates into Orthodoxy was designed to serve as a preparatory stage for Soviet annexation of Slovakia, in the conviction that the Orthodox Church would be less nationalist and more pliable, and thus was done in conjunction with the suppression of the Uniates in neighboring Ukraine.

SUPPRESSED GROUPS: JEWS

Prejudice against Jews is endemic in the region. Jews have traditionally been viewed as outsiders, and anti-Semitism remains strong in the ranks of the Soviet, Polish, and other East European communist parties. The etymological relatedness of the Russian words for peasant *(krestyanin)* and Christian *(khristiyanin)* must have provided an unconscious predisposition for excluding the Jews from national life, and most experts concur that Judaism is far worse off than any other "legal" religious group in the USSR.[32]

In Russia, as elsewhere in Eastern Europe, the Jewish community council (the *kehillah*) was traditionally the chief body responsible for ritual baths, cemeteries, and synagogue maintenance. In summer 1919, Stalin, then commissar of nationalities, decreed the abolition of the *kehillahs*. A special section of the communist party, known as the *Yevsektsiia* (Jewish section), was entrusted with the task of assailing and ridiculing the Jewish clergy and religion; the section was not abolished until 1930. In 1948–49, all secular Jewish institutions in the USSR, including theaters, were destroyed; authorities even melted down the type in the last remaining Yiddish publishing house.[33] In the 1950s, Soviet propaganda called Judaism "the most harmful and most reactionary of all religious cults."[34] Traditional Slavic anti-Semitism was reinforced by the creation of Israel.

Stalin had already created a so-called Jewish homeland in 1934 when the town of Birobidjan and its surrounding area in the Soviet Far East were designated the Jewish Autonomous Region; that, for the Soviets, was the solution of the Jewish question. But few Jews have migrated there, while many have been interested in Israel, provoking Soviet doubts about the loyalty of Soviet Jews. In a well-known episode, Stalin exiled Polina Zemschuzina, the wife of his close colleague Foreign Minister Vyacheslav Molotov after she showed too much interest in Israel during a conversation at a diplomatic party.

As in the case of the Uniates, the strong linkage of Judaism with non-Russian nationalism (in this case, identification with Israel) has marked out Soviet Jews for special repression. During Khrushchev's antireligious campaign, 1959–64, large numbers of synagogues were closed, and the practice of Judaism has become all but impossible. Rabbis cannot be trained in the USSR.

There are no Hebrew-language publications and, since 1961, only one Yiddish periodical, the monthly *Sovietish haimland*. Hebrew, because of its connection with Israel, is taught only at the diplomatic schools of Leningrad and Moscow universities, and otherwise is identified as the language of Zionism. Hence, even the newspaper of the Israeli Communist Party can be purchased only in its Arabic and Yiddish editions, and not in Hebrew.[35]

Anti-Semitism has been more or less constant in much of Eastern Europe. It played a role in the factional infighting of the early 1950s in Czechoslovakia (the Slansky trial) and Romania (the purge of Ana Pauker). Later, when East European elites were compelled to revise their policies in light of Khrushchevite de-Stalinization, the Stalinist excesses were occasionally, if spuriously, blamed on the Jews. There were reports of anti-Semitic incidents in Hungary in the 1960s, including the removal of some high-ranking Jews from the party. In Romania, the regime began encouraging Jews to emigrate to Israel around 1958. Some 650 Romanian rabbis had emigrated by 1970, leaving only nine behind and compelling the rabbinical seminary in Arad to close.[36] By late 1982, no more than 30,000 Jews were left in Romania, out of an initial postwar population of 400,000.[37]

In Bulgaria, fewer than 5,000 Jews are left today, compared with an estimated 51,500 on the eve of the communist takeover in 1944. The only legal Jewish cultural organization is the Social Cultural-Educational Organization of Jews of the People's Republic of Bulgaria, which functions under the direct surveillance of the Central Committee Propaganda Department. The Organization publishes a fortnightly newspaper, *Evreyski vesti* [Jewish News], which promotes the regime's concept of the creation of "a single socialist nation" and serves as a forum for routine attacks on Israel. A February 1985 plenum of the organization endorsed the assimilation of Bulgarian Jews into the Bulgarian nation, with not a glimmer of dissent.[38]

It is Poland, ironically, that has demonstrated the most resilient official policy of anti-Semitism—"ironically" because, as of 1982, only 8,000 Jews remained in Poland out of a prewar community of 3.5 million. As early as 1956, the Polish Communist Party blamed "Zionists and Jews" for workers' unrest, inciting large numbers of Jews to emigrate. Twelve years later, Gen. Mieczyslaw Moczar fanned the flames of an official anti-Semitic campaign in a bid for power. More than 9,000 Polish Jews were forced from public office, and the Jewish population precipitously dropped from 16,000 in 1968 to its present level. More recently, the political instability produced by Poland's economic chaos and the refusal of Polish authorities to accept an independent trade union, Solidarity, provided the occasion for yet another scapegoating of Polish Jews. The regime sanctioned the establishment of an overtly anti-Semitic organization known as the Grünwald Patriotic Union, speedily approved publication of a new newspaper, *Rzeczywistosc,* that has been loudly anti-Jewish, and, within a week of the declaration of martial law (December 13, 1981), launched a series of anti-Semitic broadcasts on Radio Warsaw in which the handful of remaining Polish Jews, whose average age was 71, were tarnished as the chief culprits responsible for Poland's myriad of economic, political, and social problems.[39]

The roots of anti-Semitism are complex, and anti-Semitism is of course no creation of communism. But the persistence of officially condoned anti-Semitism in the Soviet Union and Poland, if not also elsewhere, requires an explanation in terms of policy. The availability of Jews as scapegoats can only be part of the answer, since numerous other scapegoats are available. The traditional anti-Semitism of the Slavic world and the symbiosis of ethnic and religious identity in the case of the Jews, conveniently embodied in the pariah state of Israel, appear to provide a fuller answer. Domestically, anti-Semitism is also useful in rallying Russian nationalists of various political hues and in buttressing traditional chauvinistic nationalism in the East European states.

COOPTED GROUPS: ORTHODOXY

A complete enumeration of Chalcedonian Orthodox Churches would include six "coopted" churches (Russian, Romanian, Bulgarian, Polish, Czechoslovak, and, to an extent, Georgian), four independent churches (Cypriot, Greek, Serbian, and Sinai), two schismatic churches (Macedonian, since 1967, and Croatian, 1942–45), and three suppressed churches (Ukrainian, Belorussian, and Albanian). To these one might add the schismatic émigré wings of the Serbian, Albanian, Belorussian, and Russian Orthodox Churches and the Orthodox Church in America.[40]

The impact of nationalism on religious policy is most directly seen in the schismatic and suppressed categories. In the case of the Croatian Orthodox Church, its creation by order of Croatian *Poglavnik* Ante Pavelić in 1942 was designed to denationalize Croatia's Serbs and convert them into "Orthodox Croats." The establishment of the Macedonian Orthodox Church in 1967 similarly enjoyed the strong endorsement of the Yugoslav communist regime, which saw in the move a validation of its claim that Macedonians are a distinct nationality group and not Bulgarians, as both the Sofia regime and the Bulgarian Orthodox Church insist. As for the suppressed churches, both the Ukrainian and Belorussian autocephalous Orthodox Churches compromised themselves in Soviet eyes by their linkage with nationalist and anti-Soviet currents during the war. Both the Ukrainian and Belorussian Churches were actually suppressed twice by Soviet authorities—once at the end of the 1920s, when the cultural and social relaxation of the New Economic Policy (NEP) period was terminated, and again in 1944, as the Red Army reconquered the western borderlands. In the case of the Belorussian Orthodox Church, some 2,000 clergymen were shot or sent to concentration camps in the wake of the post-NEP retrenchment; by 1937, the church had been completely destroyed.[41] The Albanian Orthodox Church was suppressed in 1967, along with all other religious organizations in Albania, with the explanation that Orthodoxy, like Catholicism and Islam, was a foreign import and that the authentic and autochthonous Albanian *Weltanschauung* was atheism—thus hypothesizing an antagonism between religion and Albanian nationalism.

Of the remaining Orthodox churches, two (the Polish and Czechoslovak) number only a few thousand adherents each and have therefore played a negligible role in their countries' politics. These two, together with the Cypriot and Greek Orthodox Churches, the Church of the Sinai, and the Orthodox Church in America, will thus be excluded from the ensuing discussion. Those with which we shall be concerned may be divided into two groups, based on ethnic considerations. The Russian (fifty million believers in 1984), Romanian (fifteen to seventeen million in 1983), and Bulgarian (three million in 1978) Orthodox Churches are the principal confessional organizations of dominant nationality groups.[42] By contrast, the Serbian (eight million nominal adherents in 1984[43]) and Georgian (five million in 1979[44]) Orthodox Churches are the principal confessional organizations of minority groups (although, with 36.3 percent of the population in 1981, the Serbs constitute the largest group in multi-ethnic Yugoslavia).

In the Soviet Union, Romania, and Bulgaria, the communist parties set out with two clear objectives: in the short run, to tame and control the Orthodox churches and exploit them for the parties' own purposes; in the long run, to destroy them altogether. In the first five years of the new revolutionary order (1917–22), the Bolsheviks executed twenty-eight Russian Orthodox bishops and 1,215 Orthodox priests.[45] The clergy were declared déclassé and deprived of civil rights, including even the rights to shelter and rations (full citizenship was restored to them only in 1936). Many were imprisoned or exiled. Most Orthodox theological schools were boarded up, and church publications were suspended; between 1935 and 1943, almost no religious publications were issued in the USSR. The number of Orthodox places of worship also shriveled up, from a 1914 level of 54,174 to a mere 500 on the eve of the Nazi invasion (excluding territories annexed 1939–41).[46] Nevertheless, in the regime's most critical hour, the Russian Orthodox Church lent strong support to the war effort and even volunteered to sponsor a division to fight the invaders. At a time when Stalin embraced Russian nationalism to rally his people, the church showed that its nationalism was undiminished, even if the Soviets were in charge. The result was a truce, the resumption of church publishing activity, and a general revival of the church. Russian nationalism had revived an ailing institution.[47]

More than 17,000 Orthodox places of worship were reopened between 1941 and the mid-1950s, and church membership grew more than 50 percent. By 1957, Russian Orthodoxy had 22,000 churches in operation. But by 1957 there was no foreign threat and the armed guerrilla movements in Ukraine and Lithuania had been suppressed. In 1959, Khrushchev launched a determined antireligious campaign, which, by the time he left office in 1964, had reduced the number of Orthodox churches to a mere 10,000. His successors have continued to whittle away at the church, and, according to West German sources, no more than 7,000 churches were left in operation by 1975. By 1985, the number had further shrunk to 6,500.[48]

As the Soviets chipped away at the church, they also coopted its leadership by jailing the leaders who were antagonistic toward the Soviet state, supporting those disposed to cooperation, and infiltrating the hierarchy with KGB agents. A secret report drafted sometime between 1975 and 1978 by V. Furov, deputy chairman of the Council for Religious Affairs (CRA), set forth the CRA's ideal in claiming that the council (itself heavily staffed by KGB operatives) effectively "controls the Synod [of the Russian Orthodox Church]. The question of selection and appointment of permanent members used to be, and still is, completely in the hands of the Council."[49] This cooptive relationship eventually provoked a backlash, and since 1957 there has been an active movement of opposition within the church that finds itself at odds both with the regime and with its own hierarchy.

Despite this opposition, the church continues to be useful to the regime in at least two ways. First, the church supports Soviet foreign policy moves. Its frequent endorsement of Soviet peace plans, its regular denunciations of the West for stimulating an arms race, and its unblushing approval of the Soviet invasion and occupation of Czechoslovakia in 1968[50] have all been of some use to the Kremlin. More striking have been the comments tendered by Orthodox hierarchs in defense of the USSR. Metropolitan Pitirim, for instance, in an interview with the West German magazine, *Stern,* suggested that "Capitalism and Christianity are irreconcilable," venturing to add, in the best dialectical tradition, that "Communism is closer to Christian ethics."[51] Second, the church has also been useful to the Kremlin in furthering the Russification of Belorussia and Ukraine.

In Romania, the communist party initially mimicked the Stalinist model, and mass purges decimated the Romanian Orthodox Church's hierarchy. Three archbishops died suddenly after expressing opposition to the policies of the communist-controlled government, and thirteen more "uncooperative" bishops and archbishops were arrested. By weeding out the anticommunists and setting up a proregime "Union of Democratic Priests," the party endeavored to secure the cooperation of the Orthodox hierarchy.[52] By January 1953, some 300 to 500 Orthodox priests were being held in Romanian concentration camps.[53] After the death of Patriarch Nicodemus in May 1948, the party succeeded in having the ostensibly docile Justinian Marina elected to succeed him.

As a result of measures passed in 1947–48, the 2,300 elementary schools operated by the church were closed, together with its twenty-four high schools, its academy of sacred music, three of its divinity schools, and thirteen of its fifteen theological seminaries.[54] A new campaign struck the church in the period 1958–62, when more than half its remaining monasteries were closed, more than 2,000 monks forced to take secular jobs, and about 1,500 clergy and lay activists arrested. Throughout this period, Patriarch Justinian was careful to say the right things and to avoid giving offense to the government.

The church's situation began to improve in 1962, when church-state relations suddenly thawed. This thaw coincided with the blooming of Romania's independent course.[55] Romanian nationalism became indispensable to the elite in securing its position against Soviet pressure. The church, as an intensely national body that had made great contributions to Romanian culture from the fourteenth century on, was a natural ally. The result of this second cooptation was that the church was able to stage a dramatic recovery. By 1975, its diocesan clergy numbered about 12,000 and it was publishing eight theological reviews of high quality, including *Ortodoxia* and *Studii Teologice*.[56] Today, two Orthodox metropolitans, affiliated with the Grand National Front of Socialist Democracy, have seats in the National Assembly. Orthodox churchmen consistently support Bucharest's foreign policy, refrain from criticism of domestic policies, and, in what has evidently been most gratifying to the regime, periodically speak out on various historical debates, upholding the Romanian line against the Soviets (over Bessarabia) and the Hungarians (over Transylvania).[57]

By contrast with the Russian and Romanian cases, Bulgaria's communists seem to have been content, from the start, with whittling down and controlling the Bulgarian Orthodox Church and not to have sought its demolition. But the early postwar years were, all the same, unsettling to church hierarchs. During the years 1944–47, the church was deprived of jurisdiction in marriage, divorce, issuance of birth and death certificates, and other prerogatives. Catechism and church history were removed from school curricula. Antireligious propaganda was undertaken, and some priests were persecuted. The years 1947–49 saw the height of the campaign to intimidate the church. Bishop Boris was assassinated. Egumenius Kalistrat, administrator of the Rila Monastery, was imprisoned. Other clergy were either murdered or tried. In short order, the communists replaced all churchmen who refused to endorse the regime's policies. Thus, Exarch Stefan, who coauthored a book in 1948 that was considered anticommunist, was banished to a monastery in September of that year.[58]

Since then, the church and the Bulgarian communist party have had a symbiotic relationship. The party supported the elevation of the Bulgarian exarchate to the rank of patriarchate (in May 1953), profusely celebrated the 200th anniversary (in 1962) of the composition of *The Slavic-Bulgarian History* by Orthodox monk Father Paisii of Khilendar, and commemorated the 100th anniversary (in 1970) of the establishment of the Bulgarian exarchate, which it described as "a necessary step in our national-liberation revolution."[59] It also regularly celebrates May 24, the saints' day of Cyril and Methodius. The church has also been useful to the regime, by holding peace forums and in other ways making good propaganda for church-state relations. The commemoration of the establishment of the exarchate served to recall that this exarchate (which retained its jurisdictional borders until after World War One) included not merely the territory of present-day Bulgaria but also the districts of Macedonia and Thrace.

The church in Bulgaria has consistently refused to recognize either the ethnicity of the Macedonians or the autocephaly of the Macedonian Orthodox Church (the legitimacy of which depends on the distinctive ethnicity of the Macedonians) and has spoken out in defense of the Bulgarian interpretation of Macedonian history.[60]

In the Soviet Union, Romania, and Bulgaria, cooptation has meant that Orthodox church leaders serve as surrogate spokesmen for the regime's foreign policy and as defenders of its internal policies. Cooptation has meant that, in contrast to other churches, the Romanian and Bulgarian Orthodox Churches have enjoyed a certain sufficiency of institutions and publications and that the Russian Orthodox Church has enjoyed periods of respite and even institutional revival. In each case, what the church was able to offer the regime was its nationalism; in each case, the price of cooptation was submission to a degree of control by the regime.

Developments in Yugoslavia might have followed a similar course but for two factors—the Soviet-Yugoslav rift in 1948 and the fact that the Serbs do not comprise a majority in Yugoslavia (as Russians, Romanians, and Bulgarians do in their respective countries). As a result, the Serbian Orthodox Church today enjoys independence and toleration unique among Orthodox churches in communist lands.

Initially, however, the Yugoslav communists were, if anything, more brutal toward the Orthodox clergy than were their ideological bedfellows in other countries. The Partisans, according to an eyewitness, regularly made a practice of shooting down priests in the villages they occupied.[61] An official US government publication estimated that ninety-eight Serbian Orthodox priests were executed without trial in 1944–45 and that 90 percent of the Orthodox clergy were persecuted, with many being confined at Lepoglava, Stara Gradiška, Goli Otok, Sremska Mitrovica, and other concentration camps.[62] A land reform act stripped the church of 90 percent of its lands, and government agents were dispatched to confiscate church valuables and place them in state museums. In addition, the state nationalized some 1,180 church buildings. While the church had put out fifteen periodical publications prior to World War Two, the communists permitted just three *(Vesnik, Glasnik,* and *Misionar)*—a situation that did not improve until the late 1960s. Moreover, during the period 1944–64, the church was able to publish only three liturgical or religious books and not a single theological book.[63]

Patriarch Gavrilo, the head of the church, and Bishop Nikolaj Velimirović, another leading churchman, were both ill disposed toward communism in the first place. When their forebodings were confirmed by the ensuing religious persecution, they denounced the Tito regime from their exile in occupied Germany. Metropolitan Josip Cvijović, administrator of the church from 1941 to November 1946 (when Patriarch Gavrilo finally returned to Serbia), was equally antagonistic toward the communists and, after comparing communist rule unfavorably with the Ottoman imperium, was tortured and beaten.

This situation began to change soon after the Soviet-Yugoslav rift. Three considerations militated a change of policy by the regime: Tito's need to rally the people of Yugoslavia behind him to sustain his successful defiance of the Soviets; his need to make a favorable impression in the West, to which he now looked for economic aid, political support, and military hardware; and his desire to enlist the support of the Serbian Orthodox Church in the polemics over Macedonia that had abruptly begun with Bulgaria. Indeed, Tito now supported the church in its quarrel with its Macedonian clergy. Rudolf Trofenik suggested that Tito continued to nurture his dream of annexing Bulgaria for a number of years and that this consideration impelled him to oppose a Macedonian Church schism that might have alienated both the Bulgarian Orthodox Church and the Bulgarian party elite.[64] Subsequently, when Tito realized that union with Bulgaria was out of the question and Bulgarian officials became more vocal about their belief (not voiced 1944–47) that Yugoslavia's Macedonians were simply Bulgarians, he reversed himself and found it useful to back Macedonian ecclesiastical autocephaly.

For its part, the Serbian Orthodox Church remained strongly opposed to the communist regime until 1958, when, after the death of Patriarch Gavrilo, German Djorić succeeded to the See of St. Sava.[65] Patriarch German has since been chastized by Serbian émigré groups as "the red patriarch" or "Tito's patriarch"—charges he has firmly repudiated.[66] But, although he has been reticent and cautious in his public statements, he has never retreated on any fundamental points—his opposition to the Macedonian Church, his belief that Serbian nationalism is legitimate and positive, his claims to protectorship over the interests of the Serbs in Kosovo, and his open dissatisfaction with the limitations on construction permits for Orthodox churches (though the latter situation showed tangible change by the end of 1984).[67]

The Serbian Orthodox Church is highly nationalistic—probably more so than any other religious organization in Yugoslavia. Its clergy describes the church as a "bastion at the geographical frontier of true Orthodoxy, defending the Holy Sepulchre against the false and barbarous Christianity of Rome" and sees itself as the most loyal advocate of Serbian interests. The clergy also has a sense of destiny that is Serbian rather than Yugoslav. As one Serbian monk told me, "Only Serbs and Jews have a history in which God's interference is obvious."[68]

The Yugoslav regime has little use for the church's nationalism, repeatedly complains that its biweekly newspaper, *Pravoslavlje*, tends to treat Orthodoxy and Serbdom as synonymous, and has occasionally even charged that the church has been infiltrated by Chetnik and antisocialist elements.[69] On one occasion, the Belgrade weekly magazine *NIN* even referred to the church as one of the regime's "chief internal enemies"—a charge that elicited the reply from *Pravoslavlje:* "Lucky is the state if its greatest enemy is the Serbian Orthodox Church! In that case, it can sleep peacefully."[70]

TOLERATED GROUPS: CATHOLICISM

Romanian party chief Gheorghiu-Dej expressed the sentiments of all the Stalinist elites of Eastern Europe when he identified the Roman Catholic Church, in a public statement of February 22, 1948, as one of the few institutional obstacles to communization.[71] Some of the parties—the Czech,[72] Yugoslav,[73] Polish,[74] Hungarian,[75] Romanian,[76] and Albanian—tried to persuade their Catholic Churches to break off ties with the Vatican and to reconstitute themselves as "national" churches. These attempts to isolate the churches, as a prelude to subjugating them, were rebuffed in all cases, though the Albanian communist press succeeded in perpetrating the fiction that the Albanian clergy had agreed to the creation of an Albanian National Catholic Church.[77] (Subsequently, in 1967, Albania's rulers outlawed Catholicism, along with other religions, when they declared Albania the world's first atheist state.)

Throughout the region, as World War Two drew to a close, the communists proceeded with a campaign to decimate and intimidate the Catholic churches. The highest prelates were sent to prison (Stefan Cardinal Wyszynski in Poland, Josef Cardinal Beran in Czechoslovakia, József Cardinal Mindszenty in Hungary, Alojzije Cardinal Stepinac in Yugoslavia, Archbishop Gaspër Thaçi and Vincenc Prennushi in Albania, and Bishop Vincentas Borisevičius in Lithuania), just as Archbishop Baron Eduard von der Ropp of Russia had been in 1919. Archbishop Alexander Cisar of Romania was fortunate; he was merely removed from office and forcibly retired. Msgr. Evgenii Bosilkov of Bulgaria, on the other hand, was executed, after a show trial in 1952. Catholic priests in Lithuania, Latvia, Belorussia, and Bulgaria were sentenced and deported, and churches were closed down. In every country in which the communist regimes took control after World War Two, except East Germany,[78] the Catholic Church lost its hospitals, its orphanages, its charitable facilities, most or all of its schools, and much of its press. In all but Hungary and Poland,[79] Catholic religious instruction in schools was banned. In Bulgaria, permission to maintain higher schools of theology was granted on the condition that mandatory courses on Marxism be incorporated into their curricula.[80] Several of the parties simultaneously offered to put the clergy on state salary as a device to encourage ecclesiastical docility.

Catholic priests were harassed and arrested in all these countries, and murders of Catholic clergymen were reported in several of them. Clergy in Albania, Romania, Czechoslovakia, and Lithuania were sentenced to hard labor in forced labor camps, the Lithuanians being deported to Soviet Central Asia for this purpose. In Romania, a 450-man labor brigade made up entirely of Catholic priests was detained to work on the Danube-Black Sea Canal project; almost half the brigade died at the work site.[81]

In the USSR, after the imprisonment and deportation of the church's highest clerics, there was not a single Roman Catholic bishop left as of 1926. By May 1941, only two of the 1,195 churches that had been operated by Catholic clergy in 1917 were still operating.[82] The annexation of the Baltic republics and the western Ukraine brought new Catholic populations under Soviet sovereignty, and the Kremlin quickly set about the business of imprisoning its upper clergy, closing some of its seminaries, and enrolling secret police agents in the remaining Catholic seminaries to infiltrate the church and destroy it from within. The subsequent post-Stalin thaw eased church life briefly but proved to be only a tactical concession. By 1957, anti-Catholic pressure was resumed. Some 500 clergy were removed from priestly work in Lithuania alone between 1944 and 1967.

In Bulgaria, the jailing of the country's three Catholic bishops in 1952 and the subsequent expulsion of large numbers of priests, monks, and nuns virtually obliterated the church. A 1965 source included an obituary for the Bulgarian Catholic Church,[83] but after a visit by Bulgarian strongman Todor Zhivkov to the Vatican in the summer of 1975, church-state relations improved somewhat, and the pope was able to install two new bishops in Bulgaria to replace two who had died in prison (one in 1952, the other in 1974).

In Albania, of the ninety-three Catholic priests active in 1945, twenty-four were murdered, thirty-five were imprisoned or sentenced to hard labor, ten were missing, eleven were drafted, and three fled the country, leaving only ten by 1953. In the heat of Albania's anti-Catholic crusade, Albanian party chief Enver Hoxha denounced one of the leading figures in the Central Committee (in 1955) for not hating the Catholic clergy enough.[84]

In Yugoslavia, more than a third of the Catholic clergy were quickly removed from the scene. Of the 2,700 Croatian priests, more than 400 had been killed by summer 1946, another 200 had fled abroad, and several hundred were in jail.[85] The scenario repeated itself in Czechoslovakia and to a lesser extent in Hungary and Poland. In Czechoslovakia, the party moved especially quickly, expropriating church property within a month of seizing power and suppressing both the Central Catholic Agency (the bishops' executive organ) in Bratislava and the League of Catholic Women by the end of the year. The church lost its monasteries, seminaries, and theological colleges in 1950, and several bishops were either sentenced to life imprisonment or transferred to physical labor. The convents were closed and the nuns sent to labor camps, where 52.2 percent of them died, mostly of tuberculosis.[86] A priests' association of fellow travelers was set up by the regime to provide a mechanism of control and to divide the church from within. The result there, as among the Uniates in Ukraine, was the development of an underground ecclesiastical network that continues to endeavor to elude the authorities.

In Hungary, the Catholic religious orders were banned, and several bishops were placed under house arrest. Seven of the church's thirteen seminaries were closed, and the new regime required that the church submit prospective hierarchical appointments to the State Office for the Church for approval. In the past two decades, thanks to state obstructionism and pressure, the number of priests in Hungary has dropped by two thirds, dwindling to about 2,790 in 1982. Each successive year the number of priests declines by about fifty.[87]

Only in Poland, where a large and powerful Catholic Church seemed inseparable from the people, did the communist regime hesitate. Not until 1949 did the authorities create a "patriot priests" movement, and only in August 1949 were church-run hospitals, nursing homes, and orphanages belatedly nationalized.[88] This hesitation was the product of a combination of factors—chiefly the initial weakness of the Polish Communists, who had been decimated by Stalin's prewar purge and dissolution; the strength of the church; and continued armed resistance against the communists for some two to three years after the war officially ended. In connection with the question of newly acquired territories in the West, the regime found itself sympathetic to the Polish hierarchy's efforts to have the Vatican transfer jurisdiction from the German episcopate to the Polish. But otherwise the regime viewed the church with essentially unmixed hostility. Indeed, until 1956, the regime aimed at no less than the obliteration of the church. To this end it employed a variety of means, including outright slander and the imprisonment of four bishops and Primate Wyszynski in 1953. With the accession of Wladyslaw Gomulka to the party helm in 1956, the church's situation improved somewhat, though Gomulka's religious policy was uneven and unpredictable.[89]

By contrast, in the German Democratic Republic, where political development has been exceptional in several ways, the Catholic Church, which claims only 1.3 million adherents in a total population of seventeen million, still maintains some forty hospitals and 167 nursing homes, freely offers religious instruction to children on church premises, publishes two weekly newspapers, and has even been able to broadcast Sunday services on state radio. With Poland's church under considerable pressure since the imposition of martial law in Poland,[90] the Catholic Church in East Germany may well enjoy more freedom than any other Catholic church in Eastern Europe, aside from Yugoslavia.

The late 1960s—the era of détente and papal *Ostpolitik*—brought relief in a number of cases, reinforcing autochthonous liberalization trends that touched most of Eastern Europe in one way or another. Yet not all the East European states have experienced religious liberalization. The Roman Catholic Church in the 1980s finds itself distinctly oppressed in Romania, Czechoslovakia, and the Soviet Union—all countries in which the elites have been troubled by the presence of ethnic minorities whose interests have been championed by the church—and in ideologically fanatical Albania. The church enjoys greater security and the authorities show greater respect for its rights in the German Democratic Republic, Poland, Hungary, and Yugoslavia—all, with the exception of Yugoslavia, ethnically homogeneous states.[91]

If we observe, first, that in Romania official policy singles out the Roman Catholic Church (i.e., among legal church organizations) for particular discrimination[92] and second, that this church is more or less the exclusive preserve of Hungarians and Saxons, themselves the victims of a cultural Romanianization campaign, it is tempting to conclude that nationalities considerations have something to do with religious policy in Romania. One can presume that the Romanian elites are fully aware of the important role that the Catholic Church has traditionally played for these people as a bulwark against denationalization.

In Czechoslovakia, the brutal campaign launched in 1980 against the Catholic Church is only partly explained by reference to Prague's fear of a "Polish model" (see chapter 8). The antichurch campaign has been especially strong in Slovakia, and the Slovak security forces had to be augmented by agents from Bohemia for the duration of the campaign. These circumstances suggest that the traditional linkage of nationality and religion in Slovakia—made more potent by an 80 percent attendance rate at Sunday mass there—may also be a cause of the regime's worries. It is clear that the regime remains much concerned with relations between Slovaks and the numerically predominant Czechs.[93] Few Slovaks are really satisfied with their union with the Czechs, and this grudging acceptance of what was imposed by force is no doubt shared by the Catholic clergy of Slovakia. It was, after all, the Catholic clergy who promoted the

Slovak language and consciousness in the first place, fashioning a local dialect into a national language. Autonomist sentiment remained strong among Catholic clergy in the First Czechoslovak Republic (1919–39) and the clerical Slovak People's Party created by Fr. Andrej Hlinka ultimately became the vehicle for the establishment in 1939 of a quasi-independent state of Slovakia, under Nazi protection. Although, in keeping with communist hostility to all forms of nationalism, the Prague regime has denigrated Msgr. Dr. Jozef Tiso, who was president of Slovakia (1939–45), as a "clerofascist" and Nazi stooge, certain church circles view him as a nationalist patriot and have sought to exculpate him.[94]

In the Soviet Union as well, the Roman Catholic Church, while legally tolerated, appears to be severely discriminated against. While the Russian Orthodox Church, the Evangelical Church, the Baptists, the Pentecostalists, and certain other denominations have been granted the prerogative of operating regional administrative centers, this prerogative has been withheld from both the Roman Catholics and the Jews. The situation is especially severe in Belorussia and Ukraine, where there is no local seminary and KGB agents have attempted to infiltrate the ranks of the clergy.[95] The political logic here parallels that in the Slovak case in three important respects. First, the Soviet authorities believe that religiosity among Belorussian and Ukrainian Catholics is more "fanatical" and more "convinced" than among other groups.[96] Second, the Soviets perceive the link between nationalism and Catholicism in these areas.[97] And third, Ukraine and Belorussia have been specifically "targeted" by nationalities policy formulators for speedier and more intense Russification than other regions.[98] The national churches serve as bulwarks against Russification. If Ukraine and Belorussia stand at the top of the list of areas to be Russified, then the nationalistic Catholic Churches of Ukraine and Belorussia require "special treatment."

The dilemma repeats itself in Lithuania. Some 75 percent of the Lithuanian population is Catholic, and the church there has reacquired its historical role of guardian of the national identity of the Lithuanians. The authorities have indicated quite openly that they view the campaign against Catholicism in Lithuania as a campaign against Lithuanian nationalism.[99] The underground *Chronicle of the Catholic Church in Lithuania,* created in 1972, explained Soviet logic in this way:

By fighting religion in Lithuania, the atheists attempt to break the spirit of the Lithuanian nation, to deprive it of its spiritual values, to enslave the Lithuanians' personality and to denationalize the believing people. When Lithuanians will become atheists, start entering into mixed marriages, disparage their own Christian culture, then conditions will be achieved for them to submerge in a homogeneous mass of people who adopt Lenin's native language.[100]

The Catholic Church has been involved in the defense of Lithuanian national identity since the nation was incorporated into the Soviet Union. At least 250 of Lithuania's 1,300 Catholic clergy are said to have been actively involved in the anti-Soviet resistance movement of 1944–53, with two of them (Ylius and Lelesius) serving as brigade leaders. In retribution, the Soviets deported about 30 percent of the priests, four bishops, and almost all monks and nuns to forced labor camps.[101] The *Chronicle,* which enjoys the tacit support of the Lithuanian Church hierarchy, has eulogized Mindaugas Tamonis, who committed suicide to protest the Soviet occupation of Lithuania after demanding a referendum on the reestablishment of an independent Lithuanian national state. The *Chronicle* called Tamonis's protest "the cry of our generation."[102] The Lithuanian Catholic Church stands squarely against Soviet Russification efforts. For this reason, as a Belorussian party organ put it, "it is not mere happenstance that Soviet Lithuania has become one of the principal centers of [communist] criticism of Catholicism."[103] Soviet authorities are deeply vexed by what they call the church's "fables about the alleged danger that is threatening Lithuanian culture,"[104] and they are determined to remove any obstacle to their nationalities policy. Thus, religious policy must be adjusted to serve the needs of nationalities policy.

The authorities regularly interfere in the operation of Lithuania's one remaining Catholic seminary. In 1980, for instance, Petras Anilionis, a CRA commissioner, disapproved the admission of fourteen of thirty-six candidates accepted by the Kaunas seminary, subsequently forcing the expulsion of seminarian Aloyzas Volskis on the grounds of "spreading anti-Soviet rumors among the clerics." That this charge signified Lithuanian nationalism on the part of Volskis seemed implicit in Anilionis's simultaneous attack on Radio Vatican for aiming to "convert Lithuania into a country of clerical domination and exploitation."[105]

Various reports confirm that the election of Karol Wojtyla to the papacy in 1978 stirred Lithuanian religious consciousness and that the papal visit to Poland in 1979 not only contributed to the explosion of workers' unrest there the following summer but also stimulated religious dissent in Lithuania. The Czechs, themselves worried about the influence that the Slavic pope was having in Slovakia, repeatedly denounced him for fostering "counterrevolution" and clericalism.[106] In the Soviet Union, Pope John Paul II has been attacked in the Russian, Belorussian, Ukrainian, and Lithuanian regional press. In May 1982, the Soviet literary journal *Literatura ir Menas* published an abrasive assault on the pope, charging him with supporting "religious extremism" in Lithuania and calling him "the hope of reactionaries all over the world."[107] For the Soviets, the Catholic Church is a threat not merely to their program of ideological socialization but also to their policy of ethnic homogenization.

TOLERATED GROUPS: SOVIET MUSLIMS

Muslims can be found throughout Eastern Europe. Some 2,000 Muslims live in both Czechoslovakia and East Germany, 15,000 in Poland, and 35,000 in Romania.[108] But Yugoslavia, Bulgaria, and the Soviet Union (along with Albania) have the largest concentrations of Muslims in the area, and in these countries Islam has become an ethnic as well as a religious question. Different nationalities considerations have resulted in widely differing policies among the three countries with the most Muslims. In Yugoslavia, where the regime has a stake in fostering a separate Muslim ethnicity, Muslims (two million in 1981) have enjoyed considerable freedom of action and operate eighty-five mosques in Sarajevo alone (as compared with 200 mosques in all of Soviet Central Asia). Yugoslavia's Muslims have had their own theological faculty since 1977, publish a biweekly newspaper, and, since early 1979, have been publishing a monthly theological journal, *Islamska misao.*

In Bulgaria, where Muslims comprise around 15 percent of the population (700,000 to 900,000 Turks, 120,000 Pomaks, 5,000 Tatars, and 120,000 Muslim Gypsies),[109] the regime's drive to Bulgarianize its population has dictated a policy very different from Yugoslavia's. A Keston College report revealed that "Muslim villages [in Bulgaria] are reported to have been pillaged, mosques and Koran schools demolished, and countless copies of the Koran burned, [while] men and women trying to remain loyal to their beliefs have been detained in camps."[110] Regime pressure on Bulgaria's Muslims to assimilate—Turk, Pomak, and Tatar alike—has a long history, with a 1971 Bulgarian publication explicitly describing atheization as a prerequisite to "Bulgarianization" of the Turkish, Pomak, and Tatar populations.[111] As early as 1974, all Turkish language teaching was terminated. But in late 1984, the Bulgarian regime stepped up pressure on these peoples to assimilate. In early 1985, the long-time bilingual (Bulgarian and Turkish) newspaper *New Light* stopped publication in Turkish. Turks were ordered to adopt Bulgarian (Christian) names, and some Muslim villages were surrounded by tanks to compel "Bulgarianization."[112] By the end of 1985, Muslim culture in Bulgaria was shattered.

The Soviet Muslims enjoy a status somewhere between these two extremes. They are discouraged from practicing their religion, have a grossly inadequate number of mosques, and are certainly not encouraged, as

Yugoslav Muslims are, to develop a sense of Muslim identity. But they are also far too numerous—forty-four million, or 17 percent of the total Soviet population in 1979[113]—to be coercively assimilated in the Bulgarian style.

The Basmachi rebel movement of the 1920s reinforced Bolshevik apprehension of Pan-Turkic and Pan-Islamic currents and induced the Kremlin to attempt to solve its Muslim problem by depoliticizing Muslim consciousness. To accomplish that, the Soviets undertook the very opposite of what Marx had urged: While Marx had considered it both natural and progressive for people to draw together into larger regional collectivities, the Bolsheviks encouraged fissiparous rather than integrative tendencies in Central Asia; they thus encouraged the emergence of a series of new peoples—Kazakhs, Karakalpaks, Uzbeks, Chechen, Ingush, and Bashkirs—and converted local dialects into "languages," magnifying dialectal differences by conscious manipulation.[114] The Soviets have encouraged ethnic identification based on language and have systematically combated ethnic identification based on religion.

Until 1941, the Soviets attempted to suppress Islam by force. With the Nazi invasion of the Soviet Union in June of that year, however, came a reversal of policy and the legalization, in 1943, of the Muslim Spiritual Directorate for Central Asia and Kazakhstan. Although the party continues to rail against underground Muslim associations operating illegally, party policy since then has been one of toleration of "official Islam" (i.e., the officially registered Islamic institutions), combined with continued efforts at atheization.

The Soviets' great concern is the tangible anti-Russian strain in Central Asia Muslim nationalism. As one Soviet writer put it, the ideology of the "united Islamic nation" is "irreconciliable with true internationalism."[115] The difficulty is that even nonbelievers in Central Asia are apt to identify themselves as Muslims and to view any assault on Islamic religious traditions as a threat to their ethnic and cultural identity. What Soviet propagandists believe they must do to accomplish their goals is thus to deny that their campaign against religion has anything to do with Muslim national identity (though that is the heart of the issue), to insist that their concern is only the obstacle constituted by Islam to the emancipation of women and other progressive programs,[116] and to portray the identification of Islam with national identity as a "trick" of reactionary ulema.[117] Having staked out this position, the Soviets created commissions in the kolkhozes and sovkhozes for the introduction of new traditions and civil ceremonies (to displace religious traditions), organized atheism classes at the level of the collective throughout the region (8,000 such centers in Kazakhstan alone), and tried to undermine various Islamic customs by tracing them to pagan origins. But recent writings indicate that this campaign has often been sloppily carried out and that it has made no real headway in disassociating ethnic identity and Islam, and thus in dissolving the specter of Muslim nationalism in Central Asia. The late M. G. Gapurov, then first secretary of the Turkmenistan Communist Party, called in 1976 for "a stepped-up struggle against the religious psychology and especially against the Muslim cult," pointing to the fact that "Islam, like any religion, often plays the role of "custodian" of reactionary national customs and traditions and arouses feelings of national exclusiveness."[118] The Soviets, on the other hand, would like to refocus national identity on language; that would permit them to foster ethnic assimilation by the device of linguistic Russification.

In Central Asia, perhaps more than anywhere else in the Soviet Union, the linkage of religion and national identity stands out in bold relief; and perhaps nowhere else in the USSR is the nationalities motivation for religious policy so clearly discernible.

DEVIANT CASES: THE HUNGARIAN CATHOLIC AND GEORGIAN ORTHODOX CHURCHES

The importance of the ethnic factor for religious policy is underlined by the two deviant cases in this region: the Roman Catholic Church in Hungary and the Georgian Orthodox Church. The former, with no nationalist causes of substance to champion, aside from the persecution of Hungarians across the border in neighboring Transylvania and Slovakia, has, since the death of Cardinal Mindszenty in 1975, enjoyed a cooperative relationship with the regime unparalleled among Catholic churches of Eastern Europe. This church, which was able to open a Catholic Academy of Theology in Budapest in 1977, will be examined in chapter 4.

The Georgian Orthodox Church, which enjoyed autocephaly from the eighth century until 1811 and then regained de facto autocephaly in March 1917 (and de jure recognition by the Russian Orthodox Church in 1943), has fared far worse under Soviet rule than has the Russian Orthodox Church. For one thing, of some 2,500 Georgian Orthodox churches in operation in 1917, only about 200 remained open in 1984.[119] For another, Georgian Orthodox believers are unable to practice unmolested outside their republic. And the KGB rigged the election of the patriarch of the church in 1972, going so far as to destroy the will of his deceased predecessor, Efrem II Sidamonidze, (which had endorsed Ilia Shiolashvili as his successor), and to forge a new will, ensuring the election of the more pliable David V Devdariani (1972–77) as patriarch.[120] Under Devdariani, church services were increasingly being conducted in Old Church

Slavonic rather than in Georgian, and a Georgian source claimed that Devdariani, upon his enthronement as patriarch, promised that he would eventually renounce the Georgian Church's autocephaly.[121]

But if the patriarchate seemed thus unmistakably coopted by the regime, the church itself was not, and the gathering movement to resist Russification of Georgia found some support within the church.[122] Corruption and moral depravity among the Georgian clergy came to public attention in the 1970s, stirring resentment, protests, and efforts to force reform upon the hierarchy. Increasingly, Georgian nationalists came to view the struggle for their church as a part of a more general effort to preserve Georgian culture. As the Georgian dissident nationalist Gamsakhhurdia put it, "The struggle against the Georgian Church is a struggle against the Georgian language and culture. . . . Surely it must be clear that atheist propaganda today . . . fights the very idea of Georgia."[123]

Ultimately, Ilia Shiolashvili, the man the Soviets had tried to keep out of office, became patriarch in 1977. Under his leadership, the church has become somewhat more assertive. In early 1980, for instance, Ilia II Shiolashvili defied both the Kremlin and the Moscow patriarchate in signing a declaration of the World Council of Churches condemning the Soviet invasion of Afghanistan.[124] And in his Christmas message that year, the patriarch defiantly stated that "without Christianity we would not be a distinctive nation, and we would die," and went on to praise the Georgian language, warning his listeners that "where language declines, so the nation falls."[125] In August 1981, the church held a memorial service in the Cathedral of Mtskheta, the ancient capital of Georgia, to commemorate the third anniversary of the 1978 demonstrations, when Georgians successfully forced retraction of an amendment to remove a constitutional clause designating Georgian the official language of Georgia and demanded cultural, religious, and national autonomy. More than 500 persons (and perhaps as many as 1,000) participated in the service, which ended with the singing of Georgian national songs.[126]

RELIGIOUS AND NATIONALITIES POLICIES

For Marxists, religious policy and nationalities policy are parts of an organic whole; neither should be thought to be autonomous or independently elaborated. There is a considerable area in which they overlap, in which issues and problems arising in the one sphere have consequences in the other, in which policies undertaken at one level can yield a payoff at the other. Moreover, in the communist view, both are but aspects of the process of the formation of the "new man." Hence, for communism, the "resolution" of the religious "question" (i.e., the liquidation of religion) is "closely linked" with the "resolution" of the national "question" (i.e., with ethnic homogenization).[127]

This chapter has been concerned specifically with delineating the way in which nationalities considerations affect religious policy and identifying broad patterns in this policy linkage in the region. I identified six factors affecting communist religious policy. The first factor—the size of the religious organization in question, insofar as size translates into power of resistance—quite simply provides a kind of insurance against suppression; hence, while the Bulgarian Muslims are being subjected to forcible Bulgarianization, a similar policy in the USSR is obviously ruled out.

The second factor—the religious organization's disposition to subordinate itself to political authority and its amenability to infiltration and control by the authorities—defines the broad patterns of church-state interaction. In practice, Orthodox churches have been far more amenable to infiltration and far more disposed to subordination than Catholic churches, though the fiery Serbian Orthodox Church, which, in the interwar period, exercised considerable influence over state policy,[128] remains an important exception. This is the explanation for the fact that Orthodoxy has proven more apt to serve as an instrument of nationalities policy than has Catholicism. In other cases (Judaism, Islam), the identification of religion and nationalism, of cult and culture, is so close that except where the collective identity thus produced has been viewed with favor (as in the case of the Yugoslav Muslims), the religious institutions have been viewed as impediments to socialist construction and, depending on the size of the community, subjected to one degree or another of persecution.

Allegiance to a foreign authority—the third factor—arises principally in connection with the Roman Catholic Church and, as a guarantee of institutional autonomy, reinforces differences already outlined in factor 2. Such allegiance is automatically viewed as anathema by the Soviets and their East European imitators.

The fourth factor—disloyalty and support of secession and of armed resistance to reincorporation—connects a religious body directly to secessionist nationalism. The Ukrainian Uniates and the Roman Catholic Church in Lithuania have suffered the most as a result of their wartime nationalism, and the cooperation of some of the Franciscans with the *Ustaše* in war-torn Yugoslavia has since been cited as a basis for charging virtually the entire Croatian Catholic Church with wartime collaboration with the Axis. The Ukrainian Orthodox and Belorussian Orthodox Churches certainly cooperated with the Nazis. But these two churches, like the Ukrainian Uniate Catholic Church, cooperated with the Nazis *because* they had been persecuted by the Soviets; it was not the other way around.

Again, the ethnic configuration of each given country—the fifth factor—affects the religious policy that is apt to be adopted. Communist elites of ethnically homogeneous states can embrace church leaders of the past as national heroes (e.g., Martin Luther in East Germany and Fr. Paisii in Bulgaria) and find it useful to do so to reinforce national pride, communal solidarity, and "socialist patriotism." Communist elites in multiethnic states are faced with a very different situation, and vaunting religious leaders of the dominant group could prove dangerous by inciting religious organizations of minority groups to revive their own religious leaders of the past, thus stirring up ecclesiastical involvement in nationalist politics—the very thing elites in multiethnic societies want most to avoid.

Finally, the political culture of a country—the sixth factor—has a direct impact on popular attitudes and behavioral responses to activities and policies of either church or state. Political culture, an ever-evolving blend of historical memory and new influences, is the sum total of popular beliefs about politics and society and may affect attitudes toward pacifism (the East German case being illustrative), ecclesiastical cooptation, and the role of the church in relation to national culture. The presence and degree of religio-national symbiosis is likewise an aspect of the political culture.

While multiethnic societies are not necessarily unstable, illegitimate regimes in multiethnic states are, because the illegitimacy of their rule reinforces the natural desire of peoples to live apart from peoples of other languages, religions, and cultures (what is sometimes called the "right of self-determination"). Religious organizations, as vestigial political organizations, are by nature disposed to involve themselves in politics. Indeed, a Serbian monk confided to me that when it comes to being "satisfied" with the religious situation in Yugoslavia, the church would only be "fully satisfied" if it *ran* the state, if it reestablished the theocracy.[129] Religious organizations thus constitute, insofar as they manifest themselves as guardians of particular peoples, an acute threat to communist regimes in multiethnic states. One might even put this conclusion in propositional form and suggest that the greater the ethnic heterogeneity of a society, the more threatening the nationally linked religious organizations of minority groups will be to illegitimate regimes.[130]

PART II

Individual Countries

THREE

Social Functions of Religion in the USSR

Religion is a political phenomenon, both in the sense that it provides an organizational principle for uniting individuals into purposive groups and in the sense that it entails an institutionalized value system that may be supportive of or in tension with the dominant culture of the social system. To analyze religion in these terms is to become interested in the social functions of religion and, more broadly, in the functional context in which religion figures.

Talcott Parsons identified four general functional imperatives that must be fulfilled in any social system if it is to be stable: pattern maintenance, integration, goal attainment, and adaptation.[1] Pattern maintenance refers to the stabilization of behavioral and institutional norms, so that social expectations are directed toward existing patterns and frameworks. Integration refers to the harmonization of the goals of the parts with the goals of the whole—or, in the context of this chapter, the harmonization of the goals of religious organizations with the goals of the communist party of the Soviet Union. Goal attainment refers to the fact that a system cannot be stable unless it satisfies certain basic needs of political community, such as defense, sustenance, and political order. And adaptation refers to the generation of institutions capable of maintaining coherence in the fulfillment of the other functions.

In any society, these basic functions must be performed. If the formal institutions designed to satisfy these requirements fail, informal institutions will spring up; corruption in the Soviet economic sector is one example of that.[2] If the original institutions that satisfied certain demands

42

are suppressed, new ones will step into the breach; thus, for example, the suppression of the independent government in Lithuania reinforced the Roman Catholic Church's role there as guardian of the national culture. Failure to perform requisite functions for a certain sector of society will have distortive effects on the system.

In speaking of the social functions of religion, one need not assume either the truth of the particular religion or the beneficence of its functions. Indeed, some of the functions of religion may be concealed or unintended; they may be by-products of intended functions, or latent functions that, for one reason or another, are not readily associated with the ecclesiastical organization.[3] On the other hand, it is important to avoid the trap of viewing any particular religion as in some sense culturally "universal." On the contrary, every religion is culturally specific, reflecting in its origins, institutions, values, authority patterns, and sociocultural assumptions the norms of a particular social order arising at a specific time. As such, the evolution of religious "dogma" constitutes a brake on the adaptive ability of a church and on change in social norms.

In the social context, religion performs several general functions. First, religion sacralizes the norms of a particular society, legitimizing the social order and providing for the ritual expiation of guilt on the part of those who violate the social norms. Second, religion socializes its members—and, to an extent, even nonmembers in some societies—to the norms and values of the given culture. Third, religion provides a bedrock of social identity. Subscription to a particular creed is one of the most basic ways in which an individual defines himself—socially, culturally, in group terms, and nationally. Fourth, religion fosters a sense of purpose in its adherents, a sense of purpose that is typically linked to a perceived need to participate in propagating the faith. And fifth, religion provides a set of answers to the fundamental questions people typically confront.[4]

This chapter has two broad arguments: first, that a functional analysis must be dynamic—specifically, that the central tasks confronting the Soviet regime have evolved and that with this evolution the calculus of religious policy has also necessarily changed; and second, that the Soviet regime has pursued functionally ambivalent policies in the religious realm that are apt to have mixed and even unforeseeable results.

THE EVOLUTION OF SOVIET RELIGIOUS POLICY

Analyses of political change in the Soviet Union must begin with the identification of the criteria for analysis. The dual criteria I have selected are the central problems and tasks confronting the regime. As these problems and tasks change, I shall argue, the nature of the system as a whole evolves. My central assumption is that politics is an integral whole in which the cultural and social components are organically related, so that systemic complications necessarily affect more than one sector of policy.

On the basis of this starting point, Soviet political development may be analyzed in terms of four phases: system destruction, 1917–23; system building, 1923–38; system maintenance, 1938–82; and system decay or rejuvenation, 1982 to the present. The phase of system building itself breaks down into two subphases: consolidation, 1923–28, and mobilization, 1928–38. These phases are, I believe, characteristic of revolutionary mass movement regimes generally.[5]

System destruction is necessarily a short phase. The revolutionary party, newly entrenched in power, is confronted with the task of uprooting the old elites, culture, and ideas. Because of the weakness of the new regime, policies may be incoherent, locally determined, even self-contradictory. Given the foreign ties enjoyed by traditional elites, this phase is typically characterized by the threat of foreign intervention and internal "counterrevolution."

In the Soviet case, this phase was characterized by a radical egalitarianism in the army (where military ranks were temporarily abolished), in sexual matters (embracing the lifting of all discriminatory restrictions against women and at the same time the encouragement of sexual promiscuity),[6] in class relations, and in interethnic relations. It was a phase of revolutionary expansionism, with a crusading fervor that pinned great hopes on signs of workers' unrest in Hungary, Germany, and elsewhere. Because of institutional and political weakness, charismatic leadership (specifically that of Lenin and Trotsky) played a vital role in cementing loyalty to the new authorities. This era saw non-Bolshevik parties operating legally and overt competition between factions within the Bolshevik party.

The years 1921–23 were clearly years of transition. The civil war was over by 1921, and rural insurrection had been suppressed by 1922. Ukrainian anarchists, the Kronstadt rebels, and Workers' Truth (an underground communist opposition) had all been crushed by 1923. Lenin was fading out of the picture, leaving routine administration to Stalin. The Mensheviks and Social Revolutionaries—leftist revolutionary parties that had continued to meet and to criticize the government openly—were wiped out by 1923 and their newspapers confiscated. Also in 1923, a new constitution for the USSR was passed, bringing the Ukraine, Belorussia, and Transcaucasia into union with the Russian Soviet Federated Socialist Republic. In the foreign policy sphere, moreover, the failures of Comintern-inspired efforts to spread revolution in Germany in 1921 and 1923 led to the demotion of the Comintern and the realization that world revolution was not around the corner.[7]

Shaken by the anti-Bolshevik rebellion of March 1921 and constrained by economic rigors to rebuild the economy, the Bolshevik regime adopted its New Economic Policy of limited laissez faire and succeeded, by 1923, in stabilizing the ruble. With the uprooting of the old elites and the successful repulsion of foreign intervention, the chief tasks of the system building phase were the consolidation of power and the penetration of society by the regime apparatus and the building of a new society (socialist construction).

System building involves a growth in the strength of political institutions, the undertaking of postponed programs (of modernization, socialization, and social homogenization), the ripening of a cult of personality, and the subordination of the party to the cult leader (and hence also the triumph of one faction over all others).

In the Soviet case, the consolidation subphase (1923–28) saw general policy relaxation in the economy, cultural life, politics, and nationalities policy. At the Twelfth Party Congress in April 1923, for instance, party members were ordered to advance and support the cultures of non-Russian peoples—and the result was a period of literary creativity and cultural renaissance in Belorussia and Ukraine. In gender relations, this subphase saw a reversal of the assault on "bourgeois" mores,[8] but also a sweeping attack on traditional society in Central Asia, encouraging women to initiate divorce proceedings and to compete with men for jobs and organizing mass unveilings. In the educational sphere, this subphase saw the creation of the People's Commissariat for Enlightenment, headed by Anatole Lunacharsky, which assumed responsibility for supervising all schools, theaters, museums, art galleries, libraries, and media. Soviet literature in the early 1920s focused on the civil war but still displayed considerable aesthetic diversity. In particular, a literary group known as the Serapion Brothers advocated nonconformism in art and won a guarantee of "coexistence" at a special session of the Central Committee in June 1925.[9] In foreign policy, it was a period of retrenchment.

The mobilization subphase (1928–38) was the era of the so-called Third Revolution, in which Stalin launched radical programs of collectivization and forced industrialization, harnessing agencies of mass mobilization such as the Stakhanovite movement and the League of Militant Atheists. In nationalities policy, this subphase saw a reversal of laissez faire and a re-Russification of Ukraine, with renewed emphasis on the assimilation of non-Russian peoples to a common "Soviet" culture. Advocates of local autonomy were purged as "bourgeois nationalists" (e.g., in Tadzhikistan in 1934 and 1937) and the presence of Russian cadres in the borderlands came to be seen as permanent. By the end of this phase, the Cyrillic alphabet had replaced the Latin alphabet in the Central Asian languages and the use of Russian was compulsory in all Soviet schools. In the sphere of gender relations, the drive toward centralization entailed the abolition of Zhenotdel (the party agency for women's affairs) in 1930, the subordination of the political interest of gender equality to the economic interest of industrial development (and hence the encouragement of women to enter the labor force), and the reversal of the policy of condemnation of the "bourgeois" family and the invention of the concept of the "socialist" family. In the cultural-educational sphere, a new rigidity was imposed when, in 1930, Soviet philosophers were ordered to accept Marxism-Leninism-Stalinism as the only legitimate philosophy. The following year, historians were informed that there could be no questioning of any of Lenin's views or pronouncements. And in line with this, the contents of the children's magazine *Murzilka* evolved from nature stories and verse (in 1928) to such patriotic themes as the foreign menace, the army, and Stalin (in 1938).[10]

The political, economic, cultural, and social changes that came in the mobilization subphase could not be effected without terror, and in the years 1934–38, between seven and twenty-three million persons were liquidated.[11] The terror extended to the party itself, and 60 percent of the membership in 1933 was out of the party by January 1939. Between the Seventeenth Party Congress (1934) and the Eighteenth (1939), more than two thirds of the members of the Central Committee were liquidated.

The end of this phase was signaled by the passage of the "Stalin Constitution" in 1936, the beginning of the rehabilitation of Russian nationalism between 1936 and 1938, the end of the terror in 1938, and the resumption of an active foreign policy in 1939 (with the annexation of eastern Poland and the invasion of Finland).

A stable system cannot be founded on terror and mobilization; these tactics can only be tools in a transient phase of system building. The subsequent phase of system maintenance entails the creation of stable institutions and stable procedures for conflict resolution. The chief tasks are institutionalization, the stabilization of political patterns, and the reaffirmation of party control over the terror apparatus and of collective rule over one-man rule. The increasingly technical demands of a complex society produce new challenges to which mobilization-style responses are inappropriate. The Soviet response (1938–82) was to coopt new social elites and technocrats into the apparatus, at the price of access sharing and the tacit toleration of something akin to interest-group formation. Stabilization in cadres gave rise to the gerontocracy of the late Brezhnev period, as the leadership endeavored to provide assurance to its apparatchiks. Stabilization also meant stricter adherence to schedules for meetings of leading institutions of party and state, renewed emphasis on socialist legality, a repudiation of the cult of the leader, and a relaxation of demands for various kinds of "vigilance."

System maintenance cannot be a static end state, however; in fact, the original system cannot be maintained indefinitely at all because it is tied to a revolutionary vision specific to a given period. Social, economic, and cultural change cannot be averted; and in a collectivist system, such change is apt to strain the political levers of control. Hence, at a certain point, the choice is between adapting the political system (political change) and allowing it to deteriorate.

While it is decidedly more difficult to demarcate a clear boundary between the Soviet Union's system maintenance phase and its phase of system decay or rejuvenation, 1982 may serve as a useful signpost insofar as it was the year Brezhnev died and thus the year the Soviets began to confront the need for rejuvenation. The Soviets themselves are most conscious of the dilemma as it presents itself in the economic sphere. In the first sixteen months after Gorbachev succeeded to the general secretaryship of the party, the Soviet press became the forum for a public discussion of economic reform unparalleled since the early 1960s. Some writers explicitly endorsed Hungarian-style market socialism and urged the USSR to adopt it as a model. Academicians Tatiana Zaslavskaia and Abel Aganbegian of the Academy of Sciences in Novosibirsk have called for a thorough reassessment of the suitability of central planning, while Evgeni Ambartsumov, another Soviet economist, advocated a return to Lenin's New Economic Policy, with its legalization of the free market and small private enterprises.[12] In February 1986, moreover, Gorbachev told the Twenty-seventh Party Congress that the time for partial remedies was over and a "radical reform," even a "profound transformation in the economy," could not be averted.[13]

The basic problem is that Soviet functionaries, saddled with a system that cannot work, have established informal patterns (corruption) that keep it going in the absence of an institutional reformation. In the long run, such makeshift solutions build up networks of interests that distort political processes and affect the hierarchical flow of plans, instructions, and information. The assault by Andropov and Gorbachev on corruption is a result of Soviet recognition that the problem is one of the system qua system.

This latest phase has also seen a serious reexamination of the premises of Soviet policy in the developing world,[14] a reopening of debate on the nationalities problem,[15] and warnings—in a manifesto allegedly written by a high Soviet official and signed by the "Movement of Socialist Renewal," November 21, 1985—that the Soviet bloc is coming apart, that the USSR is in danger of becoming a second-rate power both technologically and militarily, and that reform should be sought in the legalization of private enterprise, a free press, freedom of speech and religion, and the right to organize political opposition.

To recapitulate: The phase of system destruction involves completion of the tasks of destroying the old order, rewriting history, and suppressing counterrevolution. The phase of system building entails the consolidation of power by the party over the society and by a faction over the party, the mobilization of the population for economic tasks, and the inception of social homogenization (Russification, atheization, Sovietization). The phase of system maintenance involves the creation of stable institutions and stable procedures for conflict resolution, the reaffirmation of party control over the terror apparatus, and the cooptation of skilled elites. And finally, the phase of system decay or rejuvenation challenges the regime to reverse corruption, reform the economic sector (improving its efficiency), open up society so as to benefit from cultural and technological advances elsewhere in the world, and terminate programs of social homogenization. Thus summarized, the model holds that, given the unworkability of collectivism, revolutionary mass movement regimes are inherently self-destructive, so that their practitioners must in time either seek rejuvenation through the abandonment of significant portions of their operational programs or reconcile themselves to steady and ineluctable decay.

In the context of these dynamics, the Soviet regime's policy toward religion evolved through a series of parallel phases. In the phase of system destruction, the party, absorbed with the task of assailing the Old Order to which the Russian Orthodox Church was organically tied, looked for all possible allies. Accordingly, it adopted the policy of encouraging small sects, even while applying pressure on the larger churches. In line with this policy, the party proclaimed freedom of religion, including the freedom of religious propaganda, and authorized the publication of a number of Protestant religious books and pamphlets, even allowing conscientious objectors to serve in hospitals instead of in the Red Army. While Russian Orthodox churches and monasteries were looted and desecrated and priests assaulted and sometimes murdered or sent to labor camps, the Bolsheviks simultaneously tried to weaken the Orthodox Church by encouraging Old Believers and members of other breakaway sects to come out into the open (in a decree of February 5, 1921). In this atmosphere, the Ukrainian Autocephalous Orthodox Church seceded from the Moscow patriarchate in 1921, and a Belorussian Autocephalous Orthodox Church emerged in July 1922.[16] This policy of religious fragmentation paralleled the policy of ethnic *razmezhavanie,* whereby the Bolsheviks attempted to divide larger nationality groups into smaller ones.[17] However, the policy of encouragement of sects was too successful, and membership in the sects grew rapidly. Thus, in 1923, the party abandoned the policy of religious *razmezhavanie* and the antireligious campaign was generalized to embrace all the sects.

In the consolidation subphase, the party moved to consolidate its authority in the religious sphere, setting up additional organizations to carry out its policy and attempting to undercut the Russian Orthodox Church by sponsoring the establishment of a schismatic "Living Church" or "Renovationist Church" (created 1922–23), with a "reformist" and "loyalist" orientation. This church was a vibrant competitor to the patriarchal church for only a few years, but remnants of it survived until the 1940s.[18]

The State Publishing House for Antireligious Literature and the weekly newspaper *Bezbozhnik* (The Godless) were created during this subphase (in 1924). In February 1925, the League of Militant Atheists came into being, headed by Emelyan Yaroslavsky. Though there was no religious NEP, except to a limited degree in Central Asia, religious policy in the mid-1920s was clearly in a premobilization subphase—as evinced in a decision taken by educational authorities in 1925, that "special implanting of antireligious views into each child is not needed."[19]

A sharp redirection came in 1928 in religious policy as in other spheres. In conjunction with the launching of the first Five-Year Plan that year, the party set in motion an intensified campaign against religion; at the same time, it called on the Soviet movie industry to undertake subtler and more effective techniques to turn moviegoers against religion.[20] In addition:

> In 1929, "Godless shock brigades," "Godless factories," and "Godless collective farms" made their appearance. These detachments of industrial or agricultural workers vowed to fulfill high production quotas, while simultaneously carrying on antireligious propaganda. [But] although they were constantly urged to be uncompromising toward religious belief, their members rarely demonstrated the requisite militancy.[21]

The League of Militant Atheists unleashed an often violent antireligious campaign, lasting from 1930 to 1935. More than 95 percent of the 100,000 places of worship that had been in operation in 1917 were shut down, and large numbers of clergy were murdered, exiled, or imprisoned. All religious publications were terminated. In 1917, there had been 46,457 Russian Orthodox churches, 50,960 priests, and 130 bishops; by 1941, the church could tally only 4,225 churches, 5,665 active priests, and 28 bishops.

In this mobilization subphase, the Islamic community lost its ostensible immunity from direct assault. As early as 1927, the regime had started pressuring Muslim women to discard their veils. In 1928, it began rounding up Muslim ulema and confiscating or destroying large numbers of mosques (some of which became movie theaters or prisons).

The earlier toleration of the Ukrainian and Belorussian Orthodox Churches was reversed, since ecclesiastical separatism was now associated in the regime's view with "bourgeois nationalism." In October 1928, the Ukrainian church was constrained to depose its metropolitan (Lypkivsky) and replace him with a more pro-Soviet bishop (Mykola Boretsky). Fifteen months later, an extraordinary church assembly accused itself of "nationalist counterrevolutionary and anti-Soviet activity," thus signing the church's death warrant. Similarly, in Belorussia, the confluence of the antinationalist and antireligious campaigns of 1928–38 led to the "complete extermination" of the Belorussian Church:

> Its three bishops, Filaret of Bobruisk, Mikhail of Slutsk, and Ioann of Mozyr, died in prisons and concentration camps. All the more prominent priests, including all the signatories of the Minsk statement setting up the Autocephalous Church (in 1922), were also arrested. By July 1937 not a single priest continued to celebrate the liturgy in Belorussia, and not a single church remained open.[22]

A new religious law, passed in 1929, withdrew the earlier right of religious propaganda. The constitution henceforth guaranteed "freedom of religion and freedom of antireligious propaganda." This law also banned church involvement in any social, charitable, or educational activity, and the organization by the churches of special meetings for children, young people, or women. It also gave state authorities broad rights of control and intervention, including the power to abolish a religious organization.[23]

Between 1928 and 1938, the Soviet regime succeeded in greatly weakening the Russian Orthodox Church and cowing other religious organizations. It thereby dislodged religious organizations from primary involvement in pattern maintenance and made possible the reintegration of the church on a new basis—a goal that would be attempted and partially realized in the next phase, system maintenance.

Besides the sheer enervation of the churches, two other factors made for a change of policy between 1938 and 1941: the rehabilitation of Russian nationalism by 1938 and the German invasion in 1941 that resulted in Stalin's needing church support. The League of Militant Atheists was closed just three months after the German invasion, and the antireligious journals were shut down. Stalin himself received Orthodox Metropolitan Sergei in September 1943 and promised to restore rights guaranteed under the 1929 law. Some bishops and priests were released from prison. There was a thaw in church-state relations until the mid-1950s, and more than 17,000 churches were reopened.

The regime endeavored to promote its candidates in ecclesiastical hierarchies and to "coopt" religious elites into partnership with the state. The result has been a distinction between "official Islam" and the underground Sufi movement; a split between legal "official Baptists" and illegal, unregistered Baptists who refuse to cooperate with the state; and a differentiation, on the part of the authorities, between "cooperative" and "uncooperative" Orthodox bishops.

The inability of the regime to accomplish a "functional synthesis" of churches with the party program in harmony with the functional imperative of integration (as defined earlier)—and, more specifically, party awareness that the churches figured as the purveyors of distinct value systems and the vehicles of independent organizational principles—underlay the continued hostility shown by the regime toward religion in the system maintenance phase. The antireligious drive of 1958–61 was an expression of this functional disharmony.

At the same time, the Khrushchev regime introduced new socialist rituals (for the naming of children and for marriages and funerals) in the late 1950s and early 1960s, believing that the rituals would assist in secularizing popular consciousness and in inculcating communist values. The initiative for the creation of these rituals was taken in Latvia, Estonia, and Leningrad at the end of the 1950s and was picked up after 1963 in several regional capitals of the Russian Soviet Federated Socialist Republic and in certain parts of Ukraine. Soviet ritual engineers drew essentially on Slavic (both Christian and pre-Christian) rituals, ignoring Islamic and other non-Slavic heritages. These engineers have also tended to prefer pagan rituals to Christian ones as a basis for deriving new socialist rites.[24] They view ritual as a tool of "culture management," as Christel Lane put it, and as a form of socialization that may promote group solidarity and inculcate certain value orientations in participants.[25]

In the 1980s, there are, in Borys Lewytzkyj's assessment, "probably more believers in the Soviet Union than twenty to thirty years ago." For Lewytzkyj, that means "the Soviet leadership has lost its struggle against religion."[26] If the regime's sole concern were to reduce the number of believers, this datum would be a sufficient basis for judgment. Yet Soviet sources suggest that the regime's religious policy has at least three other main goals: effective control of the churches,[27] attenuation of the fervor of religious devotion,[28] and disassociation of religious and national identity.[29] (In addition, the regime has endeavored to infiltrate communist values into religious rituals and publications to bring about the functional "integration" of religion and socialism[30].) These three goals, which display a close correspondence to the social functions of religion outlined at the outset of this chapter, provide a key to assess whether Soviet religious policy stands at a crossroads.

On this basis, the record is mixed. On the first goal, the Soviet regime is still far from controlling religious life, but has, all the same, succeeded in dramatically circumscribing it and in channeling some of its energies (e.g., the foreign activity of the Russian Orthodox Church) into patterns useful to communist policy needs. On the second goal, while some statistics support the unsurprising contention that urban residents are less religious than rural residents (and hence that urbanization promotes secularization), there is now considerable question as to whether religion is really in decline, in the USSR or elsewhere,[31] and research by David Powell, in particular, found that Soviet mass oral propaganda measures designed to foster secularization were failing miserably and generally only reached the "de-converted".[32] On the third goal, Soviet anxieties over the effects of the "Polish model," 1980–81, on believers in the Soviet republics of Lithuania, Belorussia, and Ukraine is itself evidence that the regime is a long way from decoupling religious and national identity.

What this brief analysis suggests is that as the regime confronts new sets of tasks and as the society evolves through a series of organically related phases of political development, the social functions of religious organizations change, too. Already in the 1920s, the destruction of the anti-Bolshevik resistance forced the Orthodox patriarch to break his links with the political opposition. More particularly, Orthodox Christianity gradually assimilated certain strands of the dominant ideology, and Orthodox theologians in the USSR now commonly preach the compatibility of communism and Christianity. Similarly, among Soviet Baptists one can find ministers who preach equality of women and men.[33]

On the other hand, as the system chokes off career channels to believers and denies them forums for the intellectual development of their faith, religious belief (especially among certain Protestant denominations) acquires the function of sustaining a kind of ghetto mentality, alienated from the mainstream of Soviet life. As L. A. Serdobel'skaia put it in 1974,

> a deliberately negative attitude toward literature, the drama, and Soviet culture is instilled in sectarian youth. Children from "Initsiativniki" Baptist families in Leningrad show no interest in reading works of creative literature. The overall level of culture and horizon of these children is noticeably lower than that of other children of their age.[34]

The regime's program of atheization has produced differences of religiosity within families, thus undercutting one dimension of family cohesion. It has also resulted in the appearance of large numbers of "vacillators" who continue to participate in religious rites but without conviction; religion only serves to connect them with their heritage or allows them to postpone a more complete reevaluation of their world view.[35]

FUNCTIONAL AMBIVALENCE

This analysis would seem to suggest that the premises of Soviet religious policy are in decay and that a reexamination of this policy on the part of Soviet authorities would not be without reason. What is the functional evidence of decay?

Soviet religious policy has targeted both the manifest (devotional) and latent (e.g., nationalist) functions of religious organizations. The connection between secularization and internationalization, thus, is often made by Soviet writers. I. M. Dzhabbarov put it this way:

> A further development of the Soviet way of life and the reorganization of the everyday life of the Soviet people on a communist basis serves as an active factor in promoting an intensification of the secularization of the entire mode of life and of family and domestic relations. Even such stable elements of everyday life as housing, clothing, food, family and marriage relations, and rites and rituals, when they become subjected to the influence of the process of internationalization and of the Soviet way of life, gradually become free of religious survivals. As a result of the internationalization of social life and of culture and everyday life there occurs a substantial weakening of the connections and then a complete break between the religious and the national moments.[36]

But, ironically, in targeting this latent (nationalist) function, Soviet religious policy has converted it into a manifest function, both in the sense of calling attention to church nationalism and in the sense of aggravating local sensitivities and driving belief and nationalism closer together.[37]

In fashioning policies to deal with religion and nationalism (both being viewed as divisive identities with extrasystemic loyalties), the Soviet authorities have marshaled a strange conglomerate of instruments, ranging from the promotion of corrupt and intoxicated priests,[38] to the ostensible toleration of neo-Nazis (including some with an Orthodox Christian cast),[39] to calls for the purification of Islam (of pre-Islamic accretions),[40] to the resurrection of pagan cults.[41] These policies may be apt to have mixed and unforeseen results (as was the case in earlier Bolshevik support for Protestant and schismatic sects). But these examples suggest something else—that there is an ad hoc quality about facets of Soviet religious policy; such an ad hoc quality is inconsistent with the concept of "culture management" and reflects persistent uncertainties in policy framing.

Yu. V. Arutiunian, a Soviet ethnographer, admitted the difficulty of framing a consistent and coherent nationalities policy in 1969. According to him, Soviet experience had prompted the conclusion that "there can be no universally valid means of improving ethnic relationships. A given technique may lead to different and sometimes even directly opposite results in different social groups."[42] The same could just as easily be said of Soviet religious policy.

CONCLUSION

This chapter has presented a case for analyzing the social functions of religion in the context of a four-phase model of Soviet political development. It argued that the dynamics of policymaking in each phase are universal across policy spheres and urged that an assessment of the successes or failures of Soviet religious policy must take into account the functions that the policy was designed to perform. And in the case of religio-national symbiosis, Soviet policy was found to be functionally ambivalent, in that it simultaneously assails and reinforces the linkage of religious and national identity.

FOUR

Catholicism and National Culture in Poland, Czechoslovakia, and Hungary

Poland, Czechoslovakia, and Hungary are all predominantly Catholic countries, ruled by communist parties since the late 1940s. They also have other features in common. All three achieved sovereignty after World War One, ending centuries of foreign overlordship. All three had the experience of being parts of traditional feudal empires (specifically, of tsarist Russia and Habsburg Austria). All three were concerned in the interwar period with questions of ethnic heterogeneity (though in the Hungarian case, irredentism had a much stronger claim on the popular mind). And in the 1930s, the proportion of the population that was Catholic was, across the three cases, nearly identical.

Yet despite these salient commonalities, church-state relations in these three countries are divergent today. In Poland, the Roman Catholic Church has obvious grass-roots strength and has been able to maintain a defiant posture toward a regime that has shown its hostility to the church by unleashing, since the beginning of the decade, a systematic campaign of harassment and intimidation. Religiosity remains intense, and candidates for the priesthood are plentiful. In Czechoslovakia, by contrast, the Catholic Church has waned in the Czech lands and only held its own in more agrarian Slovakia; it is under pressure in both parts of the country. Whereas Polish communists from the beginning ruled out, as unrealistic, any notion of drawing the Catholic Church away from communion with the Vatican,[1] Czechoslovak communists, including the Slovak party's first

55

secretary, Vasil Bilak, have recently suggested that a break between the local church and the Vatican may be a precondition for a "normalization" of church-state relations. Religiosity among Czechs is generally characterized as weak, while the training of priests is controlled and obstructed by the party. In Hungary, the Catholic Church enjoys the protection of the state, is able to operate eight high schools, and has not had to worry, in recent memory, about harassment or obstruction by the authorities. The price paid for this relationship is a generally supportive attitude toward what is, in any event, a relatively liberal communist regime.

How, given the numerous factors common to the three societies, is one to account for these strikingly different patterns of church-state interaction today? The argument that will be made in this chapter is that religio-national symbiosis plays a key role as an intervening variable between historical and present patterns. Or, put another way, the present aspect of religio-national symbiosis reflects the distillation of historical patterns and, in turn, sets limits to the possibilities in present church-state relations.

The method employed in this analysis is geneticism-monism, a specific incarnation of the dialectical method. Geneticism-monism, as an analytical methodology, was developed by G. W. F. Hegel and perfected by the Young Hegelians (Bruno Bauer, David Friedrich Strauss, Ludwig Feuerbach, Friedrich Theodor Vischer, Max Stirner, and others). Geneticism is predicated on the assumption that any phenomenon or pattern in history can be understood only if its origin and evolution are understood; consideration merely of present functions is apt to be misleading.[2] As such, geneticism is hostile to functional analysis, which reverses the priorities. The influence of geneticism can be seen in the work of Sigmund Freud, who believed that the cure of neurosis could not be accomplished merely by identifying the functions being performed by neurotic behavior but entailed an exegesis of the origins of the neurosis as such.

Monism is the natural complement of geneticism. It is the belief in the interconnectedness of reality and the reducibility of forms to each other. A monist sees art, philosophy, institutions, economics, ideas, and ideals as related, so that it becomes possible to ask, for example, whether certain art forms are compatible with certain political institutions. For a monist, the reason why social stress, even though it is focused in a specific sector, may have perturbations across cultural forms and give rise to widespread self-doubt and critical rethinking, is that all facets of human society have social meanings that express the values and orientations of the epoch.[3] Monism sets geneticism in context and ties its findings to a given political-cultural configuration. Monism is not necessarily reductionist. Marx inherited Young Hegelian monism and chose to give it a reductionist thrust, tracing changes in the "superstructure" of political institutions and art forms to changes in the economic "base." The Young Hegelians made no such assumption of unidirectionality of change; on the contrary, they thought that all spheres of society were susceptible to stress and change, producing new stresses and corresponding changes in their wake.

FACTORS AFFECTING RELIGIO-NATIONAL SYMBIOSIS

The presence or absence and the particular configuration of religio-national symbiosis cannot be presumed. In some regions, religion may be the most important formative agent of national identity, while in other regions and among other peoples it may be of secondary importance. Pašić, for instance, lists religion as the fourth most important factor in the formation of nations in the Balkans, behind political states, ethnic and linguistic variables, and cultural factors.[4] Nations may view their churches as bastions of defense of the national culture, as in the case of the Poles, Croats, Serbs, and Bulgarians, or they may view their churches as somehow antinational, as in the case of the Czechs. Or, sentiment may fall somewhere between these extremes, as in the case of the Slovaks, Hungarians, Romanians, and Germans.

Among the factors affecting religio-national symbiosis in Eastern Europe and the Soviet West, one may list the following:

Ethnic mix. Is the country ethnically homogeneous or not? If not, do the component national groups have common external foes and allies?

Confessional mix. Are there two or more rival churches, each claiming to be the authentic voice of a given group (as in the case of the Slovaks, Hungarians, Romanians, and Ukrainians), or does a single church have a monopoly on nationalism (as in the Polish, Croatian, Serbian, Bulgarian, and Lithuanian cases)? Is the dominant religion of the largest national group also the dominant religion of other national groups? Are other confessional groups indifferent to national mythology?

Previous history of church cooptation or opposition. If nationalism is identified with the governing class or party, a cooptive relationship with the church may foster religio-national symbiosis. Alternatively, foreign rule may confront the church with a choice between governmental hostility and popular hostility.

Traditional class roots of the church. Is a given religion perceived as being the legacy of the upper class (as may be the case in Bohemia), or is it viewed as also the traditional religion of the lower class (as is clearly the case in Poland)?

The specific content of the given faith. What is the dominant confession's attitude toward history, culture, authority, and conscience? How much emphasis does the dominant confession place on the good of the collective, and how much on the integrity of the individual? Croatian theologian Šagi-Bunić describes Catholicism as a "point of departure" for nationalism insofar as it engenders values caring for the community.[5] Protestantism, by contrast, is generally understood to place less emphasis than Catholicism on authority and received tradition, and more emphasis on individual judgment and conscience.

The Polish, Czechoslovak, and Hungarian cases will be used to examine and test the following hypotheses:

1. Trauma concentrated in one sphere of society necessarily affects other spheres. Insofar as trauma necessitates policy reappraisal, its effects will penetrate through several issue areas.

2. The closer the religio-national symbiosis, the more difficult it is for the state to maintain a purely confrontational attitude toward religion.

3. The experience of the Counter-Reformation created a tradition of anticlericalism that makes the church more vulnerable.

4. Confessional strength is positively correlated with national symbiosis and resistance to foreign oppression, and negatively correlated with antinational demeanor and cooptation by or alliance with foreign rulers.

5. If nationalism is oppositionist in orientation, church posture must also be oppositionist if religion and nationalism are to be symbiotic.

THE CHURCH IN POLAND: OPPOSITIONIST NATIONALISM

The Polish Catholic clergy is fond of speaking of the historical association of Christianity and Polish culture[6]—by which it means Catholicism and Polish culture. Yet Protestantism was an important social force in Poland for some 130 years (from about 1520 to about 1650); in Silesia, the population was overwhelmingly Protestant as recently as the second half of the seventeenth century.[7] Lutheran, Calvinist, Socinian, Anabaptist, and other groups spread into Poland from Germany, France, Bohemia, and Italy. Polish Calvinism had its center in Little Poland (Malopolska) after its introduction there in 1546.[8] By the end of the sixteenth century, these diverse Protestant denominations had developed a dynamic presence in many Polish towns. The failure of Polish Protestantism to leave any important mark may be traced to at least three factors. First, one may mention the lack of organization in the Protestant churches in Poland and the difficulties they experienced in trying to cooperate with each other.[9] Second, whatever its strength in the towns, Protestantism failed to take root among the peasantry.[10] And third, in contrast to the situation elsewhere, Polish Protestantism failed to produce intellectual spokesmen of the caliber of Catholic intellectuals Jan Laskii, Andrzej Frycz Modrzewski, and Stanislaw Hozjusz.[11]

The central fact in the development of modern Polish nationalism is the century of partition, from November 25, 1795, to the end of World War One in 1918. This fact not only colored Poland's attitude toward the outside world but also cemented its bond with Roman Catholicism, even though the Holy See—concerned above all with protecting its own interests, whether in annexed territories or in a sovereign Poland—assured the partitioning powers (Austria, Prussia, and Tsarist Russia) that it "accepted" the partition as "inevitable."[12] A series of autonomous or nominally autonomous national reincarnations (the Duchy of Warsaw, 1807–46; Kongresowska, 1815–17; the Republic of Cracow, 1815–46; the Grand Duchy of Posen, 1815–49; and the "Kingdom of Poland," under German auspices, set up in November 1916) helped keep alive the Polish idea. But they were no substitute for self-determination, and, in consequence, Polish nationalism took on the character of resistance and sometimes insurrection. To be a Polish patriot meant to be in opposition.

Ironically, the Roman Catholic hierarchy, in the eighteenth and nineteenth centuries, was unsymphathetic to Polish nationalism, and the Polish-Catholic equation was more important in border areas than in homogeneously Catholic areas. Even so, Catholicism has been a major component of Polish identity. Indeed, the loss of statehood encouraged Polish national consciousness to focus above all on religion and language as the mainstays of national being. Moreover, of the three partitioning powers, only the sole Catholic power, Austria, pursued a tolerant policy toward the Poles, and that prevented the Austrian Catholic ecclesiastical hierarchy from being seen as inimical to Polish cultural survival. Protestant Prussia and Orthodox Russia posed more fundamental threats.

In the Russian pale (sometimes called Vistulaland) the church fared the worst. The Russian court viewed Catholicism as a tool of Polish nationalism within Russia, and, as early as 1772, immediately after the first of the three partitions that removed Poland from the map, Catherine II forbade the Catholic clergy to communicate directly with the Holy See.[13] Some Poles tried a conciliatory tactic, aspiring to play the role of Greeks to the new Rome.[14] Fr. Staszic hoped, for instance, to use Russian political leadership and power to buttress Polish cultural leadership in Europe. Similarly, August Cieszkowski (1814–1894), a Hegelian trained at the University of Berlin, believed that the Catholic Church and the Polish nation alike had a divine mission and looked forward to a Catholic utopia he called the Era of the Holy Spirit.

Ultimately, however, persistent efforts at Russification, together with unremitting pressure on the Catholic faith, undermined the conciliatory line and reinforced the insurrectionary spirit.

In "Vistulaland," Catholic clergy were subject to control, and obstacles were erected to the promotion of Catholics in the army and the bureaucracy; the Catholic clergy lost their estates and their dioceses were reorganized. The Greek-Rite (Uniate) Catholic Church was given especially harsh treatment; during three periods (1770s–90s, 1830s, and 1860s), the Russian army was summoned to compel mass conversions to Orthodoxy.[15] As Norman Davies stated in his history of Poland:

> Papal bulls could not be published in Russia without the assent of St. Petersburg, and were often ignored or countermanded. . . . Books were burned; churches destroyed; priests murdered; services conducted according to the Orthodox rite under the shadow of bayonets. In 1839, all contact between the Uniate Church in Russia and the Vatican was severed. In 1875, the Union of Brest was itself officially annulled. By 1905, when a decree of religious toleration was finally exacted, no more than 200,000 Uniates were left to practise their faith openly. In all these religious policies, there is no doubt that the prime motivation was political.[16]

Roman Catholicism was a religion of the West, subject to a foreign prelate (the pope), and thus suspect. Russian Orthodoxy, by contrast, was under the tsarist thumb and was viewed as a pillar of imperial stability.

Indeed, St. Petersburg remained suspicious of the Polish provinces per se and therefore excluded them from even the limited grants of self-government that were extended (e.g., to the cities in 1775, to the *zemstva* after 1864). When the Poles revolted, the tsars struck back at the "Polish Church." Hence, after the Polish insurrection of 1831, which spread also to Lithuania, the tsar took reprisals against the Catholic Church, which he viewed as a den of "Latin propaganda." And after the insurrection of 1863, the tsar began shutting down monasteries and closing schools (usually monastic) in which Polish was the language of instruction. According to Davies:

> As a result of the November [1830] Rising, almost half of the Latin convents of Russian Poland were closed, while payment of the stipends of the clergy was turned over to the state. Unauthorized correspondence with Rome was punishable with summary deportation. All sermons, pronouncements, and religious publications were to be approved by the Tsarist censorship. All seminaries were to be inspected by the Tsarist police. As a result of the January [1863] Rising, the great majority of Catholic orders were disbanded. The entire landed property of the Church was confiscated together with the estates of lay patrons of Catholic benefices. The conduct of the Sacred College was placed under the Ministry of the Interior, and all business

between the College and the diocesan curias was handed over to lay police-approved delegates.[17]

Around mid-century, Russian intellectuals and authorities began extolling the "superiority" of the Russian language over all other European languages and equating the speaking of a foreign language with political disloyalty. Russification began in earnest. A Russianized Catholic Church, with the rituals in Russian, was supposed to serve as a vehicle of Russification. Accordingly, a Russian-language liturgical book was issued to replace the Polish one.[18] After 1864, moreover, Polish teachers were obliged to use Russian as the medium of instruction for all subjects, including religion, and even for teaching Polish to Polish children.[19] Field Marshal Iosif Hurko (1828–1911), governor-general in Warsaw from 1883 to 1894, was a leading advocate of the Russification of the Poles. Under his governorship, the Cyrillic alphabet was actively promoted in public places and street signs appeared in both Russian and Polish. The legacy of Russian occupation, then, was to reinforce an earlier tendency to view Orthodoxy as a foreign religion, Catholicism as the Polish religion, and tsardom as hostile to the Polish soul.

The Prussian partition initially fared better, enjoying some autonomy in the "Grand Duchy of Posen" between 1815 and 1848 and benefiting from the generally more tolerant policy toward religion.[20] German unification changed Poland's situation when Bismarck launched his *Kulturkampf* in 1873. As a result, the use of Polish in state schools was banned, except for religious instruction, and teachers were barred from joining either Polish or Catholic societies. A year earlier, under regime pressure, the primate of Prussian Poland, Archbishop Mieczyslaw Ledochowski of Gnesen (1822–1902), had agreed that *Boze cos Polske* would no longer be sung at Holy Mass. In 1873, after he resisted growing government interference in religious instruction and the operation of theological seminaries, he was imprisoned, along with ninety other Polish priests. As Davies noted, the anti-Catholic edge of the *Kulturkampf* served to identify Polishness and Catholicity, and in Silesia, the Polish national movement was now captured by such radical priests as Fr. Jozef Szafranek (1807–74).[21]

Ironically, until the *Kulturkampf* and its attendant aggressive German assimilatory efforts, Germanization had been proceeding steadily. The sharpening of policy backfired and produced resistance. Protestant Germany, like Orthodox Russia, showed itself inimical to Polish culture and nationality. The German attitude is well summed up by Max Weber's remark: "Only we Germans could have made human beings out of these Poles."[22]

By contrast, Austrian rule seemed benign almost to the point of altruism.[23] In 1869, for instance, the Polish language was put on an equal footing with German in Galicia and came to be used in all official business. In 1870, the Jagiellonian University was allowed to reinstate Polish as the principal language of instruction; two years later, the Academy of Learning (Akademia Umiejetnosci) was established in Cracow. A Polish literary, cultural, and scholarly renaissance developed under Habsburg rule, centered in the universities of Cracow and Lemberg (Lwow). In Lemberg, theaters presented plays in Polish and operas in Polish and Italian (solos generally in Italian, choruses in Polish). Earlier, in 1827, Jozef Maksimilian Ossolinski had created the Ossolineum in Lemberg for the dissemination of Polish arts and sciences. The Habsburgs permitted the founding also of the Polish Historical Society in Lemberg and, in 1884, the Polish historical journal *Kwartalnik Historyczny*.

In political terms, the Ausgleich Law of December 21, 1867, created an elective legislature and a provincial executive body for Galicia. In 1871, a Ministry of Galician Affairs was established in Vienna to defend Galicia's interests. In Habsburg theory, the Poles were considered a "historical people," alongside Germans and Hungarians, and thus entitled to greater consideration and privileges than such "unhistorical peoples" as the Slovaks and Romanians.

The Catholic Habsburg regime viewed Polish Catholicism with favor. The only difference was that instead of praying to "the Virgin Mary, Queen of Poland," Austria's subjects in Galicia were urged to pray to "the Virgin Mary, Queen of Galicia and Lodomeria."[24] And while Habsburg rule meant a policy of subordinating church to state and resulted at one point in the closing of hundreds of monastic orders, the Holy See displayed complete equanimity in regard to Galicia—and, for that matter, in regard to the Prussian and Russian occupations. The Holy See did not in fact show any particular interest in the Polish question per se during the period of the partitions, advising Poles to let the established authorities administer the affairs "of this world"; Pope Leo XIII even issued an encyclical urging Polish bishops to adopt a posture of loyalty toward their respective governments. Still, the Holy See was not indifferent to its own interests, and subsequently, in an encyclical of April 24, 1864, Pope Pius IX chastized "the [Russian] potentate who oppresses his Catholic subjects."[25]

At least two factors prevented anticlericalism (which would have sundered the religio-national linkage) from becoming a dominant trend in Galicia: First, by contrast with Germany and Russia, Catholic Austria was permitting, even encouraging, a Polish cultural renaissance and Galician prosperity; and second, by contrast with the Holy See, the lower clergy— in Galicia as well as in "Vistulaland" and eastern Germany—was closely bound with the lives of the parishioners and took active parts in the political movements of the day.[26]

The restoration of independence did not attenuate the church's oppositionist legacy. Although the constitutions of 1921 and 1935 assured the Roman Catholic Church of preeminence among the religious denominations of Poland, with the government paying Catholic priests' salaries and enforcing religious instructions at state schools,[27] during the two decades of the interwar Polish Republics (1921–39), the Catholic Church "was pushed on to the fringes of political life."[28] For most of the interwar period, the ruling class was anticlerical in character, and the establishment of Catholic Action in Poland in 1930, like the convening of the Plenary Synod at Czestochowa in 1936 (for the first time in 300 years) and the International Congress of Christ the King in Poznan the following year, was a symptom of the church's anxiety about the spread of atheism.[29]

It was the Polish political right—rejecting notions of toleration of non-Polish culture—that was most enthusiastic about the role of the Catholic Church as protector of the Polish nation. This liaison proved abortive. As the Catholic monthly *Znak* noted in 1945 or 1946:

> The problem of nationalism had especial meaning for the history of Polish Catholicism in the two decades (of the interwar period). For a large part of Polish school youth found itself under the political influence of national democracy and its student organization, Mlodziez Wszechpolska (All-Polish Union), as well as of the radical-nationalist organizations that arose in the last years before the second war. These influences led the youth to positions of radical nationalism, often of a chauvinism that called into question the rights of national minorities, linked with anti-Semitism and racism, with distinct sympathies for fascism. Moreover, those nationalist tendencies were quite usually joined with a rather strange religious formation; that was a superficial, traditional, sentimental Catholicism—a religion that did not form a world view and had a rather limited influence on mores. Odrodzenie [the Catholic academic organization], although it was an apolitical organization and jealously guarded its apolitical character, stood in sharp conflict with the circles of the "national youth," combating the latter's nationalism and anti-Semitism. For Odrodzenie, nationalism could not be conjoined with Catholicism properly understood, because nationalism was at the same time antipersonal (insofar as it subordinates the human person to the welfare of the nation) and antiuniversal (insofar as each nation is posed against other nations and insofar as [nationalism] posits the principle of struggle rather than cooperation).[30]

The Catholic Church has always been suspended between the principle of universalism and the claims of local national culture. Had the interwar republic lasted, the church might in time have become divorced from nationalism. It was the advent of Soviet-style communism that ensured the perdurance of oppositionist nationalism on the part of the church.

The seizure by the state of much of the church's holdings in land and livestock in March 1950[31] ensured that the church would not be seen as somehow part of "the establishment." The arrest and imprisonment of Stefan Cardinal Wyszynski, Czeslaw Bishop Kaczmarek, and other Catholic prelates revived the image of the suffering church and stimulated religious loyalty among the Poles. And hence, when protesting workers marched on provincial party headquarters in Poznan in June 1956, they shouted, "We want God and bread."[32] Even the suppression of all religious instruction in the schools in 1961 produced the opposite effect from that intended by the authorities; not only did the resultant network of catechistic loci thrive on Polish determination to defend their Catholic culture, but it also indirectly contributed to identifying that culture with the Polish heritage.

The communist party drew the church into nationalist concerns more directly by its efforts to rewrite Polish history through the lenses of Marxist dialectical materialism. These efforts, which downplayed the role of individuals and attempted to blot out the memory of the church's close identification with Polish culture over the centuries, stirred the church to action. In a series of pastoral letters, sermons, and official remonstrations presented to the government, Cardinal Wyszynski defended the church against historical falsification.[33]

After 1970, the church became bolder. The episcopate subsumed its concern for social justice and civil rights under Polish nationalism, linking "true democracy" with Polish traditions "since the times of the kings" and underlining the nation's "right to existence and independence."[34] In a series of sermons in 1974, Wyszynski criticized the regime for obstructing the construction of new churches, opposed the amalgamation of all youth organizations into a single Polish Socialist Youth organization, and underlined the church's concern for freedom of association, press, opinion, and scientific research. To the regime's claim that Polish interests were identical to Soviet interests, Wyszynski countered that Polish interests had a life of their own, quite distinct from those of other countries. In Wyszynski's words:

> next to God, our first love is Poland. After God one must above all remain faithful to our Homeland, to the Polish national culture. We will love all the people in the world, but only in such an order of priority.
>
> And if we see everywhere slogans advocating love for all the peoples and all the nations, we do not oppose them; yet above all we demand the right to live

in accordance with the spirit, history, culture, and language of our own Polish land—the same which have been used by our ancestors for centuries.[35]

Hence, when, at the end of 1975, the regime published its proposed changes to the Polish Constitution, one of which would have based Poland's foreign policy on its "unshakable fraternal bond with the Soviet Union," the church joined numerous intellectuals in voicing concern. Ultimately, the regime toned down the wording to read that Poland "strengthens its friendship and cooperation with the USSR and other socialist countries." In response, the Episcopal Conference issued a statement in March 1976 regarding these finalized proposals, arguing on the subject of foreign policy that nothing should be introduced into the Constitution to limit the nation's sovereignty. Curiously, the church had allied itself with the opposition in order to champion Polish freedom and sovereignty *against* its own government's position.

During the late 1970s, the Polish Church became the chief focus of opposition, defending the underground "flying university," maintaining contacts with the workers' defense committee KOR that had been set up by a small group of intellectuals, and launching a series of "Days of Christian Culture," which provided an annual occasion for probing historical and cultural issues through lectures, concerts, poetry readings, films, art exhibits, and informal discussion groups.[36] The establishment of the independent trade union Solidarity in August 1980 changed the political landscape in Poland—in some ways, permanently—and since then the church has ceased to be the focal point of opposition.

That is not to say that Solidarity weakened the religio-national symbiosis in Poland. On the contrary, what the religiously inflected workers' protest in Gdansk (July–August 1980) showed was that "after thirty-five years of socialism in Poland religious symbolism had become the only language capable of expressing the ideals of social emancipation."[37] Solidarity was also clearly a nationalist movement, in that it strove to maximize the Polish people's control over their own fate and stimulated a wave of expressions of anti-Russian sentiment. During the two years of Solidarity's legal existence, Poles reopened the question of the Soviet massacre of thousands of Polish officers at Katyn during World War Two and the discussion of the Polish resistance during the war and the subsequent Soviet occupation. Solidarity set up a working group to revise the history textbooks used in Polish schools and invited exiled Polish writer Czeslaw Milosz to come to Poland to address Polish workers.[38]

The Solidarity episode reinforced the identification of the church with nationalism in yet another way, by drawing attention to the dependence of the opposition on church support. Thus, while some members of Solidarity clearly saw religion as inseparable from the national life, others, like Adam Michnik, a member of KOR and an adviser to Solidarity, first espoused anticlerical views but then came to see the church as an essential ally in the struggle for human and national rights. The church, for its part, cautiously welcomed the appearance of the new organization. A token of the church-Solidarity alliance was seen at Solidarity's First National Congress in Gdansk in September 1981: It was opened with a mass concelebrated by Jozef Archbishop Glemp, Lech Bishop Kaczmarek of Gdansk, and Kazimierz Bishop Kus of Gdansk. Indeed, various delegates referred to the role of the church and religion in Polish society, and the official report of Solidarity's National Coordinating Commission stressed the support given to Solidarity by the church on numerous occasions.

By contrast with the progovernmental stance taken by the Holy See in the nineteenth century, Pope John Paul II repeatedly underlined the church's commitment to national self-determination and human rights. In a particularly striking move on September 15, 1981, John Paul II issued his encyclical Laborem Exercens, in which he defended the right of workers to organize unions.

Since the military coup of December 13, 1981, and the suppression of Solidarity, the church has repeatedly spoken out on behalf of Polish workers. In late January 1982, for instance, the Episcopal Conference issued a pastoral letter demanding

> a return to the normal functioning of the State, the release of all those interned, cessation of all duress on ideological grounds and of dismissals from work for political views or trade-union membership. We make it clear that the right of working people to organize themselves into independent self-governing trade unions and of the youth to form their own associations must be restored in the name of freedom.[39]

On January 21, Archbishop Glemp set up the Primate's Committee for Help to the Internees to deliver food and clothing to imprisoned members of Solidarity, dispense legal advice, provide for their religious needs, collect information on those imprisoned, and draft petitions to the authorities. Later that year, in July, the church tried again to persuade the regime to permit Solidarity to resume legal activity. Subsequently, in a homily delivered at Jasna Gora, Archbishop Glemp identified the church with the jailed Solidarity activists and drew a pointed analogy between the workers' uprising in 1980 and the January 1863 Polish uprising against Russian rule, with which the church also had sympathy. Glemp specifically demanded freedom for the jailed Solidarity leader Lech Walesa, restoration of free trade unions, release of imprisoned Solidarity activists, and agreement on a date for a second papal visit to Poland.[40]

The Polish Catholic Church is strong, both in institutional terms and in terms of its popular base. In both respects, it is the church's close identification with the defense of the interests of the Polish people—its nationalism—that is the ultimate source and guarantee of its strength. This strength does not grant it immunity to attack,[41] but it does assure the church of being consulted regularly by government authorities at the highest level. Bogdan Cywinski, a top Solidarity adviser, has called the Polish Church a Julian church, recalling the persecutions under the Roman Emperor Julian the Apostate. The Constantinian church (enjoying the favor of Emperor Constantine) became wedded to state power; the Julian church responded to duress by seeking to consolidate and deepen its links with the people.[42]

THE CHURCH IN HUNGARY: COOPTIVE NATIONALIST

The Reformation was brought into Poland by immigrants, achieved a measure of toleration in the mid-sixteenth century, and was by and large expunged by the mid-seventeenth century. With this development, Protestantism ceased to be an important factor in Polish national life. In Hungary and Czechoslovakia, by contrast, the manner in which Protestantism was combated has had, in each case, effects to the present day.

In seventeenth-century Hungary, the Counter-Reformation was pursued on the one hand by persuasion, through the cultural activities of Primate Peter Pázmány (1570–1637), founder of the University at Nagyszombat, and on the other hand through forced conversions, confiscation of the property of "heretics," and jailing of Protestant ministers. In 1672, Jesuits, accompanied by soldiers, "traveled through the country forcibly converting the [religious] dissidents. Catholic magnates confiscated Protestant churches and schools on their estates, expelling ministers and teachers."[43] But unlike the Bohemian situation, in which the Battle of White Mountain provided a symbolic reference point for the simultaneous defeat of Czech national aspirations and Czech Protestantism, the Hungarian situation involved no military confrontation and hence no symbolic military defeat.

The Counter-Reformation had its effect on the church-state relationship directly, since the Roman Catholic Church owed its triumph over Protestantism to the state. In the aftermath of the Counter-Reformation, the church found that the state had already established commissions, under Ferdinand I (1503–64), to check clerical misconduct and inspect monasteries and churches, and had proscribed the sale of monastic property without government approval. Maximilian II (1527–76) had established a Monastic Council to supervise the administration of monasteries and convents. Conflicts concerning ecclesiastical property were now to be settled by secular courts. Later, Leopold I (1640–1705) introduced the practice of submitting other decisions by ecclesiastical courts to judicial review by secular courts.[44]

The Habsburgs expected the Catholic Church to preach obedience to secular authority, and the church by and large did so. For this service, the church hierarchy was granted the dignity of princely rank on a par with the highest lay nobilities. But the Habsburgs also wanted a tame church, and between 1740 and 1792 (the reigns of Maria Theresa, Josef II, and Leopold II), the chief issues in church-state relations were state control and centralism. Maria Theresa (1717–80) barred apostolic delegates from visiting the dioceses and frowned on inspections of monasteries by foreign generals of orders. Her son and successor, Josef II (1741–90), generally subjected the church to close control, abolishing monastic schools, cutting monastic ties abroad, requiring royal approval for the promulgation of papal encyclicals and the issue of excommunications, and even prescribing the number of candles to be used in specific church services.[45] In the early 1750s, moreover, after the tax reform of 1748 abolished tax exemptions of both church and nobility, the government assumed control of, but not administrative responsibility for, the church's property; henceforth, the church needed governmental approval to purchase or acquire additional land.

The Josephinian concept of the church held that church activity had to serve government interests and follow government regulations; it effectively treated the church as a branch of the civil service. This conception was continued by Franz II (1768–1835) and influenced the thinking of Kaiser Franz Josef (1830–1916). Vienna adopted a new tactic in the 1850s, however: It decided to try to enlist the hierarchy as an "ally" of the crown. Accordingly, in 1850, new legislation expanded the powers of the bishops over the lower clergy and even freed the seminaries of state control. In line with this new approach, Vienna signed a Concordat with the Holy See in 1855, granting wide-ranging concessions to the church.[46]

This Concordat ceased to apply in Hungary after the *Ausgleich* of 1867. With its autonomy now guaranteed, the Hungarian government in Budapest abrogated the concordat and restored the religious bill drafted in 1848, during the Hungarian Revolution. It is worth recalling here that Josef II's Edict of Toleration of 1781 had allowed individuals to convert from Catholicism to Protestantism. But the Hungarian religious bill of 1848/1867—which remained in force until 1948—went much further: It guaranteed the full equality of all religions and disestablished the Catholic Church, which had been the state religion until then.[47] Thus, from 1867 to 1918, Catholicism was the state religion in the Austrian half of the empire (including the Czech lands of Bohemia and Moravia) but enjoyed no special status in the Hungarian half (which included Slovakia).

For a few decades after the Ausgleich, the Budapest government clearly favored the Protestant churches over the Catholic Church, paying subsidies to the former but not to the latter. Only in 1909 did the government agree to make a contribution to paying the salaries of the poorer members of the Catholic clergy. Education was long the preserve of the churches, but, beginning in the early part of the century, the state began paying subventions for teacher salaries in ecclesiastical schools; with the subventions came state interference and the dependence of church schools on the state. Yet the Catholic Church was still—in a curious, back-handed sense—a "quasi-established" church, insofar as all its responsible appointments, including archbishops, bishops, abbots, provosts, and canons, had to be approved by the government.[48] That was the legacy of Josephinism in Hungary.

The late nineteenth century was the high-water mark of Hungarian Protestant nationalism. Pushed to the geographic periphery at the time of the Habsburg Counter-Reformation, Hungarian Protestants bounced back under the Ausgleich and "became the rallying point of all anti-Habsburg nationalist sentiments."[49] The years 1890–95 saw a Hungarian *Kulturkampf,* a Protestant-backed legal campaign introducing civil marriage, civil register, and new regulations regarding children from mixed marriages; legalizing divorce and areligious status; and allowing Christians to convert to Judaism. Needless to say, the Catholic Church was opposed to all of this. What should be underscored is that the legacy of the Kulturkampf, which was in part anti-Catholic in inspiration, was a strong Catholic revival and the birth of a new political party, led by Count Nándor Zichy. Essentially a Catholic organization, this new party initially swore complete loyalty to the terms of the Ausgleich and pressed for reversal of the Kulturkampf and passage of a moderate social program to benefit the lower classes.

While the Ausgleich era had been characterized by liberal predominance and a liberal aspiration to narrow the public role of the churches (and especially of the Catholic Church), the era of Admiral Miklos Horthy, between the two world wars, was more conservative in tone. The Horthy government regarded the churches as important pillars of morality and gave them extensive support. Indeed, the interwar regime discouraged irreligiosity and anticlericalism, and religion was a compulsory subject in state schools.[50]

While the Holy See sought concordats in many European countries at this time, it desisted in the Hungarian case, fearing, for good reason, that it could alienate non-Catholics and possibly revive the Kulturkampf. Yet the

Catholic Church, like and perhaps more than other churches, was clearly part of the establishment. Hence, in the initial upper house of the interwar Hungarian parliament, thirty-three of the 244 members enjoyed seats by reason of ecclesiastical office (nineteen Catholics, six Calvinists, four Lutherans, one Unitarian, one Greek Orthodox, and two Jews).[51]

In interwar Hungary, which had been stripped of two thirds of its territory and population by the punitive Treaty of Trianon, revisionist irredentism was the dominant political force. All the churches were "nationalist" in the sense of supporting demands for the restoration of the irredenta.[52] Children were taught a Hungarian Credo that summoned God's authority on behalf of irredentism: "I believe in one God. I believe in one Fatherland. I believe in eternal, divine justice. I believe in the resurrection of Hungary."[53] Moreover, Catholic and Lutheran clergy proved enthusiastic apostles of Magyarization in the schools, steadfastly blocking the aspirations of Catholic ethnic minorities to establish schools in their own languages.[54]

When the communists took power in Hungary after World War Two, they found religion stronger than in Czechoslovakia but less homogeneous and arguably less independent than in Poland. Unlike Poland, Hungary saw no hesitation by the new regime in launching policies aimed at whittling down and taming the churches. The less organized and less centralized Protestant churches quickly succumbed to communist pressure and made peace. The Catholic Church put up tougher resistance.

A 1945 land reform nationalized 34.6 percent of the Catholic Church's land holdings. A decree of July 9, 1945, banned most church social organizations, including the youth organization. In September 1947, the independent Catholic press was suppressed. Between 1946 and 1948, the church lost 3,163 of its 3,344 educational facilities, along with 600,000 of its students. And beginning with the 1949–50 school year, religious instruction ceased to be compulsory.[55] Church and state were officially separated on August 18, 1949, and on June 30, 1950, the Catholic theological faculties in Budapest and Pecs and the Evangelical theological faculty in Debrecen were separated from the respective universities. Between June 6 and July 12, 1950, security forces assaulted the country's monasteries and convents, deporting some 3,820 monks and nuns, many of whom were imprisoned and, according to Steven Polgar, tortured.[56]

Hungarian Primate József Cardinal Mindszenty refused to compromise with the authorities and was imprisoned. Other Catholic clergy decided to cooperate with the Stalinist regime on its terms. A "peace priest" movement came into being in summer 1947, followed, in August 1950, by the establishment of a Peace Committee of Hungarian Catholic Clergy under the chairmanship of Miklos Beresztóczy. The following year saw the creation of the State Office for Church Affairs, entrusted with the task of bringing the churches under the authority and supervision of the regime. The bishops were compelled to entrust responsible posts to "peace priests," and less cooperative prelates gradually were forced out of office. As a result, a new pattern of neo-Josephinism was inaugurated; with time, it began to take on some characteristics of a cooptive relationship. In September 1966, under pressure from the State Office for Church Affairs, the episcopate established a Committee for Foreign Affairs of the Hungarian Episcopate; this committee provided the mechanism for state control and supervision of the foreign contacts of the Catholic Church.[57]

In 1964—by which time the Hungarian Catholic Church was only a shadow of its former self[58]—the Hungarian government of János Kádár signed a major agreement with the Vatican. The agreement provided that episcopal appointments were to be acceptable to both sides (a stipulation, earlier, of both the Habsburg and Horthy governments), that the clergy were to be bound by an oath of allegiance to the Hungarian constitution, and that the Hungarian Papal Institute in Rome was to be administered by priests acceptable to Budapest.[59]

Church-state relations became distinctly more cooperative in the 1970s. An important factor in this amelioration was the accession of László Lékai to the posts of archbishop of Esztergom in 1974 and primate of Hungary in 1976, after the death of Cardinal Mindszenty. Lékai (who died in July 1986) embraced a policy of survival rather than confrontation—a choice that inevitably sparked controversy. The government welcomed this shift and decorated Cardinal Lékai with the Order of the Banner of Rubies of the Hungarian People's Republic. The award was said to recognize his "exceptional efforts to promote good relations between the Hungarian State and the Catholic Church."[60] Indeed, governmental decorations have become commonplace, with a veritable proliferation of honorary titles, medals, sashes, orders, and decorations for cooperative clergy.[61] A more tangible token of church "cooptation" was the election of three Catholic "peace priests" (Imre Biro of Esztergom, János Kis of the Bishops' Office at Szekesfehervar, and Istvan Pregun of Hajdudorog) to the Hungarian Parliament in June 1985. Although contrary to canon law, their candidacy was expressly approved by Cardinal Lékai.[62]

Yet change has not been entirely superficial. On July 17, 1970, for instance, the Catholic news agency KNA reported that the Peace Committee was "no longer very successful" and would shift its focus from political problems to philosophical and educational issues. On January 15, 1975, a new regulation on religious instruction went into force, culminating long negotiations between the Bishops' Conference and the State Office for Church Affairs. The regulation allowed religious instruction to be conducted twice a week on church premises on a voluntary basis.[63] In 1976, Budapest lifted its proscription on the grass-roots Basic Communities, which had been meeting illegally for some time, and granted them legal recognition,[64] despite the fact that they had not proven amenable to supervision by either the government or the ecclesiastical hierarchy. Early in the 1970s, the Bible was printed in a Hungarian-language edition of 200,000 copies, and in 1980 it was announced that secondary schools would be allowed to study the Bible as literature. In 1984, there was talk of establishing a new Catholic religious order for women.[65] And according to figures provided by State Secretary for Church Affairs Imre Miklos, there were 497 theological students in Hungary in the 1983–84 academic year—a marked increase from the roughly 300 in 1963–64.

Recent years have seen a reawakening of national self-consciousness among Hungarians, as exemplified in the rediscovery of King Stephen, who brought Christianity to Hungary, and the production of a rock opera based on his life. The church has played its part in his rediscovery, celebrating the 1,000th anniversary of his birth in 1970 and drawing attention to his "religious fervor."[66] The Hungarian Church's nationalism, unlike the Polish Church's, is consistently supportive of the regime. In an interview with the Budapest periodical *Kritika* in September 1983, for example, József Bishop Cserháti, secretary of the Hungarian Conference of Bishops, drew attention to

> training in patriotism as a separate task [for both the state and the Church]. . . . I [have] always believed that the question of patriotism is primarily an ethical question. It is the statement of the purified, noble man toward his own kind, own brothers, own history and contemporaries.[67]

The bishop continued by praising church-state dialogue in Hungary and by slyly suggesting church-state collaboration in the communist project of creating the New Communist Man and Woman—naturally on the basis of church teachings and the inspiration of the lives of the saints. In Cserháti's words:

> We still suffer from the negligence or lack of Hungarian unity, the sought-after national unity. Thus, the task of the present is to form a new type of man; on the basis of the gospel, contemporary man must be told to "love your neighbor as yourself" and to "do unto others as you wish them to do unto you." In this regard, the possibilities remain unchanged: the churches are open, we are not prevented from describing an ethical humanistic vision of man from the pulpit and from inspiring people to work together to create a new Hungarian homeland. The Church can also illuminate the values from the past very effectively with their discovery, and with the introduction of

Hungarian saints and outstanding personalities, we could certainly influence the present generation positively, especially the youth.[68]

Then, on the basis of this argument for the utility of the church in buttressing nationalism and patriotism and in building socialism, Cserháti appealed for greater access to youth and for more constructive criticism of social policies.

It is only when its eyes are turning outward that the church's Hungarian nationalism assumes a critical edge. Both the Catholic and the Protestant press have amply discussed the difficulties of the Hungarian diaspora in Slovakia and Transylvania, and, according to Leslie Laszlo, "they were the first to open their columns to contributions from Magyar writers and scholars in the successor states."[69] Yet even here, the church behaves in conformance with regime policy objectives. The church has reverted to a Josephinian cast.

THE CHURCH IN CZECHOSLOVAKIA: MODUS MORIENDI[70]

Although most citizens of Czechoslovakia are nominally Catholic—with 36 percent of the residents of the Czech lands and more than half of Slovakia counted as believers[71]—the Catholic Church in Czechoslovakia is neither national nor, where the Czechs are concerned, nationalist. It is not national in the sense in which the Church is in Poland and Hungary because there is no Czechoslovak nation: There are a Czech nation and a Slovak nation, united in a Czechoslovak state. And in the Czech lands of Bohemia and Moravia, where most of the population resides, the Catholic Church, far from being nationalist, is widely viewed as antinationalist. And hence its weakness.

Two developments ensured the disassociation of Catholicism and Czech national feeling. The first was the religious reformative movement in the fourteenth and fifteenth centuries, which resulted in the emergence of the Unity of Czech Brethren. This movement, though strictly illegal for some 150 years, nonetheless became the most widely diffused congregation among the Czechs (before the 1620s).[72] Jan Hus (martyred in 1415) was the central figure in this movement; he polished the Czech vernacular and inspired an armed rebellion that was finally subdued only in the 1430s. The movement bequeathed to the Czechs the idea of a Czech national church, a "Hussite" church.

The second development that ensured the disassociation of Catholicism and Czech national sentiment came two hundred years later, with the defeat of the Czech Protestants by Catholic Austria at the Battle of White

Mountain (November 8, 1620). Ironically, as late as 1609, Kaiser Rudolf II
(1552–1612) issued a letter of toleration, legalizing both the Lutheran
"Ultraquists" (Evangelicals) and the Unity of Czech Brethren and granting them the right to build churches and schools. At that time, more than
90 percent of Czechs may have been Protestant, though most of the Czech
nobility had returned to Catholicism.[73]

Actually, the Catholic establishment had begun its Counter-Reformation
in Bohemia in the 1560s, and it was showing some results within a decade.
The years leading up to 1618 saw growing uncertainty in the rivalry
between the armed camps of Protestants and Catholics in Bohemia, leading to revolt by the former in the war of 1618–20. Ferdinand II (1578–1637),
who had become emperor in 1619, was only too glad to have done with
Protestantism—which he equated with disloyalty.[74] The war resulted in the
complete defeat of Protestant arms and the flight of Protestant King
Friedrich V von der Pfalz (1596–1632) from Bohemia. After White Mountain, Protestantism was banned, Protestants were persecuted, Protestant
nobility were driven abroad and their estates turned over to "reliable"
Catholics (including Germans, Walloons, Frenchmen, Spaniards, Irish,
and Italians), the Jesuits were put in control of all higher education in
Bohemia, and large numbers of books and manuscripts were confiscated
and burned.[75] Ferdinand II's attitude was summed up in his comment, "A
desert is better than a country with heretics."[76] Protestantism was declared to be a crime punishable by death. Accordingly, the population of
Bohemia and Moravia fell from about three million to some 900,000, as
Ferdinand's forces applied pressure to bring about the re-Catholicization
of the Czechs.[77] The resultant "Ferdinandian church" was quintessentially antinational.

The Czechs lost the right of self-rule, much of the Czech cultural
heritage was destroyed by the Jesuits, and German settlers were brought
in to fill the sudden demographic vacuum. German quickly became the
dominant language of government and business. The unity of purpose of
Habsburg political power and Catholic religious power was unmistakable
in Czech eyes. As Joseph Lehrl observed:

> Nowhere else has the corpus of Catholic teaching become so deeply embod-
> ied in the historical consciousness of a people as in [Habsburg] Austria. The
> relations between Rome and the State have always differed radically from
> those in other countries. The two were not simply parties to a legal contract
> (the Concordat), but two different expressions of the same idea, each moving
> in its own manner towards a common goal. Church and State were not two
> independent powers, but members of a common Christian entity.[78]

For the Czechs, Catholic Church and Habsburg state were two faces of a single enemy.

During the nineteenth century, when nations created nationalism by looking to their past, the Czechs reclaimed "Hussite Protestantism" as the national ideology. The "tension between nationalism and Catholicism," Alexander Tomsky stated,

> produced towards the end of the century a movement within the Church known as [the] "Los von Rom Bewegung" (Away from Rome Movement), culminating in the creation of a schismatic Hussite Church after the founding of the Czechoslovak Republic in 1918.[79]

The Czechs could not overlook the preponderance of German aristocrats among the leading Catholic Church dignitaries in Habsburg Bohemia or the church's distance from the Czech national renaissance of the nineteenth and early twentieth centuries.[80] During World War One, as the sentiment for independence grew among Czechs, the church again remained aloof. The end of the war saw an upsurge of anti-Catholic and anticlerical feeling among Czechs, who saw the establishment of the Czechoslovak Republic as the reversal of White Mountain, which was in turn blamed on the Counter-Reformation. The Czechoslovak government supported Hussite churches and festivities and viewed the creation of a schismatic Czech National (Hussite) Church with favor. This latter church, set up by a group of alienated Catholic clergymen, was antipapal and pronationalist, using the vernacular in the liturgy and introducing a variety of changes, including lay representation in parish governing bodies and the abolition of priestly celibacy. Czechoslovak President Tomas Masaryk (1850–1937), a freethinker, obtained a separation law on the French model and introduced a series of other statutes inspired by Czech anticlericalism and French precedent.[81]

Slovakia had been assigned to Hungary under the terms of the 1867 Ausgleich, and the church in Slovakia was therefore shaped by the religious and nationalities policies fashioned in Budapest. Above all, the ecclesiastical hierarchy's support of Magyarization, while wedding it to Hungarian nationalism, alienated nationally conscious Slovaks. After World War One, de-Magyarization was often associated with anticlerical overtones.[82] At the same time, however, the Slovaks found an advocate in Fr. Andrej Hlinka (1864–1938), a charismatic orator who denounced Ausgleich Hungary's policy toward Slovaks and rebelled against the hierarchy for its support of that policy. Hlinka went on to found the Slovak People's Party, which worked for Slovak autonomy and ultimately, under Hlinka's successor, Msgr. Jozef Tiso (1887–1947), found itself charged with administration of the nominally independent Nazi puppet state of Slovakia. Because of this different development, and in particular because of the activity of the Slovak People's Party and the experience of the wartime Slovak Republic, Catholicism has not become similarly divorced from Slovak national consciousness.

Though most Slovak Catholic clergy supported Tiso's quisling regime, a few joined the opposition, along with most Slovak Lutheran ministers. Protestants resented the regime's close identification with Catholicism and flocked to the resistance. As a result, the regime muzzled the Protestant press and put Protestant ministers in prison.[83]

As the war drew to a close, the provisional government promised the churches complete religious freedom. But even before the communist coup, the Slovak National Council—which consisted entirely of communist and Protestant members—ordered the nationalization of all church schools in Slovakia on May 16, 1945. Already in the first weeks of the provisional government, important publishing houses of the Catholic Church were nationalized, several church newspapers were suspended, and others were throttled by cutting off paper supplies.[84] Even at this stage, some leading Catholic personalities were being arrested, including Archbishop Buzalka and Bishop Vojtassak. It is clear, thus, that Czechoslovakia was susceptible to anticlerical programs, quite independent of the communist takeover in 1948.

Once it had carried out its coup, the communist party ordered crosses to be taken out of the schools, removed teachers and professors who belonged to religious orders, eliminated religious instruction in the middle schools, abolished the Central Catholic Agency (the executive organ of the bishops of Czechoslovakia), and banned the League of Catholic Women. In February 1949, the bishops tried to reach an accommodation with the regime; the regime demanded a declaration of loyalty and reinstatement of certain "progressive" priests. Shortly thereafter, Czech priest Josef Ployhar drew up a manifesto calling for a new Catholic movement that would be free of "foreign" (i.e., Vatican) control. That revived sentiments of the "Los von Rom" movement and was understandably viewed by the bishops as a schismatic organization. At the same time, the Uniate parishes were forcibly placed under Orthodox jurisdiction, and the term *Greek Catholic* soon disappeared from Slovak dictionaries.

As of 1945, the Roman Catholic Church had a theological faculty in Bratislava (separated from the University of Bratislava that year) and theological seminaries in Nitra, Spišská Kapitula, Banská Bystrica, Košice, Žilina, and Sv. Križ; the Greek Catholic Church had a seminary in Prešov; the Protestant Church of the Augsburg confession had a seminary in Modra near Bratislava. In August 1950, the regime closed all existing seminaries and, in their place, set up the Cyril and Methodius Faculty for Catholics in Bratislava and a theological faculty for Evangelicals. The regime also ordered all theologians to enroll in a political awareness class during summer 1950; the course included instruction in Marxism. Of some 400 Catholic theologians, only twenty-four enrolled.[85] Not until 1968 did the bishops reestablish their control over the seminary.

In 1950, police seized the monasteries and convents, locked up the 3,000 monks and 10,000 nuns in "concentration monasteries" or placed them in work camps, and launched a press campaign accusing them of participating in bacchanalian sex orgies and plotting "counterrevolution." The population had already been tranquilized by a series of strategic arrests. But in many Slovak villages, police were unable to arrest pastors, whom the villagers guarded day and night.[86]

The religious climate remained oppressive until the "Prague Spring" of 1968. Then, during Alexander Dubček's brief rule, Ployhar's "patriotic priests" organization was closed, the Catholic Church was allowed to set up its own clerical organization, and the Uniate Church was relegalized.[87] The episode, however brief, had its effects. In an internal memorandum in 1970, the Slovak administration bemoaned that religious consciousness was allegedly spreading, and explained that the Dubček episode had restored Christians' self-confidence.[88] Another official document, smuggled out of Czechoslovakia in 1974, said that the number of atheists in Slovakia was stagnant, the workers were antiatheist, and too many youths were enrolled in religious instruction; it also urged the necessity of keeping Christian girls from becoming nurses.[89]

A quarterly journal devoted to atheism was launched in 1973, and the Husak regime extended its "normalization" program to the religious sphere. Under regulations issued by the state in March 1975 and still in effect, seminarians were barred from contact with any lay persons except family, from free movement outside the seminary other than in groups and with the previous permission of the authorities, and from having any radio equipment or foreign literature on hand. Churches were barred from any activity with youth other than limited religious instruction, and 1976 saw a rapid drop in the number of children attending religious instruction, as regime pressure began to produce results. The seminary is now controlled by the Ministry of Culture, and the church is supervised by the State Office for Church Affairs. The state uses its salary subsidies to reward priests who give up religious instruction, avoid contact with youth, and preach less; as a result, there are both poor priests and rich priests in Slovakia. In this atmosphere of planned stultification, evasion is preferred to confrontation, accommodation to martyrdom, shrewdness to defiance. As Teinhold Lehmann put it in 1983, "There is no high regard in this country for the hero who is prepared to act in desperation. The goal is survival."[90]

In 1980, in the wake of the outbreak of labor protests in Poland, the Czechoslovak regime intensified its containment strategy and stepped up raids on church members and arrests of clergy. This campaign is more fully described in chapters 8 and 9 and need not be related here.[91] What may be noted is that, while the campaign is taking its toll, some reports say it has produced a backlash. Along this line, the Bratislava publication *Učitelske Noviný* ran an article in late 1982, conceding that "interest in religion, and a noncritical attitude toward it, is being revived among part of the youth."[92]

The continued resilience of Catholicism among Slovaks was clearly shown in 1985 on the occasion of the 1,100th anniversary of the death of St. Methodius, bishop of Moravia. A national as well as a religious occasion, the commemoration was supposed to be attended by Pope John Paul II, but the regime refused to allow a papal visit. The pope therefore sent a letter, calling attention to Methodius's role (with his brother, Cyril) in introducing the Slavic liturgy and "strengthen[ing] the foundations of Czechoslovak cultural history."[93] The Czech regime countered by issuing instructions to its cadres to debunk and contain church celebrations of the saint. The greatness of Methodius, it announced, "does not consist in his religious activities or adherence to the Church but in his active participation in forming the State of Greater Moravia."[94]

Nothing could better demonstrate the difference between Czech and Slovak religiosity than the attendance at the commemorative ceremonies at a monastery in the Moravian village of Velehrad on July 7: Though Methodius lived and worked in the traditional Czech lands, the ceremonies attracted 100,000 to 200,000 Slovaks, many singing religious hymns, but only "a sprinkling" of Czechs.[95] The disparity between Czech and Slovak religiosity is also borne out in official government statistics. According to figures cited by Karel Hruza, the former head of the Secretariat for Church Affairs, in a four-hour lecture about "scientific atheism," 71.6 percent of all children born in Slovakia in 1984 were baptized, compared with 31.2 percent of children born in the Czech lands; 53 percent of all weddings in Slovakia that year were church weddings, compared with only 15.8 percent in the Czech lands; and 80.5 percent of Slovak funerals were church funerals, compared with 50.6 percent of Czech funerals.[96]

CONCLUSION

This brief comparative history has emphasized the genesis of popular attitudes toward religion, tying it to considerations of nationalism. The argument, in brief, has been that a state's religious policy has a direct impact on religio-national symbiosis, which in turn shapes the environment in which church-state relations subsequently evolve. Central to this analysis has been the assumption that popular attitudes, routine policy proclivities, and even institutional resources are affected by trends spanning decades and even centuries.

The overall conclusions can be summarized as follows: First, national trauma (e.g., the partition of Poland or the Battle of White Mountain), insofar as it has direct religious consequences, is apt to become part of a religio-national mythology linking religion and nationalism. Second, the more closely linked religion and nationalism are, the less able an anticlerical government will be to assault religious institutions. The clear correlation between religio-national symbiosis and relative policy liberality under communism across these three countries provides evidence of that. Third, while the Counter-Reformation restored the numerical preponderance of Catholicism, it also created and reinforced a tradition of anticlericalism. Fourth, in Poland, Czechoslovakia, and Hungary, the role of the Catholic Church in resisting foreign domination has been directly correlated with national symbiosis and overall confessional strength. The church is strongest in Poland, where, since 1795, it has generally been in opposition—a "Julian church." The "Josephinian church" syndrome exemplified in Hungary preserves the nationalist character of the church but not its opposition role, and the legacy is a pattern of accommodation—arguably, at this stage, by necessity. The "Ferdinandian church" syndrome, as characterized by the Catholic Church among the Czechs, combines an antinational demeanor with cooptation by an antinational, foreign power. Its legacy is estrangement from the people, anticlericalism, and confessional weakness. And fifth, among the peoples whose nationalism has been predominantly oppositionist (defensive) in character—Poles, Czechs, Slovaks—the churches that were also oppositionist have retained their strength and their nationalist base.

FIVE

Church and Peace in the German Democratic Republic

The German Democratic Republic (GDR) has a well-deserved reputation for ideological orthodoxy and mimetic loyalty to Moscow.[1] Its ruling Socialist Unity Party (Sozialistische Einheitspartei Deutschlands, or SED), so the argument runs, has done better than most East European communist parties in establishing an effective political monopoly.[2] Yet, since early 1982, a de facto alliance has developed in the GDR between an independent peace movement and the dominant religious organization, the Evangelical-Lutheran Church. Moreover, this church has shown itself capable of defying the SED without—thus far—experiencing a deterioration in its relatively favorable situation. Why has the Evangelical Church supported the oppositionist peace movement and adopted an openly critical stance toward regime policies? How has the regime reacted? Why has the Catholic Church been much slower to follow suit? And what are the short-term prospects for the entente between the Evangelical Church and the opposition in the GDR? This chapter will address these questions.

THE EVANGELICAL CHURCH AND THE STATE, 1949–78

The religious situation in the GDR differs in some important respects from that in the rest of Eastern Europe and the Soviet Union. The GDR is the only communist country with a Protestant majority.[3] More important, despite the post-World War Two division of the German nation, the Evangelical Church retained an all-German institutional structure until 1969.

80

That gave the church additional resources and made a communist policy of harassment more difficult. Due both to this consideration and to the initial Soviet readiness to negotiate about Germany's political future,[4] it was not until mid-1952 that the SED introduced a Stalinist program, including the Soviet model on religious policy. This policy aimed at eliminating church influence in society. Thus, while the SED had recognized the legitimacy of church-sponsored youth organizations in 1947, these groups were later declared to be illegal rivals to the SED's youth organization and encountered systematic obstruction after 1952. Religious instruction in schools also was often hindered after 1952 and gradually shrank. In 1954, the authorities introduced the *Jugendweihe* (youth initiation) as an atheist substitute for the church sacrament of confirmation (normally administered in early adolescence). Supposedly voluntary, the Jugendweihe was actively promoted and by 1958 had made a decisive breakthrough among the youth of the GDR. The functioning of the church press was also obstructed.

In the early years of the GDR's existence, the SED strove to consolidate its rule, to neutralize institutional rivals, including the churches, and to isolate the Evangelical Church in the GDR from its West German sister church. As early as 1950, a "peace movement" was established in hopes of drawing Christian clergy and laity into active collaboration with the government. Uncooperative priests were imprisoned and, by the mid-1950s, some seventy clergymen were behind bars.[5] A 1958 agreement by the West German Evangelical leadership to provide religious care in the newly established West German army allowed the SED to attack the "NATO church" and to pressure the East German Evangelicals to distance themselves from this agreement by declaring their loyalty to the GDR and its program of socialist construction. In the view of the SED, that was a tangible step toward the attenuation of links between the East German and West German branches of the Evangelical Church.[6]

The efforts of the East German regime to break completely the institutional links between the Protestant churches of the two Germanys were crowned with success on June 10, 1969, when a Federation of Evangelical Churches in the GDR was established.[7] By this action, the Lutheran and Reformed Churches of the GDR withdrew from their institutional association with their West German counterparts. Shortly thereafter, Bishop Albrecht Schönherr, first chairman of the Evangelical Federation in the GDR, declared: "It is not our intention to be the Church *against* socialism, nor the Church *beside* socialism; we want to be the Church *in* socialism."[8] Although the Evangelical Church had reconciled itself to working within the framework of the GDR in the 1960s and 1970s, its leaders continued to speak out, albeit cautiously, on various political

questions, including the exodus of East Germans to the West, collectivization of agriculture, and especially military service. As early as 1962, when
the SED introduced universal military conscription, the Evangelical
Church took the side of conscientious objectors. Through a series of
public and private statements, it succeeded in obtaining, in September
1964, the creation of a construction soldiers' service as an alternative to
regular military service, though the church could not prevent the regime
from discriminating against veterans of the construction units when it
came to university admissions and career advancement.[9]

The Lutheran tradition of putting individual conscience above institutional discipline complicated the SED's policy toward the church, insofar
as it meant that church-state accommodations worked out with the leadership of the Evangelical Federation might be repudiated by provincial
hierarchs or even by the lower clergy. For example, while Bishop
Mitzenheim, chairman of the Conference of Church Leaderships in the
GDR, was overtly cooperating with the regime in hopes of improving
conditions for East German Christians, the other bishops would not follow
his lead. On the contrary, on September 27, 1961, they issued a ten-point
declaration on freedom and service of the church, in which they disavowed the collaborationist party (the East German Christian Democratic
Union, or CDU-East), renounced any obligation to promote socialism,
insisted on their right to speak out on social issues, and pointedly rejected
the temptation offered by Party General Secretary Walter Ulbricht to
merge the church's interest in human welfare and peace with the SED's
interest in socialist humanism and proletarian internationalism.[10]

Despite Bishop Schönherr's slogan of "Church in socialism" and the
CDU-East's opinion that the thoroughly coopted Russian Orthodox
Church might constitute an appropriate model for the East German Evan-
gelical Church, there were clear limits to the SED's ability to draw the
Evangelical Federation into an alliance. In February 1971, Paul Verner, a
member of the Politburo, incautiously told the CDU-East that

> the clergy and laity are called to further strengthen the German Democratic
> Republic in service and testimony, to preserve peace and to put every single
> person to good use. . . . The Church representatives . . . should make it clear
> in their official functions and in the Church organs that the Church cannot
> stand either between the capitalist front and the socialist one, or in "critical
> distance" to their state.[11]

Two weeks later, Bishop Schönherr used the occasion of an official state
reception to make clear that the state's position as outlined in Verner's
speech was unacceptable. Schönherr stated that the church would never
resign itself to the status of a "cult" church, that religious life encom-

passed much more than religious services, and that the church intended to maintain an active part in discussing the social issues of the day.[12]

Despite such reservations, the Evangelical Church and the SED regime achieved a kind of concordat in 1978, signaled by a meeting between SED General Secretary Erich Honecker and church leaders on March 6. Honecker pledged to end discrimination against Christians in education and employment and to lift obstacles to church construction projects. In the wake of this meeting, the Evangelical Church was allowed to take up construction and renovation of church buildings. In May 1981, the church was able to dedicate the first fruit of its construction program: a church and community center in Eisenhüttenstadt, which had been called the first socialist city in the GDR because it had remained churchless since being built in the 1950s.[13] Restrictions on broadcasting religious programs were eased. While religious services had always been broadcast on radio on Sunday mornings, after 1979 there were also monthly radio programs with church news and information. Six television programs annually, scripted by the Evangelical Church itself, were permitted.[14] More than thirty religious periodicals now appear regularly in the GDR, including five regional weeklies published by the Evangelical Church; by and large, however, they limit themselves to noncontroversial topics.

Understandably, the Evangelical Church has been reluctant to endanger the relatively propitious modus vivendi worked out in 1978. It has repeatedly distanced itself from the perception that it opposes the regime. Bishop Werner Krusche of Magdeburg said in 1976 that it seeks to occupy "the narrow space between opposition and opportunism."[15] This sentiment was echoed by Bishop Werner Leich of Thuringia in March 1983, when he declared that the church is neither a "camouflaged government party nor a camouflaged opposition party."[16] But, as the Politburo member, Verner, had made clear in 1971, the SED recognizes no space between opposition and opportunism and has no patience for the idea of "critical distance." It was therefore not surprising that, despite its accommodation with the government, the church should gravitate toward opposing government policies.

A CRITICAL DISTANCE

The central issue in the Evangelical Church's opposition to SED policies has been peace. Since the GDR regime describes itself as a peace movement, deviance from regime norms is, by definition, an act against peace. The church's conception of peace differs from the state's in two important respects: First, the church believes that truly stable international peace is inseparable from internal peace in every state, and by internal peace the church means a broad toleration of multiple world views, with respect for and safeguarding of human rights. Second, the church believes that the SED must abandon its hostile characterization of the West in the media and schools, turn away from "education in hatred," and give true information about its military policy and politics. In 1978, Bishop Krusche, who later served as chairman of the Federation of Evangelical Churches (September 1981 to November 1982), explained the differences in perception:

> The churches have their own peace policy to pursue. . . . The churches are forces for peace only as long as they safeguard their freedom, so that they do not become estranged from the real interests of the nation [and] become merely the foreign policy tools of their respective states.[17]

Discrimination by the regime against citizens who substituted service in construction units for regular military service provoked church recriminations against the government as early as 1966. Yet the church's engagement in a peace policy at cross-purposes with the regime should really be dated from 1978, when the SED introduced obligatory premilitary instruction for youths of both sexes in all schools in the ninth and tenth grades. School texts and classroom instruction were revised to sharpen hostile stereotypes of the West and thus to further Honecker's program of *Abgrenzung* (demarcation) from West Germany. To foster military discipline among the population, the regime sought to introduce "military elements" into all other classroom subjects.[18] In fifth-grade sports classes, for instance, students are instructed in the use of hand grenades.[19]

It is possible that the regime's olive branch to the church in March 1978 was extended to "neutralize" the church before launching the new premilitary training programs in September. If so, the regime miscalculated. At its national conference on June 14, 1978, the Evangelical Church Federation protested that the planned educational changes would deepen "friend/foe thinking" and, in an open rebuff to the regime, charged that the new policy could only endanger peace. The church reaffirmed its opposition to premilitary instruction in the schools at its synod in Berlin-Weissensee in September 1978, [20] and proposed that the regime replace military training in schools with "peace education" (*Friedenserziehung*), by which the church meant instruction in the duty of obeying one's conscience and in the stimulation of independent thinking on moral questions—scarcely an approach congruent with the SED's program. In May 1981, the SED issued a decree extending premilitary instruction to the eleventh grade and making it obligatory to participate in a hitherto voluntary twelve-day summer training camp. The church deplored what it termed these "tendencies toward a militarization of social life in the GDR" and the reorientation of the school curriculum to support that militarization.[21]

The increasingly critical stance of the Evangelical Church leadership since 1978 has been due, to some extent, to both lay and clerical pressures from below.[22] One of the first demands (in 1972) for the institution of a civilian service in environmental protection as an alternative to military service came in an open letter to Honecker from alienated construction-unit soldiers.[23] By the summer of 1981, demands for a "social peace service" were widespread. Yet the Evangelical bishops did not support this initiative until three lay workers of the church in Saxony had drawn up an appeal for a social peace service to substitute for both regular military service and uniformed construction-unit service (whose work was on overtly military projects) and had obtained some 5,000 signatures from all over the GDR. By the end of November 1981, all eight regional synods of the Evangelical Church had endorsed the social peace service proposal.[24]

In the 1970s, the church had begun to address directly the concerns of young people. Church-sponsored discussions of sexuality, alcoholism, rock music, life in the Third World, life in the GDR, and the militarization of society became more common. In consequence, church services, once sparsely attended, were suddenly jammed, even in rural areas, as non-believers joined believers to hear popular preachers.[25] Another aspect of this response from below has been the burgeoning of individual pressures designed to stiffen the posture of the church leadership toward the regime. The best known protest was the self-immolation of Pastor Oskar Brüsewitz in front of his church in Zeitz in August 1976. Before setting himself on fire, Pastor Brüsewitz explained that he was taking his life to protest the timidity of the church's leadership. Pastors Rolf Günther of Falkenstein and Gerhard Fischer of Schwanewitz followed suit in September 1978.[26] Subsequently, in February 1982, Rainer Eppelmann, an East Berlin pastor, created a stir with an open letter to Honecker reproaching him for the programmatic distribution of war toys in the GDR, the glorification of army life in the schools, the regular visits of kindergarten groups and school classes to barracks, the incorporation of grandiose military spectacles into all national holidays, and the continued discrimination against professed pacifists. He went on to appeal for the withdrawal of both US and Soviet troops and weaponry from the two Germanys and the establishment of a nuclear-free zone in central Europe.[27] His appeal was signed by several hundred East Germans, but the church hierarchy felt constrained to distance itself from his action. Its caution aroused indignation among participants at a February 1983 peace demonstration in Dresden, who accused the church of needless compromise with the state.[28]

As already noted, the Evangelical Church, following the lead of the laity of Saxony, endorsed the idea of a "social peace service" and advocated it in consultations with the government in 1981. A synod of the Evangelical Federation, meeting in summer 1981, demanded that the government recognize the right of East German citizens to substitute nonmilitary social service for military duty. Klaus Gysi, state secretary for church affairs, who had earlier warned the church that church-state separation meant that the church should abstain from interference in political questions, called the demand unacceptable.[29] The intransigence of the authorities toward demands that the pervasive militarization of public life be eased did not silence these demands. Quite the contrary. Specific issues like the substitution of social peace service for military duty became subsumed in a broader demand, in which believers and nonbelievers joined: that the GDR authorities pursue less belligerent policies.

THE INDEPENDENT PEACE MOVEMENT

Since the early 1980s, the East Germans have had four distinct spokesmen for "peace." One is official, one is regime-approved, and two are independent and overlapping; three are linked, in one way or another, to the Evangelical Church.

There is, to begin with, the official peace movement, known as the GDR Peace Council. The sole purpose of this organization is to popularize the decisions and policies of the regime. The logic of its position, as expressed by George Grasnick, is that under socialism

the aims of the foreign policy and the peace efforts of the governments coincide with the peace interests of the peoples. . . . The "independent peace movement" in the socialist countries . . . thus really has nothing at all to do with the interests of the peace movement, with the peace tasks of our day.[30]

Second, there is the unofficial but regime-approved Christian Peace Conference, which has a membership of about 500 and whose views are close to those of the official Peace Council. Its position is often presented in *Standpunkt*, a monthly published by the proregime section of the Evangelical Church. A typical expression of its general attitude is an article by a Rev. P. Schrimpf in the June 1983 issue; it stated that "Christians have no special expertise in political questions; therefore there can also be no specific Christian peace policy."[31] This statement is an explicit repudiation of the position taken by Bishops Schönherr and Krusche and the Evangelical Church hierarchy in general.

Third, there are numerous Basic Communities and peace seminars organized within the Evangelical Church, usually at the regional or parish level. These seminars meet on church grounds for weekends or several days to discuss such issues as "the language of peace," "nonviolent demonstrations," and "alternatives to military service." The oldest and best known peace seminar is held twice a year in Königswalde, Saxony, and is regularly attended by 400 to 500 persons.[32]

Fourth, there is the "independent peace movement"—known by its motto, "Swords into Plowshares"—which has been closely associated with the Evangelical Church from the beginning but has always been a spontaneous, grass-roots movement without an organizational structure, officers, or spokesmen. It numbered 2,000 to 5,000 activists in 1983, with an estimated 30,000 to 50,000 supporters.[33] Small groups of independent pacifists arose in East Berlin and numerous other East German cities. The regime's liberal emigration policy of 1984 seriously depleted the ranks of this movement, however, and, for the time being, it does not seem to be a viable force.

In 1980, the Evangelical Church became more outspoken on broader political topics. In January, the Evangelical Federation released a communique calling for international cooperation in a "destabilized world situation."[34] In February, the church went further and openly criticized the Soviet occupation of Afghanistan, terming it inimical to peace.[35] And in the summer, the church remonstrated against "overly long belligerent reports" by East German media about Warsaw Pact maneuvers in the country.[36] That resulted in the confiscation by the authorities of an edition of the Evangelical News Service in September 1980. At this point, the independent peace movement did not exist, and the church had not taken any decisive steps in the direction of creating a national peace forum.

Impetus for this step came from three sources. First, as already discussed, the militarization of education and of society as a whole evoked pressures from below. Second, the church itself had been caught up in the worldwide debate on human rights in the 1970s. Shortly after the GDR ratified the UNESCO convention on discrimination in education in September 1973, the church pointed to the GDR's prejudicial treatment of young Christians and stressed that it favored discussion of human rights generally. Bishop Johannes Hempel told a district synod in Saxony in October 1977 that the church would retain a "critical distance" from the SED on the subject of human rights and considered respect for human rights a criterion for assessing the legitimacy of the state and the social order it represented. His colleague Almut Engelien spoke for the church as a whole when he declared in 1980 that "there is an indissoluble connection between the security of peace, cooperation, and the realization of human rights; whatever occurs to the detriment of human rights is at the same time an assault on peace."[37]

A third source for the development of the church-backed peace movement was the GDR government's reaction to events in Poland. After the collapse of Poland's Gierek regime and the series of compromises and retreats made by Stanislaw Kania—during which the independent trade union Solidarity was established—the GDR restricted travel to Poland, tightened controls on correspondence between the two countries, inaugurated a media campaign to revive anti-Polish prejudice among the East German population, and implied that the Evangelical Church wished to follow the example of the Polish Catholic Church, which supported Solidarity. In the autumn of 1980, East German authorities banned reporting of church synods that discussed peace; church papers that printed statements on peace were pulped and reprinted with sanitized texts. The SED decided to curtail the number of contacts between the Evangelical Church in the GDR and outside churches and, in mid-November 1980, threatened the church with "administrative measures" unless it desisted from further political criticism.[38] Nevertheless, an April 1981 synod of the Evangelical Church in Berlin-Brandenburg proclaimed its solidarity with the Polish people and deplored the SED's anti-Polish campaign. The church was able to send some six tons of food for distribution by the Polish Catholic Church, although GDR customs officials frustrated attempts by individual citizens to send food packages to Poles.[39]

From November 9 to 19, 1980, Protestant parishes throughout the GDR held what proved to be the first of a series of annual "peace decades," during which thousands of youths gathered to hear the clergy speak out on peace and participate in wide-ranging discussions. In mid-1981, the church commissioned an East German graphic artist to design a shoulder patch with the scriptural words "Swords into Plowshares" (*Schwerter zu Pflugscharen*). These emblems were distributed by the church at its second annual peace decade in the autumn of 1981. The regime initally tried to give a favorable interpretation to the symbol. The East Berlin periodical *Deutsche Zeitschrift für Philosophie* commented approvingly on the shoulder patch in its first issue of 1982. A Radio Moscow commentator covering East German affairs also praised the emblem as "one of the outstanding works of Soviet art" and noted that Soviet citizens saw in it a reflection of their own attitudes.[40]

But the benevolent attitude of the communist authorities changed as a nationwide independent peace movement developed and groups of pacifists sprouted in various East German cities, taking the motto "Swords into Plowshares" as their common emblem. At the end of 1981, when some 4,000 East German youths flocked to a "blues mass" in East Berlin, State Secretary Gysi lambasted the event as a "political cabaret." On February 13, 1982, at the urging of grass-roots pacifists, the Church of the

Holy Cross in Dresden hosted a public forum to discuss peace and disarmament. Four to five thousand East Germans took part, even though the SED had discouraged such events. There, once again, the demand was raised for obligatory "peace education" in schools. In the months that followed, similar forums were sponsored in Potsdam, Eisenach, and Burg (Spreewald), involving more that 10,000 young people altogether.[41]

By early 1982, it was clear that the Evangelical Church through its involvement in a peace movement embracing Christians, secular pacifists, environmentalists, and dissident Marxists,[42] was gaining a following among East German youth as a whole—a dangerous development from the vantage point of the SED. The church's ability to draw Catholic youths into its activities showed that its influence was not limited to its own denomination. Its Biblical slogan appeared to have captured the conscience of an entire generation. Bishop Hempel was repeatedly applauded as he took the regime to task at the peace rally in Dresden:

> Why are peace rallies forbidden in the GDR? We should stand up for peace. Is security assured through military balance and strength? We must introduce an obligatory "peace education." Three hundred thousand persons demonstrated in Bonn against nuclear missiles. I mean they put themselves on the front line so that their missiles would not fall on our heads . . . and the question which should follow is: Shouldn't we also finally begin to count up our own missiles?[43]

The Evangelical Church had seemed to some observers to be too cooperative with the regime in 1980 when it joined the SED in opposing the modernization of NATO forces and in calling for the ratification of the SALT II agreement. But now it not only denounced the SED for its educational policies and for fanning the flames of anti-Polish prejudice, but also called for a reduction in the number of Soviet SS-20s in Eastern Europe.[44] The "Swords into Plowshares" motto was clearly becoming double-edged, and the SED had no patience with criticism of the Warsaw Pact or its policies.

Therefore, at a session of its Central Committee, the SED decided upon a propaganda counteroffensive in late November 1981, with the slogan "Peace must be defended—peace must be armed." This slogan appeared on billboards throughout East Germany in the early months of 1982. To the chagrin of the SED, however, the campaign boomeranged and only served to further alienate youths attracted to the independent peace movement. Moreover, the regime's condemnation of the peace service alternative did not discredit the proposal but only aroused outspoken protest.

In early 1982, the SED set out to suppress the "Swords into

Plowshares" patch. State Secretary Gysi explained that the patch had been "misused to proclaim views hostile to the state and involvement in an illegal political movement."[45] Wearing the shoulder patch in public was declared a misdemeanor, and East German police began stopping young people in the streets and compelling them to rip off their patches. Some wearers of the emblem found they could not buy bus tickets or were otherwise harassed.[46] Bishop Krusche fretted that all this was creating a "neurotic atmosphere" in the country, while East Berlin clergyman Manfred Stolpe asked, "Why must you shoot at sparrows with cannons, at butterflies with howitzers?"[47] In Thuringia, Chief Church Councilor Dietrich von Frommannshausen declared: "Whoever attacks the symbol 'Swords into Plowshares' attacks the Church itself."[48] And Brandenburg Bishop Gottfried Forck called on the regime to reverse itself, to publish an apology in all newspapers for attacks on the peace emblem and rehabilitate it. Gysi's reply: "What we need is for the Church to obey the law."[49]

The SED thereupon altered its tactics somewhat. Instead of dealing with the church as a unit, it reverted to the old tactic of trying to drive a wedge between the church hierarchy and the lower clergy. The SED summoned church representatives to confidential meetings with party authorities to pressure them into passivity. At the same time, pacifist youths were arrested in Dresden and Jena and a young engineer in Berlin was sentenced to eight months in prison for insisting on being allowed to do his military service in the construction unit.[50] As for the church's concern about the proliferation of "enemy" images in the classroom and the media, the proregime monthly, *Standpunkt*, argued that since the SED's policy was directed against "imperialism and its most aggressive organizations and forms," it must be viewed as a "good policy" compatible with peace and therefore "compatible with the Christian commandment of loving one's enemy." Besides, the journal argued, "communist policy endeavors to bring about a just, exact, and scientifically founded image of the enemy."[51]

In May 1982, the Evangelical bishops decided to withdraw the emblem and not distribute it at peace forums. But it also decided to retain the "Swords into Plowshares" slogan for the church's work for peace and to use it as the theme at the third annual peace decade, November 7–17, 1982. The decision to withdraw the patch, which was announced only in late September at the Halle synod, provoked surprise and criticism. Lower clergy and youth were also dismayed by the church's declaration that the emblem should no longer be displayed in public, even though some 7,000 youths had worn it defiantly at meetings in Brandenburg in June.[52]

But although the church had withdrawn the patch, it continued to defend it as a legitimate symbol of its peace work. For example, Bishop

Heinrich Rathke, one of forty foreign visitors attending the Conference of Romanian Churches for Disarmament and Peace in Bucharest (June 1984), spoke out there in defense of the slogan, while Bishop Hempel told a synod, about the same time, that the authorities had no business suppressing the patch.[53]

Meanwhile, popular support for the church's peace forums grew, as shown in preparations for the 1982 peace decade. Almost every town and village had local clergy and peace groups involved in organizing discussions, meetings, and church services. Pacifists from East Berlin collected signatures on a petition calling for a ban on the import and sale of military toys. Clergy once more emphasized that the church's work for peace was a "vital matter of conscience."[54]

Whatever doubts an outside observer might have had regarding the firmness of the various parties in what was unmistakably a major controversy—dividing the regime on the one side from the youth and the church on the other—were cleared up in 1983. The SED expelled about twenty East German pacifists from the country early in the year and arrested several peace demonstrators in Berlin in September 1983.[55] At the same time, the regime mobilized its supporters in the CDU-East to champion military service under socialism as a "peace service . . . which is in complete harmony with one's conviction and faith as a Christian."[56] In early October, Halle Pastor Lothar Rochau, well known for his pacifist work, was sentenced to three years without probation for the "establishment of illegal groupings."[57] Eight more pacifists, all from Weimar, were behind bars by the end of January 1984; and shortly thereafter, theologian Wolf Quasdorf, another active pacifist, was imprisoned, ostensibly for "illegal contacts" in pursuit of emigration.[58] Meanwhile, East German authorities continued their surveillance of unofficial peace rallies, obstructed access to them by pacifist youths, and photographed those attending.

The SED also discovered that it could maintain good relations with West Germany and whittle down opposition at home through a policy of granting exit visas generously but selectively. Suddenly, after waiting for years to be allowed to leave the GDR, persons who had been fired from their jobs and given work by the church were allowed to emigrate. In 1983, for example, six East German pastors from Berlin-Brandenburg were allowed to emigrate with their families. Officials began pressuring pacifists and other dissenters to leave the country, so that, by May 1984, more than 20,000 East Germans had settled in West Germany. The church began to become alarmed at this sudden tide. In April 1984, its leadership appealed to Christians to stay in the GDR to maintain a Christian presence.[59]

The Evangelical Church continued to try to stake out "the narrow space between opposition and opportunism." It made clear that, despite its willingness to withdraw the peace emblem as a concession to the government, it could compromise only on form and not on substance. On the last day of its September 1983 synod in Potsdam, the sixty Evangelical delegates present unanimously passed a resolution calling for a moratorium on the installation of new missiles in Europe, whether by the Soviet Union or the United States. The church thus reaffirmed its support for arms negotiations, steadily voiced since September 1979; but now it specifically called on the Soviets to translate into deeds their expressed willingness to destroy some of their SS-20s as a gesture for promoting confidence.[60] The synod also submitted a set of concrete proposals to the authorities, urging them to sign a nuclear freeze agreement; promote the United Nations disarmament campaign within the GDR; declare that the possession or use of nuclear arms is a crime; attempt, within the context of existing treaties, to ban new short-range nuclear weapons from GDR territory; and strengthen personal contacts between Germans living in East and West Germany in order to reduce mutual fear and promote peace.[61] The synod also accused the SED of hypocrisy in welcoming the church's peace efforts directed at NATO countries and their allies while disparaging its peace efforts directed at the GDR and other Warsaw Pact countries. Such a two-faced policy could not enjoy any credibility, the synod added. As if to impress the authorities with its self-confidence, the church retained "Swords into Plowshares" as the symbol for its fourth annual peace decade, November 6–16, 1983.

The regime may well have decided that, while it too does not want to compromise on substance, it may have to compromise on form if its policies are to be effective. At any rate, it allowed the publication in *Standpunkt* of theologian P. F. Zimmermann's endorsement of the church's call for a reduction in "enemy images" as a prerequisite for peace.[62] In another surprising move, it allowed publication in October in the party organ, *Neues Deutschland*, of a letter to Honecker that spoke of being

> filled with horror at the thought that with stationing of American nuclear missiles in Western Europe, a move that we all condemn, corresponding nuclear missiles will also be introduced on our territory and that we and our children will have to live with the immediacy of nuclear missiles. You, yourself, have often expressed the view that more arms do not mean more security.[63]

The letter was signed by an Evangelical pastor from Dresden-Loschwitz, two members of the parish executive committee, and five parishioners. As if to make certain that the new tactic was not missed, the SED repeated it with the publication in *Neues Deutschland* (November 3, 1983) of a letter lamenting the spread of hopelessness about peace prospects among both Christians and non-Christians.

Some observers expected the flight of a number of young pacifists to West Germany in 1984 to cripple the church's peace decades. On the contrary, attendance in 1984 and 1985 was as strong as ever, with persons of all ages getting involved. In 1984, the church began to broaden the focus of the gatherings and devoted greater attention to environmental issues— another sensitive subject for the regime.[64] For all this criticism, however, the church has found that in a number of areas—the education of youth, the militarization of society, and the absence of a civil service alternative to military service, for instance—the regime has shown no sign of willingness to compromise. In this context, Bishop Hempel told the Greifswald synod in September 1984 that the state should reexamine its policy toward the churches.[65]

The involvement of the Evangelical Church of East Germany in the cause of international and domestic peace has led it to express more insistently its conviction that there is only one German nation[66] and only one German Evangelical Church (albeit organized in two separate institutional frameworks). The church has accordingly called attention to the "complicated and unresolved question of the German nation," deploring the SED's vilification of the Federal Republic.[67] In January 1982, Magdeburg Bishop Krusche, then chairman of the Evangelical Federation, called for the withdrawal of both Germanys from their respective defense pacts as a prerequisite to political reunification.[68]

The engagement of the Evangelical Church of West Germany in the peace movement there has led to common actions with the church in East Germany. In September 1979, a letter was read at Sunday services in both East and West Germany, expressing concern over deterioration in East-West relations. On March 17, 1980, church officials of the two branches met with State Secretary Gysi in the first meeting of any GDR official with West German Evangelical bishops since 1969. After the meeting, the West German Evangelical chairman, Bishop Eduard Lohse of Hanover, said he hoped that such contacts could be revived, while Bishop Schönherr characterized the meeting as a "sign of the present growing respect" between the church and the state in the GDR.[69] At that time, the GDR government seemed to welcome cooperation between the two Evangelical branches.

By the autumn of 1980, however, church contacts with West Germany seemed no longer acceptable to the GDR.[70] Travel by East German clergy to West Germany was curtailed; Western correspondents were not allowed to cover East German church synods directly; and the church press was subjected to tougher censorship. Yet on August 19, 1982, the West and East German churches again issued a joint document, this time setting forth their shared views on the responsibility of the church in working for peace. In a critical passage, the two branches spoke out for pluralism and compromise:

> In view of the continuous and ongoing rearmament and the increasing threat of the total destruction of human life contained therein, it has now become a question of political rationality to develop concepts to attempt to achieve the safeguarding of peace, and thereby the preservation of life, through other than military means. Security is conceivable today only in the context of a system that takes opposing interests into equal consideration and that requires peaceful compromise.[71]

Although secularization of East German society has steadily reduced the membership of the Evangelical Church,[72] the church has a resilience and qualitative strength that it has not enjoyed in more than a quarter-century. Its services and seminars are well attended. Those attending appear fired by a sense of purpose and look to the church for social and moral leadership rather than for ethical guidance narrowly defined.[73] More and more, those who are discontented in East German society look also to the church for protection.[74] Indeed, the church's broad credibility among youths concerned with problems of peace regardless of belief— Protestant, Catholic, agnostic, atheist—poses a threat to the ideological and political monopoly that the SED strives to maintain. The SED gives every appearance of having accepted the church as a legitimate institutional actor, at least for the foreseeable future. By 1980, the party had almost completely abandoned its earlier atheistic propaganda and had adopted a posture of relative openness with respect to religion. The SED had even gone so far as to describe religion as a necessary part of socialist society having "objective roots" in the first phase of the construction of communism.[75] To what extent that represents a true change in religious policy, as opposed to a tactical retreat, is not clear.

THE CATHOLIC CHURCH—CONSCIOUS ESTRANGEMENT

Given the outspokenness of the Evangelical-Lutheran Church, it may seem surprising that the Roman Catholic Church has adopted a relatively quiet posture. Certainly in terms of philosophical orientation, the Catholic Church in East Germany has been more estranged from the communist system, indeed consciously so, than the Evangelical Church. Thus, whereas Evangelical Bishop Schönherr signaled his church's openness to dialogue by adopting the expression "Church in socialism," Catholic Bishop Joachim Wancke (of Erfurt) deliberately kept authorities at arm's length with his chilling phrase, "Church in a secularized, materialistic environment."[76] But rather than propelling the Catholic Church into the arms of the pacifist opposition, this policy of conscious estrangement has tended to keep the church aloof from the social issues of the day, as if the price of social engagement were some degree of accommodation to the social order.

In part, the difference between the Evangelical Church and the Catholic Church is one of style. While the Evangelical Church has organized peace decades and public forums and addresses social issues in the open, the Catholic Church has tended to prefer to advance its position secretly and in private correspondence with the authorities.[77] Only rarely has the Catholic hierarchy spoken out in public. In 1974, for instance, a pastoral letter criticized discrimination against Christians in the schools. In 1978, the Catholic bishops registered their opposition to the introduction of premilitary training in the schools. In March 1981, another pastoral letter remonstrated against the "propaganda of hate," while Bishop Wancke took up the subject of the militarization of society in a series of sermons in early 1982. A second difference between the two churches is in resources. The Catholic Church, which has about 1.2–1.3 million adherents in the GDR, simply cannot command the audience and the attention that the Evangelical Church, with six times as many members, can. But the differences in orientation go even deeper, reflecting the differences between the Protestant and Catholic cultures. Catholicism has traditionally sought to find accommodation with secular power and has erected its edifice upon the triad listed by Dostoyevsky's Grand Inquisitor: miracle, mystery, and authority. And for the Catholic Church, respect for ecclesiastical authority and respect for secular authority go hand in hand. It was in this spirit that Pope Gregory XVI condemned the Polish November Uprising in his encyclical of 1832:

> These terrible calamities have no other source than the maneuvers of certain purveyors of fraud and lies who use the pretext of religion to raise their heads against the legitimate power of princes.[78]

Protestantism, by contrast, not only arose as protest against authority, but has consciously shifted emphasis from mystery and authority to individual conscience and prudence.

The Catholic Church's most dramatic protest of recent vintage against the SED may well be attributable to direct pressure from the outspoken Polish pope, John Paul II. On October 28, 1982, the pontiff received the bishops of Berlin, Dresden-Meissen, Schwerin, Görlitz, Magdeburg, and

Erfurt-Meiningen in a private audience and, according to the official record, called their attention to the church's responsibility to address questions of peace and other questions of interest to the community generally and the youth in particular.[79] Just two months later, the GDR bishops issued a pastoral letter, expressing alarm at the militarization of East German society and calling for other forms of alternative service.[80]

Later that year, Joachim Cardinal Meisner, chairman of the Berlin Bishops' Conference, met with State Secretary Gysi for private talks. During these talks, Meisner reiterated church concern about the implications of a 1980 school ordinance that requires East German teachers "to further complete communist upbringing"[81]—a phrase that seems to imply atheization and to minimize the parents' right to exercise judgment in the upbringing of their children.

CONCLUSION

The social behavior of churches reflects their character as vestigial political organizations and agents of cultural mores and practices. Hence, churches are concerned both with the behavior of society broadly and with the education of individuals. For the communists, these two aspects are equally political, and to them, religion appears to be a strictly political phenomenon.[82]

Both the Evangelical-Lutheran and the Catholic Churches in East Germany are aware of the extent to which they figure as political actors. The Catholic Church appears more comfortable than the Evangelical Church with this role, and less attracted to a posture of opposition. But the Evangelical Church, while it may be at home with a posture of opposition and protest and seems to see itself as a voice in the wilderness, remains deeply ambivalent about the broader, theological implications of its work for peace.

SIX

Factionalism in the Croatian Church-State Relationship

Among the possible approaches in studying church-state interaction is one that endeavors to treat both church and state as active subjects and is sensitive to factional divisions within both of them. From this standpoint, it is clear that just as there can be a regime religious policy, so too the churches can have policies toward the regime, and the resulting relationship will reflect the interplay of the two policies.[1] To the extent that state and church are factionalized, their respective policies will be not only the subject but also the product of ongoing debate and continuing interfaction struggles.

Sensitivity to factionalism is not a black-and-white issue. All the same, it may be possible to group Western writings on church-state relations under communism into four general categories. In the first category are works treating both church and state as unified (nonfactionalized) entities—either explicitly (by denying factionalism) or implicity (by ignoring it as analytically unimportant). This category is by far the largest, and thirty-eight of fifty-three works I have surveyed fall into this category. This general approach is characterized by the adoption of linear periodization schemes for understanding church-state relations; the description of the interests, difficulties, and opinions of the church as a whole; and the presumption of unified purposes and goals on the part of both church and state.[2] The second category embraces writings that are sensitive to the existence of diverse currents in individual churches but treat the communist state as a monolith. Divisions within the church are frequently interpreted as being the result of church difficulties or as a source of symptoms

97

of weakness and hence as something abnormal.[3] In the third category are works sensitive to the existence of diverse currents in the state, but tending to treat churches as monoliths, with monolithic interests.[4] Finally, there is a small cluster of works that evince sensitivity to the existence of factions within both the church and the state.[5] This chapter is undertaken in the belief that the presence of divisions within both church and state is an important subject of scrutiny, with the potential to affect church-state relations tangibly. In particular, a regime's religious policy cannot be assumed to be a cohesive and consistent whole, since even its formulators are divided among themselves.

Yugoslavia, a multiethnic federation, is also multiconfessional. Of its principal nationalities, the Serbs, Macedonians, and Montenegrins are traditionally Orthodox; the Turks and Bosnia's "ethnic Muslims" are Muslim; and the Albanians of Kosovo are mostly Muslim. Only the Slovenes and Croats are predominantly Catholic. When one speaks of Yugoslav Catholicism, therefore, one is speaking of the Slovenian Catholic Church and the Catholic Church among the Croats (*Katolička crkva u Hrvata*), which includes Croats living in Bosnia-Herzegovina or elsewhere in Yugoslavia.

I have limited my investigation essentially to the Catholic Church among the Croats for three reasons. First, the Catholic Church among the Croats—or, hereafter, the Croatian Catholic Church—is, in fact, a conceptual entity that views itself as a whole, albeit a divided one. Interactions within the Croatian Catholic Church are more frequent than are church interactions between Croatia and Slovenia. Second, some of the issues that divide the Croatian Church are simply not salient in Slovenia. And third, the national question is manifested quite differently among the Croats and the Slovenes. Although the church has been quite readily identified with the mainstream of Slovenian nationalism during the past 100 years, the Slovenian Church hierarchy, unlike the Croatian hierarchs in ethnically mixed Croatia,[6] has not often been at odds with the political authorities. It has, therefore, not adopted an oppositionist role, this role being unnecessary in compact, politically more pluralistic, and ethnically homogeneous Slovenia. That means there is an entire dimension of religious policy that is absent when it comes to Slovenia.

As of February 1981, there were 6.8 million Catholics in Yugoslavia, comprising about 31 percent of the country's total population, served through a network of 2,780 parishes. The Catholic Church could count 4,177 priests (2,741 diocesan and 1,436 in religious orders), 6,394 nuns, and (in 1978) 288 lay brothers. There were 401 Yugoslav priests working in other countries as of 1979, principally in Germany, Australia, Argentina, and other countries having large Croatian communities. In 1978, there were 368 seminarians, 430 students of theology, and 72 novices.[7]

The Catholic Church in Yugoslavia consists of eight archbishoprics, fourteen bishoprics, and two apostolic administrations. Unlike the churches in other communist countries, it has had no trouble keeping these seats filled. These various subdivisions are organized into five church provinces: (1) Zagreb, which includes the diocese of Djakovo and the Greek Catholic diocese of Križevci (60,000 believers); (2) Split-Makarska, which includes the dioceses of Dubrovnik, Hvar, Kotor, and Šibenik; (3) Vrhbosna (Sarajevo), which includes Sarajevo, Banja Luka, Mostar, and the dioceses of Skopje and Prizren; (4) Rijeka-Senj; and (5) Ljubljana, which includes all Slovenia.[8] The Catholic Church operates theological faculties in Zagreb and Ljubljana and theological higher schools in Djakovo, Split, Sarajevo, and Rijeka. The largest religious order in Yugoslavia, the Salesians, numbered 103 members in 1978. The Franciscans, who operate seminaries in Sarajevo and Makarska, were second, with ninety-four members. There are also Jesuits, Dominicans, Carmelites, Trappists, Paulines, Carthusians, and other religious orders.

Religious belief in Yugoslavia has been more tenacious among Catholics than among Orthodox. A survey conducted among the population of the Zagreb region in 1972 showed that 93.4 percent identified themselves as members of the Roman Catholic Church, while only 5.7 percent said they were atheists. Moreover, 58.8 percent of the women and 43.6 percent of the men said they were practicing believers.[9] Somewhat surprisingly, while 93.4 percent had declared themselves to be Catholics, identifying with the church as an institution, only 80.1 percent said they believed in God. Comparing Catholic and non-Catholic regions, recent surveys in Split and Vojvodina found that 30 percent of young Croats attend church regularly and only 30 percent are atheists, while 70 percent of Vojvodinan youth are atheists. Similarly, opnion polls reported by *Ilustrovana politika* (February 23, 1982) revealed that in traditionally Catholic regions, one third of the youth are religious, one third atheist, and one third either passive believers or uncertain. In traditionally Serbian Orthodox regions, on the other hand, only 3 percent of the youth felt religious, while 90 percent claimed to feel positive aversion toward religion.[10] Another measure of the strength of Catholicism among Croats and Slovenes was provided by a 1979 church survey, which found that close to a 100 percent of rural children in both Slovenia and Croatia attended religious instruction regularly, while in the cities, 40 to 50 percent of children up to age fourteen attended.[11]

DIVISIONS WITHIN THE ESTABLISHMENT

The "establishment" consists of the League of Communists of Yugoslavia (LCY), its governmental apparatus, the party's umbrella organization known as the Socialist Alliance of Working People of Yugoslavia

(SAWPY), and the Marxist intelligentsia concerned with religion. Strictly speaking, there are no party bodies concerned expressly with religious policy. This sphere is formally allotted to both the governmental apparatus and SAWPY, which means that there is an overlap of jurisdiction, already the groundwork for potential intraestablishment differences. In Croatia, for instance, the government's Office for Religious Affairs was headed for several years by Dr. Ivan Lalić, while the Commission for Social Questions of Religion of Croatia's regional SAWP organization was for some time presided over by Stjepan Cerjan. In addition to these institutions, a number of prominent Marxist sociologists, including Ivan Cvitković, Esad Ćimić, Zdenko Roter, Zlatko Frid, and Branko Bošnjak, have been actively concerned with religious questions.

This institutional description is only partly related to the actual differences of opinion within the elite, for although there appear to be two broad opinion groups in the regime, these groups do not correspond to the division between the governmental and SAWPY apparatus. There appears to be some correlation between the degree of Marxist orthodoxy, on the one hand, and generational differences and republic of assignment, on the other. Specifically, the older generation, in particular veterans of the partisan struggle, tends to be more clearly antireligious and to operate on the presupposition that there is no room for religion in Marxist society, that religion is a reactionary vestige of precommunist society, and that religious institutions will gradually die off under Marxist rule. In addition, members of the Croatian party apparatus per se (as opposed to the Bosnian, the Slovenian, or the federal apparatus) tend to be more concerned about fissiparous nationalism and the influence of the church in supporting Croatian nationalism; they are therefore also apt to adopt a hard-line attitude toward religious organizations. Among those in this first group (orthodox Marxists), I would include Jure Bilić, president of the Croatian Assembly; Jakov Blažević, former president of the Croatian Republic and one-time prosecutor of Archbishop Alojzije Stepinac (in 1946); Milutin Baltić, Croatian secretary of the Central Committee LCY; Dušan Dragosavac, also secretary of the Central Committee LCY; Branko Puharić, member of the presidency of SAWP-Croatia and director of Radio-TV Zagreb; Zlatko Uzelac, minister of the interior of Croatia; and the editorial staff of *Slobodna Dalmacija* (the Split daily). This group has no interest in genuine dialogue with churches; it equates public activity on the part of the churches with "illegality" and "criminality" and sees no future for the churches under communism.

A second group might be called the passive contract Marxists to indicate that they are willing to adopt a passive attitude toward religion, provided that the religious organizations adopt a passive attitude toward society and politics. This orientation implies some notion of legitimate spheres and is reflected in the party's embrace of the idea that religion is the "private affair" of the individual—an idea that has generated little enthusiasm among a clergy loathe to be expelled from the moral and public life of the community. Among those in this second group, I would include Aleksandar Fira, former president of the Federal Commission for Religious Affairs; Radovan Samardžić, longtime secretary of the Federal Commission for Religious Affairs; Nenad Ivanković, specialist on religious questions for the Croatian weekly, *Danas*; Todo Kurtović, former president of SAWPY; Ivan Lalić, long president of Croatia's Office for Religious Affairs; Mitja Ribičič, the former head of the party; and the editorial staffs of *Danas* and *Vjesnik*, the Croatian daily. These persons are not as apt as orthodox Marxists to assume that religion will necessarily wither away. While they are less antagonistic toward Christian-Marxist dialogue than the first group, they have yet to display any real enthusiasm for it, either.

In addition to these two opinion groups within the regime, there is a third opinion group within the establishment: the aforementioned Marxist sociologists. They start from the premise that religion will be around for some time, perhaps indefinitely, and can in fact make a positive contribution to the building of self-managing socialism.[12] Srdjan Vrcan, one of their number, warned recently that approaching religion as if it were doomed to an early death could have serious negative political consequences.

Policy is not formulated by any one of these opinion groups alone, but is a product of the deliberations of the first two groups in consultation with the third. But while the position of the orthodox Marxists is relatively steady, the passive contract Marxists fluctuate in their pronouncements, in part at least in response to the degree to which they feel threatened by the church.

The orthodox Marxists proceed from Lenin's statement that "Marxism views all religions and churches, all religious organizations whatsoever, as organs of bourgeois reaction, which serve to buttress the exploitation and stultification of the working class."[13] It follows, as a Yugoslav writer recently put it, that "religious institutions and organizations endeavor to hold people in subjection. . . . Marxism, whose main task is the development of the class struggle (as Lenin says) cannot be neutral vis-à-vis religion, just as religion is also not neutral in that struggle. . . . The relation of the League of Communists, as a workers' party, toward religion is founded on the principles of Marxist theory and on revolutionary praxis in the struggle for class and national liberation."[14] In line with this view, the church is criticized for striving to strengthen its position among its people, for proselytization, for the revival of forgotten religious rituals, and for taking up the defense of the rights of believers.[15]

The orthodox Marxists in the Croatian party (Baltić, Bilić, Blažević, Dragosavac) can regularly be seen denouncing various church prelates. In mid-1981, for instance, Baltić told a Bosnian audience that the leading clergymen of the Zagreb archdiocese were "the prime movers behind the movement of hostility toward our social communities, behind nationalism and the sowing of hatred between nations, clericalism and fascist obscurantism." He charged that they were identifying themselves with "exhausted and bankrupt hacks."[16] Intermittent reports have surfaced of the harassment of Croatian children attending religious instruction, both in Croatia itself and in West Germany among Croatian emigrants. Authorities of the Yugoslav consulates in West Germany have, in fact, instructed Croatian parents to withdraw their children from religious instruction; in some cases, parents whose children had received such instruction in Germany were deprived of their passports upon return to Yugoslavia.[17] Construction and renovation permits for churches have frequently been held up. On occasion, issues of the church news organ *Glas koncila* and other church periodicals have been banned. The orthodox Marxists have been particularly concerned about church support of Croatian nationalism, recognizing that it is a source of the church's strength. To cut the church off from the people, the orthodox Marxists believe, it is necessary to break the connection between Catholicism and nationalism. Thus it is no coincidence that both in 1971 and in 1981, the launching of an antireligious campaign against the Catholic Church was linked to regime nervousness about Croatian nationalism. In 1971, the campaign coincided with the purge of Croatian liberals in the party and the shutting down of the nationalist cultural society Matica hrvatska, and in 1981 with the trial and imprisonment of several leading Croatian nationalists (Vlado Gotovac, Dobroslav Paraga, Franjo Tudjman, and Marko Veselica).

But since the church cannot be expected to resign its commitment to Croatian nationalism, party hard-liners—many of them (notably Baltić, Dragosavac, Uzelac) actually ethnic Serbs from Croatia, a group that has long been disproportionately overrepresented in the Croatian party—have tried to taint that commitment by associating it with fascism. In this endeavor, the party has made full use of the ambiguous role of the church in World War Two. It has claimed that Zagreb Archbishop Alojzije Stepinac, who was imprisoned in 1946 after a rigged trial on trumped-up charges of collaboration with the fascist *Ustaše,* not only consorted with "renowned cutthroats" but also identified with two prominent Ustaše intellectuals (Dragiša Vasić and Milo Budak). It has also claimed that

Kvirin Klement Bonefačić, bishop of Split and Makarska 1923–54, was a fascist.[18] Church demands that the Stepinac case be reopened and the evidence dispassionately reexamined are rejected, with the observation that demands for his rehabilitation are reflections of the desire to spread religious and ethnic hatred.

The passive contract Marxists have often gone along with the orthodox Marxists—which then produces difficulties for the church. In late 1971, however, when a new configuration of forces brought an end to the regime's liberal religious policy of the 1966–71 period, many of the passive contract Marxists were alarmed and many lost their jobs as part of the general purge of the liberal leadership. Police searches of Franciscan monasteries, the imprisonment of certain clergy, and the imposition of a one-year ban from writing on Živko Kustić, editor of *Glas koncila,* were symptoms of the new alignment within the party.[19] More recently, on the other hand, they seem to have gone along with the orthodox Marxists' characterization of Zagreb's Cardinal Kuharić as bearing much of the blame for the frequent conflicts and tensions in church-state relations since 1973 and as viewing the church as a shadow government. At the beginning of 1983, some ten priests were in jail in Yugoslavia.[20] In 1981, government authorities actually authorized the destruction of a Catholic sanctuary in Vepric (along the Croatian coast). In January 1983, when Dominican Fr. Prcela reacted strongly in a Sunday sermon to a Split student newspaper article that depicted the Virgin Mary as taking birth control pills and Christ as a hashish addict, Yugoslav security forces arrested Prcela for infringing on "freedom of the press."[21]

Yet the passive contract Marxists seem also to have acted as a brake on the orthodox Marxists on occasion, their most powerful argument being that secularization is already eroding religious consciousness and that an oppressive or highly restrictive antireligious policy can only strengthen the churches by stimulating resistance. Such was the argument made by Nenad Ivanković, *Vjesnik's* authoritative commentator on the Catholic Church, in a November 1981 article. Ivanković, speaking on behalf of the passive contract Marxists, called for a toning down of the press campaign against the church, arguing that the exaggerations and crude oversimplifications in several newspapers had been counterproductive. Ivanković charged that "part of the press is reporting only the negative cases, while many positive facets [of the church's activity] are passed over in silence." He urged a more sober attitude as a precondition for a "constructive relationship between Christian religion and Marxism (the consequence of [which] should be the common construction of socialism in our country), which presumes a dialogue or actions that lead to a dialogue."[22] Similarly, though both Baltić and Bilić had accused Kuharić of fascistic leanings, Samardžić admitted in private conversation that Kuharić could not by any stretch of the imagination be considered a fascist.[23] When, moreover, orthodox Marxist Blažević tried to add fuel to the antichurch campaign by giving a press conference at the Twelfth Party Congress (June 1982), the Yugoslav press largely ignored him. Blažević said that his conference at the congress had been suppressed and that several journalists present had been instructed to treat his statements as only "personal opinions."[24]

In July 1982, Blažević obtained an interview with the new Croatian weekly, *Danas*. In a vitriolic interview, Stepinac's former prosecutor claimed that the church was not respecting the 1966 protocol signed between the Vatican and Yugoslavia, that Pope Pius XII had been a fascist, and that Pope John Paul II was "more dangerous" than Pius XII because he (allegedly) supported Italian irredentist claims against Yugoslavia and aspired to a leading role in the world arena.[25] Ivanković, spokesman of the passive contract Marxists, shot back in the next issue of *Danas* that Blažević did not represent the mainstream of the party and specifically repudiated the various claims made by Blažević, citing evidence to the contrary.[26]

The passive contract Marxists, less interested than the orthodox Marxists in assailing the church clerics in open confrontations, put greater emphasis on weaning youth away from the church. The infusion of the educational system with elements of atheism and mandatory study of Marxism at the university level is designed to serve this purpose. Thus, in an address to a group of teachers in early 1982, Ivan Lalić, president of Croatia's Office for Religious Affairs, said it was unrealistic for the Catholic Church hierarchy to ask that Yugoslav schools be "neutral" regarding religion, since schools must always be tools of the state and since the state is always the tool of the ruling class, which in Yugoslavia is, according to Lalić, the working class.[27] (Lalić did not mention, of course, that most Croats and Slovenes, including members of the working class, are believers.) Though that is tantamount to saying that atheism is official public policy, which is to say that atheism is imbued with political value, regime spokesmen have recently insisted that the endorsement of atheism is not tantamount to endorsement of atheization, and that it would be desirable to see the depoliticization of both theism and atheism.[28]

In the mid-1960s, the third current appeared in the establishment, seeking stability and setting a positive role for religious organizations. This current was more or less the exclusive domain of the Marxist sociologists, and, while they continue to champion Christian-Marxist dialogue today, the heyday of such dialogue was 1966–71. It was terminated by the suppression following the Croatia crisis. Branko Bošnjak may be credited with having played a central role in stimulating processes of dialogue. His invitation to Gustav Wetter, the Vatican's leading Marxologist, in summer 1966 to attend the Korčula Summer School was not only accepted but was followed by a public dialogue in Zagreb (March 28, 1967) between Bošnjak and Catholic theologian Mijo Škvorc of Zagreb, before an overflow crowd of 2,500 people. Bošnjak's suggestion that the distinction between "Marxist" and "Christian" was less important than that between "humanist" and "nonhumanist"[29] made it clear that the possibility of coexistence had been opened. As Ivica Račan would later put it, "Religious conviction is not an absolute obstacle to participation in the building of socialism,"[30] and hence, as Sarajevo sociologist Ivan Cvitković wrote in 1980, "in the political emancipation of man from religion, the socialist state does not seek the abolition of religion."[31] The criticism of religion should be superseded by the criticism of social relations in general. The high point of Christian-Marxist dialogue—which in Yugoslavia has always been Catholic-Marxist dialogue, since the Orthodox and Protestant churches have had no interest in such dialogue[32]—came in September 1971. At that time, the Institute for Social Research of the University of Zagreb and the Center for Conciliar Research, Christianity Today, cohosted an international conference attended by more than 200 participants, including more than eighty from Yugoslavia and five from Poland.

Despite recent church-state frictions, dialogue is not dead. That would appear paradoxical as long as church-state relations are viewed as the bipolar confrontation of monolithic institutions. But the apprehensions of the party have not caused the sociologists to lose their interest in dialogue. Roter in particular, a longtime champion of dialogue, sharply criticized antireligious prejudices that portray religion and communism as enemies and argued, in an article for *Delo* (November 28, 1981), that there should be more dialogue, not only on the elite level but also between ordinary people.[33] And in January 1983, Split sociologist Srdjan Vrcan called, in the pages of *NIN*, for a cessation to regime malignment of the church and to the authorities' treatment of believers as potential enemies.[34] Another token of this continued interest in dialogue was the broadcast over Yugoslav television on December 7, 1982, of a program on religion and socialism hosted by Cvitković, with both Marxists and clergymen taking part in the discussion. Among the clergy were Dr. Tomo Vereš (a Dominican from Zagreb), Bishop Vekoslav Grmič (of Maribor), and Fr. Marko Oršolić (of Sarajevo).[35]

DIVISIONS WITHIN THE CHURCH

Although the Roman Catholic Church is united by a common vision, a common pastoral mission, and an absolute submission to papal authority (under the doctrine of papal infallibility), it is feudal in structure, and the several archbishops in Yugoslavia enjoy complete autonomy. They are organized into a Bishops' Conference chaired by the archbishop of Zagreb, Franjo Cardinal Kuharić, but the bishops are ecclesiastical equals and neither Kuharić nor any other Yugoslav archbishop has predominance over the others. In addition, the various religious orders in Yugoslavia are self-conscious entities, jealous of their prerogatives and jurisdictions. Because of these and other factors, the church has been prone to internal divisions, rivalries, and frictions. *Glas koncila,* the de facto organ of the Zagreb archbishopric, and other church periodicals have not been immune to criticism from within the church. Thus, for instance, at a press conference in April 1970, the Yugoslav bishops chastized their own Catholic press for insufficient objectivity and insufficient support for the position of the church and the bishops; *Glas koncila* was singled out as a source of particular dissatisfaction.[36] Even lower clergymen have occasionally defied their church superiors. In October 1971, for instance, sixteen young priests from Zadar sent an open letter to their archbishop, accusing him of placing absolute obedience to him ahead of all other principles, employing priests lacking educational qualifications, closing church organizations that defied him in any way, and refusing to render an account of his work or of the finances of his archbishopric.[37]

Three salient divisions are found in the Croatian Catholic Church today: a rivalry between the diocesan clergy and the Franciscan order in Bosnia-Herzegovina, a personal rivalry between the archbishop of Zagreb and the archbishop of Split, and a contest of wills between the independent Theological Society Christianity Today (TDKS) and the ecclesiastical hierarchs in Croatia. All these rivalries have political importance, both for internal church politics and for church-state relations. The latter two rivalries in particular have offered the authorities the opportunity for manipulation, in the spirit of *divide et impera.*

Although the rivalry between the Franciscans and the diocesan structure dates back to the fourteenth century,[38] their contemporary rivalry centers on the staffing and control of parishes. In recent centuries, the Franciscans have usually been recruited directly from the villages they serve, while the diocesan system has brought in "outsiders." In Mostar (in Herzegovina), the bishop himself was usually a Franciscan. In 1964, however, a non-Franciscan bishop of Mostar, Dr. Petar Čule (appointed 1942) obtained permission from Rome to take over four of the thirty-five parishes operated by Franciscans in his diocese (diocesans already controlled thirty-four parishes). When the diocesans arrived at their assignments, the people refused to accept them; the bishop tried to blackmail the parishioners into submission by denying them the sacraments, but gradually the Franciscans returned to their posts. In June 1975, Pope Paul VI signed a decree instructing the Franciscans to vacate not only the four previously mentioned parishes but an additional thirteen as well. Fr. Rufin Šilić, superior of the Franciscans' Herzegovinan province, refused to sign the decree and was subsequently dismissed, along with the other five members of the provincial board. The Bosnian Franciscans condemned the dismissal and added that the 1975 decree stood in violation of both the Vatican II Declaration on Religious Liberty and the UN Declaration of Human Rights.[39]

Recently, the bishops of Sarajevo and Mostar have experienced an increase in priestly vocations, which has provided a stimulus to continue their rivalry with the Franciscans. In 1977, the archbishop of Sarajevo, in a spate of self-confidence, dared to send a diocesan priest to occupy a new parsonage in Kraljeva Sutjeska, in the middle of Franciscan territory. He was greeted by an armed contingent of parishioners who blocked his access.[40]

Some observers, including a contributor to *Komunist*,[41] have suggested that the Franciscans contrived to produce reports of miraculous appearances of the Virgin Mary in the Herzegovinan village of Medjugorje in 1981 (see chapter 8) and the village of Gala near Sinj in 1983. Whether or not the reports were the work of the Franciscans, it is clear that the Franciscans believe they stood to gain the most from the ensuing religious euphoria over Medjugorje. While the Bishops' Commission of the Mostar diocese (in which Medjugorje is located) has urged a cautious attitude regarding these claims, the Franciscans have openly endorsed the authenticity of the Medjugorje apparition (though the Franciscan provincial distanced himself from the reports about Gala).[42]

The second major division within the Croatian Catholic Church, the rivalry between Cardinal Kuharić of Zagreb and Archbishop Frane Franić of Split, is actually an intertwining of three separate issues: first, the historic rivalry between the ancient seat of Dalmatian Catholicism in Split and the "new" Croatian capital of Zagreb (allowing Franić to feel that tradition would justify his being chairman of the Bishops' Conference and cardinal rather than Kuharić); second, a personal rivalry rooted in differences of temperament between the ecclesiastically moderate but tolerant Kuharić, who places little stock in any "dialogue" with the regime, and the ecclesiastically very conservative and not particularly tolerant Franić, who nonetheless has declared himself on a number of occasions in favor of dialogue;[43] and third, an associated conflict of antidialogue and prodialogue clerical currents, which can look respectively to Zagreb and Split for inspiration.

When it comes to Christian-Marxist dialogue, Kuharić, his auxiliary bishop, Djuro Kokša, and their coworkers in the Zagreb Cathedral Chapter (Kaptol) are skeptical. From their point of view, "there is no point in pursuing a Christian-Marxist dialogue whatsoever; the Marxists are bent on atheizing society. The reason that the Marxists make concessions to the church is not any sort of mellowing, but simply that the church is a *fact*. What we must do is make the Church a *bigger fact*."[44] They emphasize the "poison" in the political atmosphere and attribute it to the regime. Hence, the SAWPY Commissions for Social Questions of Religion—which a commission official told me were "useful" to the churches as well as to the party[45]—are, for Kaptol, "of no use to the church whatsoever; they are only trouble."[46] Although Kuharić recently declared himself "open to sincere and truthful dialogue with every person and institution, expecting that the collocutor will show good will and the disposition to seek positive solutions to concrete and serious problems in mutual relations,"[47] he is actually profoundly skeptical of the sincerity of the regime and complained in 1980 that it had an active program of atheization that was turning people against religion.[48] At the same time, Kuharić has shown himself skeptical of the benefits of "self-managing socialism." He and his associates have repeatedly called for greater respect for human rights; at the solemn celebration in the Zagreb Cathedral of his elevation to the College of Cardinals, Kuharić told an overflow congregation of 15,000 believers, twenty-five bishops and archbishops, and more than 300 priests that no system should protect itself by locking up its political dissidents (a clear reference to the cases of Gotovac, Paraga, Tudjman, and Veselica) and demanded respect for human rights in Yugoslavia.[49]

By contrast, Dr. Franić, who was installed as archbishop and metropolitan of Split upon the reestablishment of the metropolite of Split-Makarska in November 1969, displayed an interest in dialogue quite early, accepting an invitation to lecture on theology and revolution in November 1970 at the Seminar for Political and Sociological Research at the Law School in Split, and reciprocating with an invitation to Srdjan Vrcan to lecture at the High Theological School in Split. Politically, Franić has tried to portray himself as absolutely loyal and has, in his own words, "stated on numerous occasions that self-managing socialism—if one takes atheism out of it—is, at this historical moment, the best social system."[50] In 1973, Franić published a book, *Putovi dijaloga,* in which he went so far as to construe Marxism as useful to Christianity. "It is our opinion," he wrote, "that dialectical-historical materialism will end up playing a positive role with respect to Christianity, because under the criticism of that materialism, Christianity must purify itself and renew itself spiritually."[51] Franić offered the suggestion that the church seek to differentiate between what is essential to Marxism and what is inessential, as a basis for dialogue.

Although Franić has been criticized in the regime press all the same for his outspoken criticism of atheism and for his suggestion (in 1979) that guarantees for religious practice in Yugoslavia be strengthened,[52] other clergymen have likewise sought to encourage dialogue-minded elements in the establishment. Among this number are Sarajevo Friar Marko Oršolić, and Zagreb Dominican Dr. Tomo Vereš.

The third source of discord in the Croatian Church hinges on the status and role of Zagreb's Theological Society Christianity Today (*Teološko Društvo Kršćanska Sadašnjost,* or TDKS). Created in 1968 by the then archbishop of Zagreb, Franjo Cardinal Šeper, the organization was charged with filling the vacuum in religious literature that had been created by the restrictive party policies of the late 1940s and 1950s. TDKS published theological studies, liturgical manuals, catechisms, Biblical texts, and church documents; it also took over publication of the journal *Svesci,* created a monthly family review called *Kana,* and established a news agency (AKSA) for the Croatian Catholic Church, which has published a weekly bulletin since April 1970. TDKS became known as an ecclesiastically progressive center (in the Vatican II sense) and began organizing congresses and symposia, including two international theological congresses. In 1977, however, as a result of new legislation that gave a tax break to "self-managing" organizations, the board of directors of TDKS unilaterally decided to change the institution's status, reorganizing its juridical form. The name of the institution, like its staffing and purpose, remained the same, and it continued to respect church authority.[53] However, the juridical reorganization had been carried out without consulting the bishops, and that was in itself a breach of discipline.

Franić has been a leading critic of TDKS. Hostile both to the democratic and "progressive" currents that emerged from the Vatican II Council and to Western democracy, which he views as the breeding ground of secularization, Franić recently defined the church as "a *hierarchical* community of faith, hope and love."[54] In his 1980 New Year's sermon, he rejected the notion of any democratization in the church, whether on the Western model or on the Yugoslav, condemning talk of democratization as "the greatest schism and heresy of the age, more dangerous to the church than was Protestantism in its time."[55] Franić was therefore hostile toward TDKS even before its juridical reorganization in 1977. In addition, Franić felt a personal antipathy toward Kuharić's predecessor in Zagreb, the creator of TDKS, Franjo Šeper.[56] But other clergy in Yugoslavia, notably the Jesuits, were also hostile to the organization's ecumenically liberal organization. After 1977, Šeper (by then in Rome), Kuharić, and Franić all expressed misgivings about the society's having passed from church jurisdiction to state jurisdiction. There have been, thus, three issues entangled in the controversy surrounding TDKS: its breach of discipline in reorganizing itself without consulting the bishops, its progressive theology, and its alleged subordination (denied by its officials) to the party apparatus.

The controversy quickly became heated, so that when, in its May 1978 issue, *Glas koncila*—whose editor, Živko Kustić, was associated with TDKS—published an article defending the theological society, Franić banned the dissemination of the issue in his archdiocese. Three months later, Kustić quit the society, after a falling out with its secretary.[57] By 1982, the bishops of Djakovo and Split had forbidden priests under their jurisdiction to associate with TDKS. In the archdiocese of Split and the diocese of Dubrovnik and conservative Mostar, priests associated with TDKS, regardless of their place of permanent assignment, were forbidden to say mass.[58] Despite this gathering clamor and his theological differences with the society, Archbishop Kuharić continued to give the society the passive support it needed to continue its work.

Franić became more sharply critical of TDKS during 1982. He told a *Vjesnik* journalist in a July interview that TDKS had seceded from the church, was no longer subject to the hierarchy, and was now under the "influence" of the party. Franić further suggested that TDKS be split in two to create a "faithful" publishing house, leaving the "political" society to do as it might please.[59] That provoked a heated rebuttal in the pages of *Vjesnik* by TDKS spokesmen, who maintained that "the TDKS of which Archbishop Franić speaks does not exist, or if it does exist, it is not *this* theological society." But by calling Franić's views "absurd" and tendentious "personal opinions," by claiming that Franić "has no right to judge the association" on the basis of those opinions,[60] and by daring to take its case directly to the regime press, again without consulting the bishops, TDKS further alienated important sectors of the hierarchy.

At its autumn convocation, September 27–29, 1982, the Bishops' Conference of Yugoslavia, meeting in Djakovo, condemned TDKS for its breach of discipline. It also employed a papal decree ("Quidam Episcopi," issued March 8, 1982) aimed at the politically subverted Czechoslovak priests' association Pacem in Terris to take TDKS to task for syndical activity outside the control of the bishops. The episcopal communique, issued in Djakovo, September 30, 1982, also upbraided the society for its insinuations in the *Vjesnik* rebuttal,[61] and declared that no clergyman was allowed to be a member of TDKS. Archbishop Franić quickly suspended the few priests in his archdiocese who were connected with the association, and so did the bishop of Dubrovnik. Archbishop Kuharić refrained from any parallel action.[62]

A FACTIONAL MODEL OF CHURCH-STATE INTERACTION

It should be clear that an account that described church-state relations as if one were dealing with two undifferentiated actors would, at least in the Croatian case, obscure fundamental features of the religious policy context. To understand processes occurring simultaneously at several levels, with crisscrossing interactions, it is necessary to adopt a factional model of church-state interaction. In this model, we might describe the Croatian Church as consisting of four opinion groups: the theologically moderate, politically noncollaborationist clergy, among whom Kuharić of Zagreb is the leading figure; the theologically conservative, politically traditional but dialogue-minded clergy, among whom Franić of Split is the leading figure; the Bosnian Franciscans, who organized a proregime priests' association, *Dobri pastir*, but who have also traditionally been deeply involved in the development of Croatian nationalism;[63] and the theologically and politically progressive clergy in TDKS. The establishment might be described as consisting of three opinion groups: the orthodox party officials, who have no interest in genuine dialogue; the passive contract Marxists, who are prepared to live and let live, provided the church abandons any claim to political engagement, including its association with the defense of national and human rights; and the liberal Marxist sociologists, who believe there is something positive to be gained from Christian-Marxist dialogue. Obviously, these opinion groups will interact with each other in different ways, so that relations at one level might be improving even as relations at another are worsening.

What emerges from a close scrutiny of the church-state interaction in Yugoslavia is a complex picture. When officials of church and state engage in mutual vituperation, when clergymen are denounced in the mass media as fascists and imprisoned for things said in sermon, relations are described as negative. When officials of church and state are mutually supportive, consult with each other, attend each other's formal occasions, and speak well of dialogue, then relations are described as positive. When the picture is too complex to lend itself to simple description, it is referred to as mixed, having both positive and negative elements. These assessments are based, then, on policy actions, public speeches, newspaper articles, and evaluations by the participants in interviews with the author.

What we find is that the theologically moderate and politically non-collaborationist hierarchy and clergy have predominantly negative relations with the orthodox party officials (who are perennially distinguishing them from the allegedly more progressive clergy elsewhere) and mixed relations with the passive contract Marxists and—within the church—the Bosnian Franciscans and TDKS. The politically dialogue-minded clergy have mixed relations with both regime opinion groups (Franić himself being criticized repeatedly over the years, sometimes for what had earlier earned him praise) but predominantly positive relations with the dialogue-minded Marxist sociologists. That part of the Croatian Catholic Church whose relations with the state are worst is the Bosnian Franciscan vicariate; over the past few years, several Bosnian fathers have been imprisoned for alleged political crimes, ranging from the singing of *Ustaše* songs, to calling the present system a system of slavery, to writing secessionist poetry, to maintaining contact with émigré Croatian terrorist organizations, to making up the miraculous appearances of the Madonna in 1981 and 1983. On the other hand, the Franciscans in Dobri pastir have been eager to maintain dialogue with the regime; so even here the picture is complex. By contrast, TDKS, which has mixed relations not only with the noncollaborationist clergy but also with the theologically conservative hierarchs (like Franić), has had positive relations with both the passive contract Marxists and the sociologists and mixed relations with the Orthodox Marxists. But the kind of "support" TDKS enjoys from the regime invites skepticism. For instance, in an interview with *Svijet* (December 27, 1982), Jakov Blažević, well known for his prosecution of Stepinac and his attacks on Kuharić, claimed that "in Croatia . . . the organization of counterrevolution is steadily growing under the leadership of the divisive prelate of Kaptol," i.e., Kuharić. But he praised "the resistance which is offered to that [leadership] from the very ranks of Catholic functionaries and priests"—a clear reference to TDKS.[64] TDKS, however, does not view itself as a focal point of struggle against clerical counterrevolution, and its members resent such a characterization.

What emerges out of the heterogeneity of opinion on each side is a mixed policy. The members of the various regime-supported clerical associations and certain other dialogue-minded clerics actively seek dialogue. The Bosnian Franciscans include not only clergy deeply hostile to the system and vocally outspoken about it but also others deeply engaged in trying to foster church-state dialogue. Their common characteristic is defiance of the archbishop and the diocesan church. The noncollaborationist clergy, finally, has pursued a policy of defense of church rights, believers' rights, national rights, human rights, and even the rights of prisoners, and has spoken out boldly against infringements of these rights.[65] The April 1981 declaration of the Yugoslav Bishops' Conference, though pledging loyalty, was subjected to months of criticism for precisely this claim that believers' rights and church rights were being violated by regime officials.[66] At the same time, the church's Philosophical-Theological Institute in Zagreb did not hesitate to host an international symposium on human rights, December 3–4, 1982, thereby defying the regime; theologians from Rome and Munich joined local Zagreb theologians in a discussion of human rights in the teaching of the church, in international documents, in Marxism, and as practiced in the USSR and Yugoslavia.[67] And conservative and liberal clergy alike have resisted the regime's efforts to pin the blame for church-state frictions on the church. For instance, in a recent article for *Glas koncila,* Rudolf Brajčić repudiated Nenad Ivanković's suggestion in *Vjesnik* (December 11, 1982) that part of the clergy was engaged in an antiatheist campaign and dismissed the very concept of antiatheism as sheer nonsense.[68]

But if the establishment also practices a heterogeneous policy, this heterogeneity is somewhat muted by the relative powerlessness of the Marxist sociologists and by the agreement of the orthodox party officials and the passive contract Marxists on three essentials: that religion is a "reactionary" phenomenon; that religious organizations should play no public role of any importance; and that the Catholic Church is the most resistant religious organization when it comes to attempted regime manipulation. Hence, despite certain countervailing currents (most particularly in the late 1960s, the heyday of "dialogue"), the Yugoslav communist party's policy (the policy of the orthodox Marxist and passive contract Marxist coalition) can be fairly characterized as a systematic effort to contain and erode the influence of the church. Thus, the party's recent encouragement of the construction by the Serbian Orthodox Church of a shrine to victims of the *Ustaše* camp at Jasenovac may well be motivated, as one source suggested, by the desire to see a permanent architectural indictment, in the middle of Croatia, against Croats and their church for serious war crimes.[69] And even if some establishment figures continue to speak well of dialogue, one is entitled to ask how meaningful such dialogue can be when the regime itself by and large abstains from it.

The adoption of a factional approach to the study of church-state interaction illuminates several related facets of what is shown to be a complex relationship. First, the model highlights the fact that religious policy in Yugoslavia is the product of a divided leadership and thus provides an explanation of why some spokesmen may speak in conciliatory terms and even hint at dialogue in the midst of a fierce antichurch press campaign. As basic a subject as the requirement that communist party members not only abstain from all religious ceremonies but also keep their children out of church, even for baptism, was assailed in the party press itself in July 1983.[70] And if policy is the product of divided minds, then change in policy is apt to reflect more than simply a change of mind on the part of an amorphously defined regime. It may, in fact, reflect a change of personnel resulting in a change in the balance of forces within the establishment. Second, the model shows that just as different factions within the political establishment may have different goals regarding religious bodies, so too different factions within the church may have different objectives regarding political authorities. Third, the model highlights some possibilities: for factions in the church to use alliances with certain sectors in the elite to obtain concessions (as happened during 1970–71 in the Zagreb archbishopric, and as TDKS may have attempted to do more recently); for church hierarchs to frame public statements in such a way as to appeal to one or another group within the establishment (i.e., to the Marxist sociologists or to the passive contract Marxists); for the dialogue-minded faction in the establishment to pursue very different avenues (e.g., through Franić and his circle, the priests' associations, or even TDKS); and for the orthodox Marxists to play the church factions against each other. Indeed, regime hard-liners, in 1983, showed signs of wanting to drive a wedge between the Slovenian and Croatian bishops, between the Franciscan Order and the Bosnian diocesan church, and between church liberals and the church hierarchy.[71]

CONCLUSION

In discussing church-state interaction, broad descriptions of the "problems of the church" and the "objectives of the regime" may tell us much. But such simplifications necessarily leave important parts of the picture in the shadows. They obscure considerations, for instance, of problems of one wing of the church (e.g., Bosnian Franciscans) that may constitute an opportunity for another wing of the church (e.g., the diocesan church in Bosnia). They also obscure considerations of the infighting that underlies what are sometimes rather loosely presented as "regime objectives." The Catholic Church is as much a political actor as the state, both because its social and ethical concerns are fundamentally political and because it is itself a body subject to internal factional politics, internal rivalries, and struggles over resources and policies.

The extension of factional analysis to church-state relations opens the door to treating not only the regime's religious policy but also the church's regime policy as a political question, a matter of policy conflict in which some voices speak more loudly than others. It also provides a theoretical basis for understanding systematic inconsistencies in church-state relations as a permutation of factional politics.

SEVEN

Organization Theory and the Bulgarian and Serbian Orthodox Churches

Organization theory is concerned with explaining "the structure, functioning and performance of organizations and the behavior of groups and individuals within them."[1] It presumes a division of labor according to some hierarchial principle and highlights the importance of individual motivations, associational group loyalties, and organizational structure for policymaking within organizations. Derived above all from the study of business corporations, organization theory professes to offer insights relevant to the study of organizations generally.[2]

Otto Luchterhandt recently observed, quite correctly, that there is tangible variation among both the religious policies of the East European states and the organizational structures set up to conduct these policies.[3] This chapter will argue that these variations are related; that, more specifically, organizational arrangements, both formal and informal, have direct consequences for religious policy; and that, conversely, differing policy orientations are reflected in differing organizational structures.

While organization theory attributes some importance to formal structure and bylaws, it is more concerned with the actual goals and procedures of an organization; these goals and procedures reflect the private objectives of key individuals or groups in the organization, or they may be the product of informal consensus, factional infighting, the exigencies of the moment, or a combination of these elements.[4] According to Philip Selznick, every organization spawns an informal structure that modifies the formal goals of the organization. Or, to put it differently, in every

115

organization, the formal goals are scuttled, deflected, garnished, or in some other fashion modified by the informal structure.[5] This informal structure includes the norms adopted by organization members to handle routine matters; these norms may embrace such things as the controlled use of sarcasm, the approach to and handling of the media, and the existence within the organization of informal cliques. The informal structure may have, but does not necessarily have, a deleterious effect on the achievement of the goals of the organization. As Selznick notes,

> running an organization, as a specialized and essential activity, generates problems which have no necessary (and often an opposed) relationship to the professed or "original" goals of the organization. The day-to-day behavior of the group becomes centered around specific problems and proximate goals which have primarily an internal relevance. Then, since these activities come to consume an increasing proportion of the time and thoughts of the participants, they are—from the point of view of actual behavior—*substituted* for the professed goals.[6]

Against this, however, one must balance the very real importance that organizational structure can have. It makes an enormous difference whether, for instance, an organization operates according to the rules of "democratic centralism," choking off innovation from below, or whether innovation is permitted or encouraged. Peter Blau has found that as organizations increase in size, structural differentiation increases, but at a decelerating rate, and that increased differentiation results in an increased need for coordination across bureaus.[7] Hence, it turns out that formal structures exhibit regularities independent of the motives of the individuals in organizations in question.[8] The differences between the organizational structure for conducting religious policy in Bulgaria and its counterpart in Yugoslavia are considerable—in both informal and formal terms—with tangible consequences for the respective regime's policies toward the Bulgarian and Serbian Orthodox Churches. Similarly, the subdivision of activities in an organization creates psychological predispositions that affect decision-making and policy-execution behavior.[9] That reinforces the situation already created by formal and informal structures, and is indeed related to them. Along this line, one may ask, for instance, what it means for practical policy that the Bulgarians have given jurisdiction over their Committee for the Problems of the Bulgarian Orthodox Church and the Religious Cults (hereafter, the State Committee on Religion) to the Ministry of Foreign Affairs.

Finally, an organization cannot be described in abstraction from its environment—political or otherwise. Any organization has a specific clientele, formal or informal, and interacts with it. One aspect of this situation is the tendency of a regulating agency to cater to its charge, under certain circumstances. The intermittent tendency of the Serbian party apparatus to cater to the Serbian Orthodox Church on the controversial matter of the Macedonian Orthodox Church serves as an example of this tendency.

THE BULGARIAN ORTHODOX CHURCH'S ROLE IN FOREIGN POLICY

The Bulgarian Orthodox Church's utility to the regime in foreign policy, reflected in its subordination to the Ministry of Foreign Affairs, is a good part of the explanation of the relative prosperity of this church in comparison with other religious organizations in Bulgaria and some other religious organizations in Eastern Europe.

Even before the church-state relationship was formalized through adoption of the Law on Religious Communities (February 24, 1949), there were prospects for reciprocal accommodation. Some Bulgarian Orthodox clergy, for example, expressly welcomed the communist takeover of September 9, 1944, as promising liberation for the church, while Archimandrite Jonah, in particular, was gratified with the separation of church and state.[10] The communists too seemed uncharacteristically favorably disposed toward the church. Georgi Dimitrov, general secretary of the Bulgarian Communist Party, attending an Orthodox Church millennial commemoration of the founding of the Monastery of the Holy John of Rila in summer 1946, told those there assembled:

> Our Orthodox Church deserves historical merit for preserving the national feeling and self-awareness of the Bulgarian people. Through the centuries of its most difficult sorrow, in struggle for the liberation of our people from the foreign yoke, the Bulgarian Orthodox Church has been the guardian of the national spirit of Bulgarians. . . . One can say, without any hesitation, that there would be no democratic Bulgaria today . . . if in those times of dark enslavement of the past, we had not had our monasteries . . . which preserved the national feeling and the national hopes, as well as the national pride, of Bulgarians, and helped to save them from disappearance as a nation. . . . We, our Fatherland Front, and especially we communists, express our recognition of and gratitude for the patriotic clergy of the Bulgarian Orthodox Church. I want to emphasize openly that I, as a Bulgarian, am proud of our church.[11]

Rather than confront the church with unambiguous hostility, the communists hoped to subvert it with a left-wing League of Orthodox Priests of Bulgaria, to bring it within the sphere of influence of the already subverted patriarchate of Moscow rather than the patriarchate of Constantinople (from which the church was already estranged), and to use the church's nationalism as a building block in communist-sponsored, "supranational," pan-Orthodox ecumenism.[12] A series of visits between the hierarchs of the Russian and Bulgarian Orthodox Churches, 1945–46, was a first step in this direction.

There were, of course, those in the church who opposed the new order and resented the confiscation of church lands; some refused to join the League of Orthodox Priests. Those considered uncooperative were recruited for hard labor or otherwise removed from responsible positions.[13] By October 20, 1948, an intimidated Holy Synod (embracing the nine metropolitans of the church) released a pastoral letter endorsing the measures taken by the regime and explicitly allowing church members to join the Fatherland Front; further, it pledged "not to undertake any special propaganda among the children and not to create any religious organizations for them."[14]

In the meantime, the communist party had introduced a new constitution for Bulgaria (on December 4, 1947), which stated (in article 78): "It is forbidden to misuse the church and religion for political ends."[15] Yet that is precisely what the communist regime proceeded to do.

The Law on Religious Communities of 1949 entrusted the supervision of the churches to a branch of the Foreign Ministry. Aside from a brief period from March 1954 to February 1957,[16] the State Committee on Religion has remained under the wing of the Foreign Ministry ever since. While its staff is relatively small (fewer than thirty-five members), the Bulgarian committee, like its counterparts in Poland and Romania, is empowered to issue directives to all state organs, where they become involved in religious matters. But as predicted by organization theory, separate offices have a tendency to develop their own interests and goals and even to pull in opposite directions. And hence, while the State Committee, representing the party consensus, has let it be known that it does not intend to apply coercive pressure toward atheization,[17] the Bulgarian secret police (DS) has remained overtly hostile to all religious organizations, including the Bulgarian Orthodox Church, and has at times perpetrated certain provocations designed to undermine the church.[18]

According to the 1949 legislation (still in force),[19] individual confessions must apply to the Ministry of Foreign Affairs for recognition; they may operate theological schools provided the curricula conform with stipulations set by the minister of foreign affairs. Article 12 gives the ministry control over hierarchical and official appointments, by empowering it to "recommend" to the leaders of specific churches the removal of church officials or ministers considered undesirable, adding that "if the official concerned is not removed from office by the leaders of the confession, he will be discharged through administrative channels." Article 13 requires that church budgets be submitted to the ministry for authorization and explicitly provides that "the financial activity of the confessions is subject to control by the financial bodies of the state." Article 15 requires that all pastoral letters, circular letters, and other documents and communications be cleared with the ministry in advance, while article 25 authorizes the foreign minister to represent the churches in matters concerning foreign property or the religious interests of Bulgarian citizens outside Bulgaria. These articles established the groundwork for converting the Bulgarian Orthodox Church into a bureau of the Foreign Ministry.

Other articles are designed to minimize or control the religious character of the churches, prescribing aspects of church rituals, declaring that the education of children lies outside the legitimate sphere of religious organizations, and barring the churches from any social commentary except commentary supportive of the party (articles 18, 20, 28). The law foresaw a special role for the Bulgarian Orthodox Church, expressing, in article 3, the hope that this church would be, "in its form, content and spirit, a people's democratic church."

Finally, foreign contacts of the churches are carefully controlled by the ministry. According to article 22:

> the confessions can maintain relations with other confessions, institutes, organizations or officials having their seat or residence outside the country, but only after previous authorization by the minister of foreign affairs.

Moreover, the churches are not permitted to accept aid or gifts from foreign countries, except with the express permission of the ministry (article 24). Thus, in its dealings with foreign bodies, the Bulgarian Orthodox Church is constrained to behave like any other bureau of the apparatus: Its delegates must be approved; its contacts, visits, and exchanges must be approved; the public statements of its officials must conform with state policy, as befits a "people's democratic church"; its documents and circulars require advance clearance; it is permitted no independent financial dealings; and the foreign minister retains final authority over all its foreign activities. As befits a bureau of state, the church was required to add a course in Marxism to its curriculum at the Theological Faculty in Sofia.

The results are not surprising. Just three months after passage of this law, *Tsurkoven vestnik,* the official organ of the church, published an article by Archimandrite Jonah, promising that "the church gives its moral support to every initiative of the People's Democratic state."[20]

Accordingly, at the prompting of the ministry, the Holy Synod created a special office to conduct ecumenical activities and promote peace. It also joined the Moscow-inspired Christian Peace Conference (based in Prague) and (in 1961), together with the Russian Orthodox Church, the World Council of Churches. The Bulgarian Church patriarch has, at times, accompanied the Bulgarian party secretary on official visits to Third World countries. He has also acted as an intermediary for Sofia on occasion—in 1984, for example, when Patriarch Maxim sent a letter to Pope John Paul II appealing to him to intercede to secure the release of Sergei Antonov, the Bulgarian airline official arrested for complicity in the plot to assassinate the pope in May 1981.[21]

Maxim's predecessor as patriarch, Kiril (d. 1971), was vice-chairman of the Bulgarian National Committee for the Defense of Peace and a member of the Soviet-backed World Peace Council. He was active in the Christian Peace Conference and advanced Bulgarian foreign policy objectives.[22] Maxim has followed in Kiril's footsteps, becoming likewise vice-chairman of the Bulgarian Committee for the Defense of Peace. For his contributions to the state, Patriarch Maxim has been awarded the Order of the People's Republic of Bulgaria (first class) and the Thirteen Centuries of Bulgaria Order. In October 1984, the Bulgarian newspaper *Sofia News* published a long tribute to the patriarch on his seventieth birthday, praising him for "his patriotic and social activities in defense of peace" and describing him as "an eminent religious and public figure who has dedicated his life to the good of the Bulgarian people."[23]

The church has intermittently organized and hosted international conferences on peace, beginning with a large interconfessional conference on October 5, 1952, chaired by Kiril, who was then metropolitan of Plovdiv. Two-and-a-half months later, the future patriarch delivered a "propeace" speech at the Second World Congress of Peace in Soviet-occupied Vienna. Recent conferences hosted by the church include a meeting of the Christian Peace Conference in Sofia (November 12–16, 1979), the Tenth National Peace Conference (March 13–14, 1980), the World Parliament of Nations for Peace (September 23–27, 1980) in which some 2,600 delegates from 134 countries (including 130 religious leaders) took part, an international conference in 1981 against the production of the neutron bomb, and an international conference in 1982 concerning necessary steps to avoid nuclear catastrophe. The church also played an active role in the 1983 Budapest Conference on Disarmament.[24] Obviously these conferences were organized not merely with the approval but also with the active participation and assistance of the Ministry of Foreign Affairs. They represent a cog in the Bulgarian foreign policy machine.

Internally, the church has likewise functioned as a bureau of state. For example, in a circular letter of May 3, 1963, Patriarch Kiril endorsed the Warsaw Pact's policies and line regarding defense and peace; a letter of the Holy Synod regarding bacteriological weapons was read from the pulpit in all Bulgarian Orthodox churches. The church has also steadfastly held to its position that there is no "Macedonian" people anywhere and hence no Macedonian minority in Bulgaria (a position taken also by the Sofia regime); that there is no justification for the existence of a "Macedonian Socialist Republic" within the framework of federated Yugoslavia, since Macedonians are "really" Bulgarians; and that the ecclesiastical jurisdiction exercised by the Macedonian Orthodox Church legitimately belongs to the Bulgarian Orthodox Church.[25] It was, no doubt, partly with this church position in mind that Party Secretary Todor Zhivkov told a conclave of party officials and church hierarchs, gathered to celebrate the 1,300th anniversary of the Bulgarian state (in June 1981), that there is "no contradiction between the interests of the Bulgarian people and [those] of the country's church."[26]

The publishing activity of the church reflects its mission. Hence, in contrast, say, to the Romanian Orthodox Church, the Bulgarian Church did not publish any new theological books in the 1970s. Instead, it brought out two books on nationalist themes: *The April Uprising and the Bulgarian Orthodox Church* (1977, 584 pages), devoted to the anti-Ottoman rebellion of 1876; and *The Church and the Resistance of the Bulgarian People against the Ottoman Yoke* (1981, 392 pages), focusing on the War of Liberation of 1878.[27] The church's official news organ, *Tsurkoven vestnik,* regularly devotes space to historical themes related to church activity or national development and carries articles and editorials with such titles as "Aggression against the Freedom and Independence of Cuba" and "Let Us Help Korea."[28] In reward for its faithful service to the state, the church was allowed, after years of difficulty in obtaining Bibles, to publish 30,000 Bibles in Bulgaria in 1980. A second edition was permitted in 1982.

What emerges from this brief analysis is that the formal goals of the Bulgarian Orthodox Church—to preach the gospel, to spread the faith, and to tend to the needs of believers—have been partly scuttled (as per restrictions on religious instruction), partly deflated (with the gospel harnessed to criticize NATO armaments and defense but not Warsaw Pact armaments), and amply garnished. Moreover, these formal goals have been modified by the State Committee on Religion (a formal state structure) and the informal structures it has spawned within the church. Finally, the cooptation of the church into the Foreign Ministry has made it amply clear to church leaders that the price of relative coddling is general subservience and loyal activity in foreign policy. And hence, as the church monthly, *Duhovna kultura,* put it in 1984, "the Bulgarian Orthodox Church will continue to cultivate in its youth a love for our socialist motherland, [and] will make its contribution . . . towards the consolidation of the age-old fraternal friendship with the Russian people and with the other peoples of the Soviet Union."[29]

DECENTRALIZATION IN ORGANIZATIONS

The most obvious difference between the Bulgarian policymaking environment and the Yugoslav is the dramatic decentralization that characterizes the latter. According to organization theorists, decentralization has certain advantages and debilities, compared with more centralized structures. On the positive side, decentralization increases flexibility, encourages initiative, and makes middle-level jobs more attractive to talented personnel. Decentralization also provides some assurance that decision makers will be acquainted with local circumstances—presumably, better acquainted than the central authorities would be. On the negative side, the central authorities may have trouble keeping control over local and republic authorities or even keeping sufficiently informed about their activities. One writer has suggested that perspectives adopted by officials in charge of decentralized units "may be too limited. They may think too much in terms of local advantage and not enough about the good of the organization as a whole."[30] Moreover, as the Yugoslav case amply demonstrates, when decentralization becomes sufficiently advanced, there may be difficulty in attracting talented people to the center.[31] Moreover, institutional jurisdiction affects lines of communication, and they in turn influence decisions.[32] That religious policy in Bulgaria is highly centralized, whereas in Yugoslavia it is simultaneously decentralized to the eight federal units and entrusted to two parallel hierarchies (making for sixteen autonomous and potentially competing offices of religious affairs) is bound to make for differences—and does. And since decentralization of authority also leads to decentralization of information processing, coordination across federal units may become a problem.[33] In the Yugoslav case, evidence of the decentralization of information processing may be seen in the frequent exhortations for better coordination, in the regular lamentations about failure of policy implementation and delays in determining failure, in Serbia's complaints about withholding of information in Kosovo, in decentralization of the media, and—where religious policy is concerned—in the different attitudes of the Serbian and Macedonian apparatuses toward the dispute between the Serbian Orthodox and Macedonian Orthodox Churches.[34]

Organization theory, thus, suggests at least two further conclusions: first, that the more decentralized an organization is, the less coherent its policy will be, so that in highly decentralized environments, the policies of individual subunits may be in conflict with each other; and second, that in decentralized organizational environments, policy formation will reflect the needs, interests, perceptions, and experiences of subunit actors rather than those of the central authorities.

THE SERBIAN ORTHODOX CHURCH IN A DECENTRALIZED ORGANIZATIONAL ENVIRONMENT

Religious policy in Yugoslavia was centrally directed from the late 1940s to the beginning of the 1970s. Under legislation enacted in March 1959, the direction of religious policy was entrusted to the Committee for Religious Affairs, set up as an autonomous organ under the Federal Executive Council.[35] The Socialist Alliance of Working People of Yugoslavia (SAWPY), the mobilization arm of the party, was also concerned with religious matters, as it still is today. In addition, a separate office was set up in the Ministry of Internal Affairs to monitor religious developments.[36]

With the passage of the new Constitution in 1974, previous federal legislation on religion was suspended, and, aside from a few guarantees of religious practice and a declaration to the effect that religion should not be misused for political purposes, the Constitution left legislation in this sphere to the eight constituent federal units (six socialist republics and two autonomous provinces). The Slovenian republic and the province of Vojvodina were the first to pass laws regulating religious practice. Curiously, in the republic of Croatia, the prevalent opinion at first was that a special law on religion was not necessary, because it was redundant and implied that believers needed additional regulation to that applied to Yugoslav citizens as a whole. A Croatian party minority, which favored passing special legislation and was backed by like-minded officials in the other federal units, eventually forced a reversal of this position. Croatia eventually followed suit and passed legislation on religious practice.[37]

While there is some variation across federal units with regard to provisions regarding religious instruction, religious publications,[38] and the founding of government-supported priests' organizations (specifically mentioned only in the Croatian, Macedonian, and Serbian laws), all the laws guarantee freedom of religion, describe religion as a "private affair," and permit the establishment of schools and seminaries for the training of clergy. All require religious organizations to obtain permits before building churches, and all ban social and economic activities on the part of religious organizations.[39] Churches are expected to abstain, generally, from sponsoring or organizing nonreligious activities, including activities of a cultural, educational, or recreational nature.

More important, from the standpoint of organization theory, is the fact that the Constitution allows the federal units to organize policy at the level of the republic or autonomous province. Religious policy is, in fact, conducted through two parallel structures: the republican (and provincial) Offices for Relations with Religious Communities and the republican (and provincial) Boards for Questions of Religion of SAWPY. The offices are typically chaired by a member of the Republic Executive Council and report directly to the council. The boards, which seem to play a less prominent role in the day-to-day management of the authorities' relations with religious organizations, operate as part of a generally powerless organization, dominated by members of the communist party and lately suffering from serious problems of morale. Even aside from the recent general discontent within the Socialist Alliance, there is a more specific complaint that its Boards for Questions of Religion have not enjoyed the necessary autonomy; there have also been suggestions that the federal board should report directly to the SAWPY Federal Conference (its supreme body) rather than to the conference's Section for Sociopolitical Relations.[40] Be that as it may, the result of this system is the federalization of religious policy and the creation of a situation in which the church-state climate may be cordial in some parts of the country (e.g., Slovenia and Macedonia) even while there are serious frictions in other federal units (e.g., Bosnia-Herzegovina and Croatia).[41]

In addition to these offices and boards, the federal and republican Social Councils for International Relations take up the subject of religion, in surveying the foreign activities of religious organizations based in Yugoslavia.[42]

By contrast with Bulgaria, nothing in the legislation, the organizational structure, or the behavior of party officials in Yugoslavia suggests a cooptive relationship with the churches. Whereas the Bulgarian regime has found it could put the Orthodox Church to work in its foreign policy, the Yugoslav regime views religious organizations strictly in terms of internal policy considerations—and in this respect, the regime sees only problems. In what typifies the Yugoslav approach, Franjo Kozul told a 1984 session of SAWP-Bosnia:

We emphasize unambiguously . . . that there is no possibility of any kind of partnership with any church or confession ever. A partnership between the so-called clergy and the secular state is a thing of bygone centuries, but not of our time.[43]

Partnership, of course, can only be premised on common interest, and neither the regime nor any of the churches have found sufficient common interest to move toward a new relationship.

Decentralization has, in fact, undercut the coherence of religious policy in Yugoslavia in several ways. To begin with, different republics have developed quite different religious policies. The Serbian Orthodox Church has an important presence in six of the eight federal units—all but Slovenia and Macedonia. The reception it has experienced in these federal units has varied widely. While Serbian Orthodox clergy are rarely mentioned favorably in the Yugoslav press—another contrast with Bulgaria—they seem to have fared better in Serbia and Vojvodina than in Croatia and Bosnia-Herzegovina. Thus, for example, it was the Bosnian newspaper *Oslobodjenje* that, in September 1981, published a series of articles attacking the deceased Serbian Orthodox theologian Bishop Nikolaj Velimirović.[44] The Serbian daily, *Politika,* did not reprint the series. Indeed, the religious climate in Bosnia and Croatia has been generally cooler since Tito's death than in the other federal units, and that seems to have affected the major denominations in these two republics, i.e., Catholicism, Orthodoxy, and Islam.

A second source of policy incoherence, again a factor of decentralization, is a growing tendency (an "informal structure") of party spokesmen to ignore the supposed ("formal") ban on interrepublican criticism. According to long-standing agreement, officials in any given republic are normally expected to refrain from criticizing developments and phenomena in other republics (especially where nationalism is concerned) but to lead the criticism of "anti-self-management" phenomena in their own republic. This principle has been breached repeatedly in recent years, and, where the Serbian Orthodox Church is concerned, criticism seems to come most frequently from the Croatian party and the Croatian press, even though the church is less important in Croatia than in several other federal units. In 1981, for instance, *Vjesnik,* the Croatian daily, called Bishop Nikolaj Velimirović "the symbol of Greater Serbian chauvinism and the sharpest anticommunism within the Serbian Orthodox Church."[45] Again, in 1982, the Zagreb weekly, *Danas,* wrote that "the dean of the Orthodox Theological School in Belgrade, Atanasije Jevtić, inaccurately and maliciously [mis]represents the situation in Croatia"; it reproached him for mentioning only the suffering of Serbs under the wartime Croatian regime of Ante Pavelić and thus not also mentioning the suffering of Croats, Jews, Gypsies, and others.[46] And in spring 1985, a session of the Commission for Ideological and Theoretical Work of the Central Committee of the Croatian party organization gave vent to criticism of the Serbian Orthodox Church's allegedly "reactionary" political activity. This criticism was occasioned by two letters; one from the Holy Synod of the church to Milka Planinc, chair of the Federal Executive Council, expressing dissatisfaction with the incumbent secretary of the Federal Office for

Relations with Religious Communities (Radovan Samardžić), and an open letter signed by several dozen Orthodox priests, urging Serbian Orthodox Patriarch German to adopt a "bolder" stance toward the authorities, since "something must be done for the Serbian Church and its people."[47] The national arena in which this should have been taken up—if at all—would have been in the *Serbian* Office for Religious Affairs, *not* in a Croatian party agency. This suggests that no one in the Serbian party wanted to do so, and that the Croatian party felt at liberty to ignore the ground rules of religious policy. Both imply incoherence in religious policy.

As for the Serbian party, it took a clearly protective, if also superordinate, stand toward the Serbian Church during the period when Aleksandar Ranković was vice-president (i.e., up to July 1966).[48] And it is surely no coincidence that the establishment of the Macedonian Orthodox Church—which the Serbian Church long opposed—took place within a year of Ranković's fall. More recently, moreover, while the Macedonian party would clearly like to see the Serbian Church accept the secession of the Macedonian clergy,[49] the Serbian party has not pressed the Serbian Church on this score. Even where the sensitive subject of Kosovo is concerned, it has been suggested that the Serbian party may consider itself in need of the support of the Serbian Church in trying to defuse interethnic friction in this heavily Albanian-populated province.[50]

A third source of policy incoherence has to do with decentralization below the level of the republic. Local authorities sometimes take advantage of their proximity to developments to take precipitous action. Since local authorities may be more doctrinaire than their republican superordinates, this tendency can work to the disadvantage of the church.[51]

And finally, decentralization may encourage party members to seek modification of religious policy, whether de jure or de facto, for private reasons. Some 27 percent of party members admitted recently that they had had their children baptized[52]—a breach of regulations for which a party member, Marija Car, was noisily expelled from the party in 1983.

The political balance among moderates and conservatives differs from republic to republic, as do the local confessional makeup and the particular policy agenda. Since priorities, regulations, perceptions, and actors all differ from unit to unit—natural in any organization—decentralization of authority has tended to bring out differences of policy, even if the rhetoric sometimes obscures them.

CONCLUSION

The operations of the religious affairs offices in Bulgaria and Yugoslavia differ markedly. These differences are reflected in the organizational structures, both formal and informal, in the two countries, and have direct consequences for the activity of the Bulgarian and Serbian Orthodox Churches. Cooptation has brought the Bulgarian Church prominence, a steady diet of panegyrics, and a kind of prosperity—but at the cost of its independence. The Serbian Orthodox Church is, from time to time, insulted in the secular press,[53] has at times had difficulty in obtaining permits for church construction, and is repeatedly advised to keep its nose out of social concerns; yet, within this context, it has preserved its independence.

Organization theory calls attention to the organizational structure and internal workings of organizations, and highlights their importance for organizational outputs. It also underlines the important distinction between the "formal" and "informal" operations of an organization. The framework outlined at the beginning of this chapter was borne out in the analysis of the policy environments in which the two churches function, suggesting that organization theory may well be a useful tool in examining the operational underpinnings of church-state interaction.

PART III

Current Trends

EIGHT

Religious Ferment, 1978–84

Eastern Europe is being swept by a wave of religious ferment without precedent in the postwar period. Although the roots of this ferment must be traced back at least twenty years, it is clear that the Polish pope and the Polish example have much to do with the recent intensification of religious fervor throughout the region—and, in consequence, of religious persecution on the part of the regimes. Concentrated in Catholic areas (Poland, Slovakia, Croatia, Lithuania, and western Ukraine), the religious revival has also penetrated into non-Catholic and religiously mixed regions (chiefly East Germany, Hungary, Romania, and Soviet Georgia, but also the Russian heartland). It presents the communist authorities with a challenge as trying and as complex as the multifaceted economic woes currently afflicting the region, and perhaps as politically potent as the crisis of legitimacy brought into focus by the appearance of the independent trade union Solidarity in 1980–81.

The religious revival has many sources. First, the unevenness of religious policy from country to country (with Gomulka easing up on the Polish Catholic Church, for example, at the same time Khrushchev was unleashing his antireligious campaign of 1958–63) encouraged clergy and congregations in the various countries to contemplate the possibility of change, whether for the better or for the worse, and in this way encouraged them to undertake organized action to affect their fate.

Second, the unevenness of religious policy over time has stimulated hope and self-confidence where policy has eased (Poland, Hungary, Yugoslavia, and, to a limited degree, Romania), while the use of antireligious campaigns (as in Czechoslovakia, the USSR, Yugoslavia, and elsewhere), insofar as it may be of intermittent intensity, has actually reinforced religious devotion.

Third, the mushrooming of religious *samizdat* since 1970 has provided the religious population, mostly the Catholic population, with an authentic forum and, in the process, encouraged religious practice. Chief among the religious *samizdat* one might mention *The Chronicle of the Lithuanian Catholic Church, Aušra, Dievas ir tevyne,* and (since 1985) *Juventus Academia* in Lithuania; *The Chronicle of the Catholic Church in the Ukraine* in Ukraine; *Teologičke texty, Informače o cirkvi, Naboženstvo a Sučasnost, Vzkršeni,* and an apparently new publication, *Una Sancta Cattolica-Advent,* in Czechoslovakia; *Beszelo* in Hungary; *Spotkania* and *The Cross of Nowa Huta* in Poland; and *Vestnik Istiny* and *Maloyaroslavets* among Soviet evangelicals.

Fourth, the editors of several legal religious publications in the East have shown an increased confidence in their ability to stake out independent, if circumscribed, paths. The examples of *Glas koncila, Družina, Crkva u svijetu,* and *Pravoslavlje* in Yugoslavia and *Slowo Powszechne, Tygodnik Powszechny,* and *Wiez* in Poland show that this process has made headway in at least two countries.

Fifth, instead of backing the churches against the wall, repressive policies had the effect of stimulating the development of "catacomb churches" and grass-roots religious movements, thereby involving lay people more actively than they might otherwise have been involved. These phenomena have developed in Czechoslovakia, Hungary, Lithuania, Russia, and Ukraine.

Sixth, reports of an apparition of the Virgin Mary on December 22, 1954, on a mountain in a rural district of Ukraine catalyzed the emergence of an intensely religious and intensely nationalist and anti-Soviet, neo-Uniate movement, known as the Pokutnyky, in Ukraine.[1] Claiming that the Second Coming had already occurred—in Ukraine—the Pokutnyky movement became a source of profound disquiet to the regime, spreading its influence throughout western Ukraine and beyond, opposing conscription into the Soviet army, and allegedly even portraying the Ukrainian nation as a new "chosen people."

Seventh, there is the availability of religiosity as an obvious form of protest against an oppressive system. The communists appear to view it in this light themselves, and recent antireligious press articles in Russia, Estonia, and the German Democratic Republic (GDR) have portrayed the fascination of even atheist youth with religious paraphernalia as a symptom of rebellion and even of dissent.

Finally, religious currents in Eastern Europe have been reinforced by the "Polish syndrome," long symbolized by the late Stefan Cardinal

Wyszynski, powerfully invigorated by the election of Karol Cardinal Wojtyla of Krakow to the papacy in October 1978 under the name John Paul II, and stirred by the triumphal visit in June 1979 of the Polish pope to his homeland, which has provided much of the catalyst for recent change. That the emergence of an independent trade union, Solidarity, and of independent farmer and student unions in Poland invite emulation elsewhere in Eastern Europe (emulation that was specifically invited by participants in Solidarity's first National Congress in September 1981) itself encourages the emulation of other aspects of Polish society, especially the privileged position of the Catholic Church. Not surprisingly, some East European elites (the Czechs, the Romanians, and the Yugoslavs) responded to this challenge by setting in motion furious anti-religious campaigns. Others (the Hungarians) have nervously underlined and reiterated the "understanding and cooperation" prevailing between church and state within their jurisdiction.

THE POLISH EXAMPLE

The partition of Poland among Austria, Russia, and Prussia, accomplished between 1772 and 1795, is perhaps the most important historical root of the Polish Catholic Church's present strength. From 1795 to 1918, the church was the Poles' sole bastion against Germanization at the hands of Prussia and Russification in the East. The church played an important role in sustaining the Polish national heritage and became important as a symbol of Polish identity, in opposition to Prussian Protestantism and Russian Orthodoxy. The Catholic clergy was identified not with an oppressive regime, as clergies were elsewhere, but with resistance to oppressive regimes; it took part in the Polish uprising of 1863. The Soviet occupation of Poland after World War Two replicated this pattern. Once again, the church figured as the most important institutional obstacle to cultural assimilation, and thus, when the party endeavored in 1976 to incorporate into the Polish Constitution an explicit reference to Poland's "friendship and cooperation with the Soviet Union," which was widely viewed as making a mockery of Polish sovereignty, opposition by the church and the intelligentsia defeated the move.[2] In the postwar period, as in the nineteenth century, a church policy of resistance and opposition led to a strengthening of the church, so that, by mid-1981, the Polish regime found itself consulting with the church as with a partner. The symbiosis of Catholicism and Polish nationalism has resulted in the fact that 99 percent of Poles regard themselves as Catholics, even though only 93 percent are baptized.[3]

In the wake of the imposition of martial law in Poland on December 13,

1981, the Warsaw regime launched, in increments, a campaign of harassment, blackmail, slander, and false arrest against the church. Code-named Operation Raven, the campaign resulted in the jailing of priests in Gdansk for leading violent street demonstrations, of a priest in Otwock for "membership in a terrorist group," of a priest in Koszalin for delivering an "anti-Polish sermon," and of others. The campaign also brought a raid on St. Martin's Franciscan Convent in Warsaw in May 1983 by men armed with police clubs who beat several lay volunteers, and the investigation of Rev. Henryk Jankowski, an adviser to Lech Walesa, and Rev. Jerzy Popieluszko in autumn 1983 on charges of abusing religious freedom and making antigovernment remarks.[4] Polish police ransacked the homes of Fr. Popieluszko and Fr. Stanislaw Malkowski, gave Cardinal Glemp a list of sixty-nine "extremist priests" to be reined in, and, according to Keston College, were suspiciously implicated in the accident-related death of a Dominican priest whose car had been tampered with.[5] The Central Committee of the Polish United Workers' Party justified itself in October 1983 by accusing the church of "undermining the state's authority and taking control of the youth," and Gen. Wojciech Jaruzelski, the party's general secretary, charged in March 1984 that the church was harboring political opposition.[6] British sources said the campaign was designed to undermine the church's authority and to foment divisions within the ranks of the clergy and demoralize it.[7] The campaign also may have contributed to Glemp's evident decision to distance himself from underground Solidarity,[8] thus safeguarding church interests; to make certain concessions to the regime in personnel policy (specifically, agreeing to transfer the pro-Solidarity priest, Fr. Mieczyslaw Nowak, from working-class Ursus to a rural parish);[9] and to work to revive church-state dialogue.[10]

The "Polish syndrome" has entailed at least six factors. First, the Polish Catholic Church has championed human rights generally (a stance also adopted by the churches in Lithuania, Czechoslovakia, the GDR, and Yugoslavia), supported what the regime calls "partial interests" (e.g., the interests of farmers or workers), and used the pulpit to present the church's version of events. Second, the church has engaged in political debate, in particular in the controversy over constitutional revision in its sundry aspects, 1975–76 (while the Catholic Church in Yugoslavia had similarly articulated its positions during the Yugoslav constitutional debate, 1971–73[11]). Third, the church has demonstrated its ability to win concessions from the government, especially with respect to media access (an ability which the churches in Yugoslavia, Hungary, and the GDR have also demonstrated). Fourth, the church has had direct contact with the democratic opposition[12] (a tactic also followed by the churches in Lithuania and Czechoslovakia). Fifth, the church has become involved in support of fellow Catholics abroad, specifically in Czechoslovakia.[13] And sixth, the primate has been able to present himself as a national leader—a role that might be emulated in Eastern Europe only by Croatian Cardinal Franjo Kuharić, and there only in Croatia and parts of Bosnia.[14] It was precisely the fear that the "Polish syndrome" might spread that prompted communist authorities in Czechoslovakia, Lithuania, and Yugoslavia—the most vulnerable areas—to launch antichurch campaigns in the past six years. The church in Poland has also come under intensified pressure recently, as has been noted.

THE POLISH POPE AND THE POLISH CRISIS

From the moment Krakow's Karol Wojtyla was elected pope in October 1978, it was apparent that there was going to be some sort of impact on Eastern Europe. Just five weeks before his election, Wojtyla had denounced communist censorship as "the weapon of a totalitarian system which places blinders on the eyes of the Polish people" and had underlined the right of Christian citizens "to express their views publicly."[15] Now, as pope, he quickly accepted an invitation from the Polish episcopate to visit his homeland and pressed to have the proposed visit coincide with the 900th anniversary of the martyrdom of St. Stanislaus, the archbishop of Krakow who was put to death by King Boleslaw Chrobry in 1079 and became the patron saint of Poland. Pope John Paul II launched a Polish edition of *L'Osservatore Romano,* the Vatican newspaper; stepped up Vatican broadcasts to Eastern Europe (with Croatian broadcasts twice a day since May 1, 1983, for example); and brought in Franjo Šeper, former archbishop of Zagreb, and Msgr. Andryss Backis of Lithuania to assist him in Rome. In November 1981, the Vatican opened the Cyril and Methodius Institute of Slavic Studies in Rome, followed, in October 1983, by a historical and contemporary archive and study center for Bulgarian affairs. During the latter month, the Vatican also canonized Fr. Leopold Bogdan Mandić (1866–1942), a Croatian capuchin father.[16]

When the new pope returned to Poland in June 1979, the triumphal visit took on the character and dimensions of a national celebration. In the nine days of the visit, tens of thousands, even hundreds of thousands of Polish and East European Catholics crowded to see him at the various stops along the way. At the shrine to the Madonna at Czestochowa, he was interrupted by ebullient applause sixty-one times, and on three occasions the applause turned into song, with the pope joining in. Earlier, in his first Christmas message to his home diocese of Krakow since becoming pope, the pontiff had seemed to invite the workers to stand up to the Polish government. "St. Stanislaus," he had told members of the diocese, "defended the contemporary society against the evil that threatened that society, and he did not hesitate to stand face to face with the ruler when the defense of the moral order required it."[17] Now, during his visit, he talked in Warsaw about the Soviet Union's refusal to come to the Poles' aid during the ill-fated Warsaw uprising of August–October 1944, when the Red Army halted across the river from Warsaw and watched the Nazis suppress the rebellious Poles. In Czestochowa, the pope even appeared to call into question the legitimacy of the communist party's power monopoly and demanded that the church enjoy complete freedom as a social actor. Nervous Polish authorities instructed Polish television to avoid any panning shots that would show the size of the crowds attending the pope's talks; and, according to certain West German sources, television broadcasts of the visit were notably "poor and scanty in the eastern and northern parts of Poland, where broadcasts can be picked up in Western Belorussia and Western Lithuania; and the Bialystock station was temporarily 'out of order' allegedly as a result of Soviet pressure."[18]

Some 3,500 Czechs and Slovaks tried for two days to cross the border into Poland. Others from elsewhere in Eastern Europe got through and joined in the celebration. Elsewhere there were reports of large encampments of Lithuanians and Belorussians along the border with Poland.[19] Cardinal Koenig of Vienna predicted that the visit would trigger a "psychological earthquake" in Poland,[20] and an anxious Andrei Gromyko, the Soviet foreign minister, would openly fret that the pontiff's visit would have "the same effect on the [Polish] masses as the Ayatollah Khomeini had in Iran."[21] Western analysts would in fact subsequently credit the visit with having given the Poles a sense of their clout and power, and with having thus provided the spark for the workers' strikes that erupted in Poland the following summer. The visit provided a poignant answer to Stalin's old question, "How many legions has the pope?"

The transformation of the Polish political landscape after August 1980 conferred a new role on the Polish Church. With the appearance of Solidarity, which inherited the role of rallying point for opposition and dissent, the church came to see itself as a mediator between the communist party and Solidarity, between state and society. This new role, as Cardinal Wyszynski's successor, Jozef Glemp, observed, seemed if anything to increase the prestige and influence of the church.

The church has been deeply enmeshed in the groundswell of communal Polish consciousness that accompanied these post-August developments. There were reports of Catholics behaving arrogantly toward Poland's Lutheran minority, even seizing their churches.[22] At the same time, the church has been solidly behind the new process of reclaiming the heroes of the past and, in April 1981, announced that the cardinal of Krakow would take part in the 100th anniversary celebration of the birth of the Polish anticommunist Gen. Wladyslaw Sikorski and would receive Sikorski's ashes (being shipped in from London) and place them in the crypt of Wawel Cathedral.[23]

SLOVAKIA'S "SECRET CHURCH"

During the 1970s, church-state relations elsewhere in Eastern Europe had fallen roughly into three patterns: siege (Czechoslovakia, Lithuania, and Ukraine), modus vivendi (Hungary, the GDR, and Yugoslavia), and cooptation (Romania, Bulgaria, and Russia). John Paul II's new *Ostpolitik,* launched with considerable fanfare, excited considerable attention in East European capitals. Even the Yugoslavs privately fretted lest the pope plan a visit to nationalistically prone Croatia, and publicly observed that "the offensive of the Polish Church has [had] its effects."[24]

Czechoslovakia was, perhaps in part for reasons of proximity, the first East European country to feel the repercussions of the Polish religious syndrome. And although Prague launched a wide-ranging antireligious campaign in early 1970 as part of its program of reversal of the policy effects of 1968,[25] the regime undertook a more specific suppression of the Catholic Church soon after Wojtyla became pope.[26] This anti-Catholic campaign gathered momentum as the Polish crisis developed, and Catholic clergy was decimated by a wave of arrests.

Western sources confirm that an underground network of Catholic priests and nuns, concentrated in Slovakia but having adherents also in the Czech lands, formed in the early 1970s, in response to the intensified wave of repression, and that it numbers 10,000 to 25,000 priests and believers.[27] This "secret church" finds itself in opposition not only to a regime bent on its liquidation but also to sectors of the church hierarchy that have been subverted by the regime (though it enjoys the blessing of both the Vatican and Prague's Cardinal Tomašek).[28] The "catacomb" status of these church members represents a significant difference from the Polish case, for in Poland the church was never driven underground. In Czechoslovakia, masses are regularly said in private homes, and nuns pursue their calling clandestinely, living together in private apartments.

Despite recurrent warnings from the regime that "religion warps the character of a person" and produces schizoid and antisocial behavior,[29] religiosity has shown tenacity in Czechoslovakia. In recent years, it has shown especial strength among youth.[30] A number of Franciscans, including Jan Barta (who had been released in 1968 after seventeen years in prison and who died in December 1982), attracted a widening circle of young people eager to discuss God and religion. Moreover, among the various denominations, it is Catholicism, to which 60 percent of the country's population adheres, that has been the most dogged in resisting regime pressures. Western journalistic distortion notwithstanding, it is not the dissident movement Charter 77 (now suppressed) that has been most vexing to the Prague regime, but rather the Catholic Church, and it was the waxing tacit alliance between Chartists and the Catholic opposition at the end of the 1970s that ultimately shook the regime's confidence.[31] The regime noted with dismay a concurrent rise of anticommunist Slovak nationalism in areas where the catacomb church (also known as the Oasis Movement) is most active and took umbrage at a pastoral letter distributed in Slovakia in which Polish clergy expressed a sense of "responsibility" for fellow Catholics in neighboring Slavic countries. The Bratislava daily, *Pravda,* signaled party displeasure by denouncing movement adherents in Slovakia as a motley group of "clerofascists," "neoseparatists," and "politically disoriented individuals . . . under the spell of mystic romanticism . . . who are incapable of recognizing what is at stake." The "secret church," *Pravda* went on, represents a direct threat to socialism in Czechoslovakia.[32] Worse yet, from the regime's standpoint, the catacomb church showed signs of feeling encouraged by events in Poland. In mid-December 1980, *Pravda* published an unusually long article accusing the Polish Catholic Church of having been behind the organization of Solidarity and of actively assisting the "secret church."[33]

The Czechoslovak communist party responded decisively, stepping up repression and targeting the Oasis Movement for liquidation. Underground priests were rounded up by the dozen, tried on charges of antistate activity, and jailed. The movement itself was infiltrated by regime agents. Persons returning from trips to Poland were interrogated and placed under surveillance. The Slovak secret police were augmented by the temporary assignment of some 300 agents from the Czech lands. Tactics have run the gamut from harassment to the "disappearance" of certain priests. With one of the toughest drunk-driver laws on the books (no minimum alcohol level is spelled out), the authorities have adopted a practice of stopping priests in their cars after mass—and after communion wine—and having them take breath analyzer tests for drunkenness; some priests have lost their driver's licenses. In other ploys, priests have been disqualified from exemption from military service and drafted into the army, while others have been forced to retire, allegedly because of poor eyesight or health defects. In Moracec, in Bohemia, witnesses reported seeing some 150 armed police with dogs search a priests' home and confiscate religious literature. Forty security officials were said to have forced their way into a Dominican abbey elsewhere in Bohemia in October 1981. There were at least two unexplained deaths of active Catholics during 1981, and two Catholic lay volunteers were arrested in August 1982 and subsequently imprisoned for illegal distribution of religious literature.[34]

In 1983 and 1984, several Catholic priests were stripped of their state licenses to practice,[35] and a number of Franciscan fathers were jailed.[36] In a surprising development, Fr. Štefan Podolinsky, who had been arrested on charges of "obstructing state supervision of the church," was cleared of all charges in his trial in Banska Bystrica in August 1983 and released. Still, pressure on young people suspected of belonging to clandestine religious orders has continued, and the Catholic seminary in Bratislava has been instructed to include a course in atheist philosophy as part of its curriculum.[37]

A commentary in the Slovak daily, *Pravda,* in July 1982 pinpointed the nature of the regime's concern by excoriating the linkage of religion and nationalism in Poland.[38] In so doing, the article also conceded that the regime was far more concerned about religiosity among the largely Catholic Slovaks (whose church attendance has recently been estimated to be as high as 80 percent), than about religious currents in Bohemia and Moravia, where church loyalty is far less strong.[39] It is for this reason that the recent antireligious campaign in Czechoslovakia has been concentrated in the eastern, Slovak territories.

Pope John Paul II responded to this pressure by ordering Czechoslovakia's Catholic priests to withdraw from the regime's Trojan horse, Pacem in Terris, and by forbidding priests to join associations with political orientations. Frantisek Cardinal Tomašek, seconding the pope's demand, withdrew the church's authorization for the regime-subverted newspaper, *Katoličke noviný,* to advertise itself as an organ of the church.[40] Responding to the assaults on Pacem in Terris, which produced an immediate plunge in the organization's membership, the Prague daily, *Rude pravo,* charged that "this step cannot be characterized otherwise than as an attempt at gross interference in the affairs of citizens of this country. We cannot permit Catholic priests committed to Pacem in Terris to be persecuted for their peace-oriented and patriotic activities."[41] The pope followed this up by naming two new bishops, Dominik Hrusovsky and Jaroslav Skarvada, neither of whom is trusted by the regime, which soon fretted that Hrusovsky intended to press for the canonization of Msgr. Josef Tiso, the wartime president of Slovakia.[42] Before 1982 was out, there had been violent clashes between police and people in the Slovak town of Velki Krtis, where authorities endeavored to prevent any religious instruction from taking place.[43]

Under these circumstances, talks between Archbishop Poggi of the Vatican and Czechoslovak state authorities in April 1984 quickly ran aground—as was signaled by *Tribuna's* denunciation, shortly after the meeting, of one of the century's most "reactionary" popes.[44]

THE MIRACLE AT ČITLUK

In Yugoslavia, the echo of Poland has been perhaps even more striking. A sharp reversal of the policy of accommodation was abruptly set in motion in January 1981. Ironically, as late as December 1979, when Cvijetin Mijatović, then ceremonial head of state, visited the Vatican, church-state relations were painted in roseate hues, and it was generally thought that church-state relations in Yugoslavia had found a stable modus vivendi. Instead, a sharp attack on the deceased Alojzije Cardinal Stepinac by Croatian President Jakov Blažević in late January inaugurated a polemical campaign against "clerofascists," "separatists," Croatian "nationalists," and "neo-Ustaše" in the Croatian Catholic Church, with Stepinac serving as the regime's chief foil in the campaign's early stages.[45]

Evidence suggests that the campaign was prompted by fears that the church in Croatia would attempt to emulate the Polish Church. Indeed, there were some ominous stirrings in church circles in the wake of Wojtyla's election and later at the time of his visit to Poland.[46] By the beginning of 1981, however, the church seemed quite clearly to have adopted an oppositionist posture toward the state. Four things pointed to this probability: first, a petition submitted by forty-three leading Catholic clergy and intellectuals in Croatia demanding amnesty for political prisoners (submitted at the end of 1980); second, the Christmas sermon delivered by Zagreb Archbishop Franjo Kuharić in which he demanded greater respect for human rights, political equality for Christians, and greater church access to Catholics in prisons, hospitals, and the military; third, a sermon delivered by Kuharić on February 10, 1981, ridiculing the regime's long-standing insistence that Stepinac was a fascist and demanding a reconsideration of the evidence; and fourth, the Croatian Church's active promotion of Stepinac as a candidate for canonization.[47] None of these elements, taken separately, represented either disloyalty or the launching of an oppositionist offensive; but, taken together, they were threatening to the weak collective leadership that succeeded Tito in May 1980.

The anti-Stepinac campaign became overtly an antichurch campaign on March 5, 1981, when Branko Puharić, a leading member of the Croatian Socialist Alliance of Working People, delivered a major indictment of the Catholic clergy. In particular, Puharić denounced what he described as an ideology of political opposition. "The political consequences of this ideology," said Puharić, "places the Church in the position of the political fighter for the rights of the believers, while trying to politicize the believers themselves in the direction of opposition activity and struggle for political change of the existing system."[48] And political opposition, Puharić amplified, could only be founded on hostility to the socialist system.[49]

By July, Yugoslav party leaders openly admitted their anxiety lest the Croatian Catholic Church follow in the footsteps of the Polish Church. Milutin Baltić, secretary of the Central Committee Presidium of the Croatian party, warned the Croatian clerics not to aspire to imitate the Polish Church in its involvement in politics, explaining that the Polish context was entirely different and implying that the Croatian Church was infiltrated with traitors. Baltić further accused Archbishop Kuharić of counterrevolutionary activity.[50] Franc Šetinc, Baltić's counterpart in the Slovenian party, added that the "Polish recipe" was irrelevant to church-state relations in Yugoslavia because Poland was not Yugoslavia. The clergy remained unrepentant, however, and on April 30, 1981, the Yugoslav bishops issued a statement demanding complete freedom of religion in Yugoslavia. The statement was quickly denounced by the authorities.[51]

This situation took a strange turn on June 24, 1981, when the Virgin Mary allegedly appeared in Čitluk, in Bosnia, to six girls from the nearby village of Medjugorje. The children claimed that they saw the apparition repeatedly over a period of several days and that the Virgin divulged five secrets to them. That stimulated a massive stream of enthusiastic Catholic pilgrims into Čitluk and provoked intense nervousness, both among the Orthodox Serbs and Muslims of Bosnia-Herzegovina and on the part of the regime. Despite efforts by the authorities to discourage them, the pilgrims jammed the town on the first anniversary of the appearance.[52] Five years later, the youngsters were still reporting daily apparitions, with hundreds, sometimes thousands, of pilgrims flocking to the village every day. As if that were not bad enough, shortly after the alleged apparition, Medjugorje's parish priest, Father Jozo Zovko, told parishioners in a sermon (as reported by *Svijet* in its August 17 issue):

> Jesus said: the Lord has sent me to deliver from the prisons the captives, the prisoners, the convicts, to set them free. . . . So did he not come to liberate me, since I am a captive? and you, who are a prisoner, since you have been enslaved for 40 years?—so that this evening or tomorrow you can kneel down before him and say: remove the chains, untie the knots, loose the links which confine my life, since I have been fettered by evil sin.[53]

The authorities promptly put Zovko behind bars, on a three-and-a-half-year sentence (later reduced to one-and-a-half years), surmising that "forty years" referred to the period of communist rule. Party authorities immediately began to blame Kuharić and the church hierarchy for having "concocted" the miracle—an accusation that is at odds with the cautious reaction of Kuharić and Mostar Bishop Pavao Žanić to the reports from Čitluk.[54]

In the meantime, another front was opened with the alleged creation of an underground pietist movement by certain promonarchist Serbian Orthodox priests. This "Orthodox Christian Community," said to be a Chetnik front organization, was openly modeled on an earlier pietist movement created during the war by Bishop Nikolaj Velimirović, a Chetnik. But the authorities saw political ambitions in the mystic pietist professions of the movement and, in late summer 1981, rounded up its leading figures, including Orthodox priests Petar Lukić and Cviko Mojić. As evidence of their pro-Chetnik sympathies, the authorities cited a recorded message from Velimirovic, which the priests were said to have played for their adherents.[55] *Oslobodjenje,* the news organ of the Bosnian communist party, launched into a seven-part series devoted to Velimirović, the new Orthodox Christian Community, and their alleged nationalist intolerance, while Živomir Stanković, chairman of the Serbian Assembly's Commission for Relations with other countries, warned that the Serbian Orthodox Church had been infiltrated by Chetnik and antisocialist enemy émigrés.[56] By mid-1983, moreover, there were reports of religious revival and ecclesiastical "politicization" along the entire Dalmatian coast, in both the Catholic and Orthodox Churches.[57]

PACIFISM AND OPPOSITION IN EAST GERMANY

The Polish crisis has also had an impact on church-state relations in East Germany, where it gets at least some of the credit for the regime's termination of the church-state détente negotiated by Evangelical Bishop D. Albrecht Schönherr over the course of the 1970s.[58] Even prior to the election of the Polish pope, there had been a revival of interest in the churches among East German youth,[59] dating from the early 1970s, that both compensated for an absolute decline in overall church membership and encouraged the churches to maintain a stiffly independent stance toward the regime. This policy was reaffirmed in January 1981 when Bishop Schönherr, then chairman of the Federation of Evangelical Churches in the GDR, told members of the Evangelical Academy in Tutzing:

> Two things must be ruled out, namely the danger of total adaptation and the danger of total refusal. The danger of adaptation is great because it is

precisely a church that has become powerless which could be enticed through power to sacrifice the freedom and the richness of its preachings for the pottage of having a chance to survive. The danger of refusal consists in the wrong conviction that a basically atheist and totalitarian regime always and everywhere produces only wrong things.[60]

But the Evangelical Church was scarcely satisfied with its status, and in an April 1976 report, Bishop Schönherr would complain that "freedom of conscience and faith is no longer unequivocally guaranteed for those citizens who cannot embrace the Marxist-Leninist world view."[61] The Evangelical Church, drawing courage from the Helsinki Conference (1975) in which the communist states of Europe pledged to respect human rights, convoked an ecumenical congress a few months later to review the results of Helsinki. The Berlin regime decided to appease the church at that juncture and promised at its Ninth Party Congress (1976) to respect the equality of all citizens, regardless of religious affiliation. Thus, encouraged by the Helsinki Conference, invigorated by its resilience among youth, and strengthened by a church-state détente negotiated in early 1978, the church began to show signs of increased stridency.

Early in 1980, the church spoke out against the Soviet invasion of Afghanistan and criticized the belligerence of reports by East German media of summer maneuvers by the Warsaw Pact.[62] East German Prof. Eberhard Poppe shot back with the accusation that the church was supporting NATO's line:

the imperialist forces keep trying to affect citizens with religious ties and religious communities in the GDR through anticommunist agitation in "Christian" garb and ideological diversion so as to push them into opposition to the socialist state and to socialist development.[63]

Despite this and similar warnings, the church raised new demands—for increased contacts with West German evangelicals and abrogation of the new foreign exchange requirements for Western visitors. It also protested compulsory military service, suggesting the institution of a social service substitute; criticized state policies in education and other areas; and lent its support to the budding pacifist movement in the GDR. The authorities confiscated one offending edition of the Evangelical News Service, banned a regional church newspaper containing other critical remarks, and put the church on notice that it would not tolerate a political church on the Polish model. Finally, as the Polish crisis unfurled and GDR authorities grew nervous, the regime stiffened censorship of church publications.[64] Numerous sources confirm that East German authorities were worried that the Evangelical Church might serve as a rallying center for opposition in the GDR and conceivably stimulate a movement similar to the opposition movement in Poland.[65] A Keston College correspondent even suggested that the Soviets may have specifically advised the East Germans to muzzle their churches or face Soviet retaliatory measures.[66]

Unintimidated by the pressure, the church found itself inexorably drawn into the Polish crisis. A high point of this process may have been reached in April 1981 when a synod of the church in the eastern region at Berlin-Brandenburg proclaimed its solidarity with neighboring Poland and set itself squarely in opposition to the regime's encouragement of traditional anti-Polish prejudices, adding, for good measure, that reciprocal visits between people of the GDR and Poland should be allowed to resume.[67]

The East German Catholic Church was slower to adopt a clear oppositionist stance, chiefly because, as a smaller organization, it felt more vulnerable.[68] Pressure from two distinct sources combined to change this situation, however. First, there was growing ferment among the congregation itself, leading to the formation, in 1969, of a lay activist organization known as the Halle Action Circle and composed of both clergy and laity. This organization, finding itself drawn into the peace movement initially succored by the regime itself but increasingly out of its control, protested the church's silence on the issue of war and peace. In an open letter of March 5, 1982, the circle charged that "many Christians can no longer overlook the troubling silence of the Catholic Church in the German Democratic Republic with respect to the contemporary peace movement. Is this church still 'in the village'?"[69] Second, Pope John Paul II explicitly urged the church in East Germany to become more involved in social issues; and Bishop Gerhard Schaffran of Dresden-Meisen, chairman of the Bishops' Conference of East Germany (as of 1982), divulged, in May 1982, that he felt pressured by the pope's exhortations.

Actually, the East German Catholic Bishops' Conference had issued a statement as early as 1978, condemning the militarization of East German society and specifically criticizing an educational system that aimed at implanting a disposition to view the world in terms of friend and foe, militance, struggle, and intergroup hate.[70] This statement was submitted to the Socialist Unity Party (SED) and circulated in the West; it was not, however, disseminated in East Germany itself. In early 1983, the church, pressured thus from above and below, overcame its diffidence and assailed the regime's militarism in a pastoral letter read to congregations in all East German Catholic churches. The letter repudiated the communist notion that arms buildup in the East is justifiable and charged that weapons of mass destruction are "in every case immoral in themselves." The letter called for controlled disarmament, endorsed conscientious objection to military service in East Germany, and chastized the East German authorities for an increase in militaristic socialization in the schools.[71] That this new but still tentative stridency in the East German Catholic Church is linked both to popular religious ferment and to the vigilant attitude of the Polish pope seems to be beyond question.

NEW WORRIES IN BUCHAREST AND BUDAPEST

The link to the Polish pope is more difficult to establish in the case of Romania, though the fact of a religious revival there is unmistakable. There has been an upsurge in attendance at church services among Orthodox, Catholics, and Baptists, and Romanian President Nicolae Ceauşescu recently conceded that religious feeling is once again on the rise in Romania.[72] At the same time, the long-suppressed Romanian Uniates reemerged and have renewed their campaign for recognition.[73] Bucharest's concern at these developments is clearly reflected in the renewed assaults on the non-Orthodox churches, with the regime forcibly closing down a number of churches and arresting "recalcitrant" clergymen. The threat that the example of the Polish church poses to Romania is the same as that posed to East Germany: It offers a possible model for emulation and may thus encourage the religious establishment to become both more vocal in defense of human rights (including workers' rights) and more critical of specific regime policies.

Romania, like the USSR, Bulgaria, and in a certain sense Hungary, has tried to achieve a relationship in which the largest Christian church is subservient to the state. Recently, however, perhaps encouraged by clerical defiance in other communist countries, five Romanian Orthodox priests drew up a "Testimony of Faith" addressed to the Romanian patriarch, demanding

> the implementation of the right to give children a religious education and the organization of a young Christian movement; individual ecumenical freedom without any constraints; the right to have access to the information media, radio and television; the release of Father Calciu from prison; the reintroduction of the "Lord's Army" movement [a moral renewal movement which operated legally from 1923 to 1947 and which may still have as many as 400,000 members underground]; and the recognition of the Uniate Church as the sister and supporter of Orthodox spiritual life.[74]

Shortly thereafter, two of the priests who drew up the statement were beaten up by the local militia. A third was taken into custody, threatened with torture, forced to sign a confession, and stripped of his license to do priestly work (and thus of his salary as well). A fourth was also dismissed from his job. Clearly, in Romania, the clergy does not have the right even to request a change in its status quo. Over the course of 1983, Bucharest stiffened its antireligious stance. Ceauşescu called for more effective atheist instruction in schools, and educational institutions from the primary level up to university level have been ordered to comply.[75]

Yet, despite these rumblings from the ranks, the Romanian Orthodox hierarchy has by and large accommodated itself to the regime. The result has been that alienated members have left the church and joined Protestant organizations, especially the Baptist and Pentecostal faiths. Today there are some 450,000 new Protestants in Romania; two thirds of them are Baptists—more than in all other East European countries combined. As Vladimir Socor recently noted,

> owing to the sense of mission they have brought to the service of their faith and the determination they have displayed in resisting regime pressures, the Baptists' visibility and their impact on the Romanian religious scene has been far greater than their number might suggest. They have been especially active in proselytizing, in disseminating throughout the country Bibles received from abroad, and have engaged in a constant tug of war with the authorities for permission to acquire or build prayer houses and churches.[76]

Change in the religious atmosphere has penetrated even Hungary. In some ways, this development is the most surprising of all, since Cardinal László Lékai has shown himself to be completely willing to cooperate with the authorities. But it was precisely this cooperation that gave impetus to a grass-roots movement of Basic Communities that arose in the course of the 1970s and may number as many as 4,000 cells.[77] Concentrated in Hungary's larger cities, the Basic Communities have drawn young people and intellectuals into a movement outside the ordinary parish framework and have inevitably clashed with the Hungarian Catholic Church authorities. The young priests who organized the communities have not only worked hard for religious renewal but have been inspired by an antihierarchical orientation that has led them to repudiate the notion of absolute obedience to the cardinal and to champion conscientious objection to military service.[78] The communities complain, in particular (according to the Hungarian *samizdat* periodical, *Beszelo*), that "the Church has made concessions that it should not have made" and that "the concessions made by the state are mere formalities that did not make any substantial change in the situation of the Church."[79] The hierarchy responded by assailing the more radically independent priests and, in a move reminiscent of communist "salami tactics," attempted to distinguish between "good" and "bad" Basic Communities, neutralizing the "good" in the process.[80] Two of the more independent-minded priests, László

Kovacs and Andras Gromon, were noisily suspended from priestly duties in October 1981 in a warning to the movement to curb itself.

Instead, the movement dug in its heels, prompting the Hungarian authorities to put pressure on the cardinal to take action against Fr. György Bulányi, the acknowledged leader of the movement. Finally, in June 1982, the Hungarian bishops' conference released Bulányi from his duties, criticizing him for views "contrary to the fundamental teaching of the Catholic Church."[81] In so doing, the bishops were motivated in part by pressure from state authorities. Bulányi rejects the idea that the hierarchy may act as "policeman" for the state, and therefore urges that individual conscience must take priority over state orders funneled through the bishops. Bishop József Cserháti calls this kind of thinking "Protestant."[82] More particularly, Cserháti accused Bulányi and his adherents of believing that they can "get on without the hierarchy, bishops and the Pope."[83] Bulányi, in turn, defended pacifism, upbraided Cardinal Lékai for holding that "military service is a holy duty,"[84] and promoted the Basic Communities as models for a "countersociety" based on selfless love. He also called into question the wisdom of Lékai's "small steps policy," which Bulányi claimed has led to the atrophy of the church's spiritual influence in society. The pope may agree with Bulányi. At any rate, on at least two occasions, the pope told the Hungarian bishops to adopt a more resolute stand in defense of church rights, especially with respect to religious instruction. Eventually, in March 1983, Cserháti, secretary of the Hungarian Catholic Bishops' Conference, called for greater freedom for the church.[85]

It is known that the election of Karol Wojtyla to the papacy in 1978 caused "considerable agitation," both among Hungarian party officials concerned with religious affairs and among Hungarian Catholic Church leaders. Both groups feared that the Slavic pope might exert an influence that would undermine the Hungarian modus vivendi.[86] At the same time, there has been a strong revival of interest in the Bible among Hungarians, both Catholics and non-Catholics, and some 50,000 Catholics took part in a recent pilgrimage. The conclusion is inescapable that religious ferment has spread to Hungary, too.

RELIGIOUS OPPOSITION IN LITHUANIA

Partly as a backlash evoked by Khrushchev's coercive antireligious campaign in the late 1950s and partly as a concomitant of related processes of dissent, religious sentiment has gained ground in the past two decades in the Baltic republics, Belorussia, Central Asia, Siberia, Transcaucasia, more especially in Ukraine, and even in the Great Russian heartland.[87] This religious renaissance has affected the Russian Orthodox, Buddhists,

Baptists, Muslims, Jews, Pentecostals, Roman Catholics, and, especially during the 1968 Prague Spring and the brief period of liberalization in Poland (August 1980 to December 1981), the adherents of the underground Uniate (Greek Catholic) Church in Ukraine.[88] Among the symptoms of this revival have been a jump in the number of young people converting, the widespread fashion, especially among young people, of wearing crosses and religious necklaces, and the "tenacity" of church rituals, such as infant baptism.[89] TASS, the official Soviet news agency, conceded in late 1980 that enrollment in the country's theological seminaries had increased, specifically mentioning the three seminaries run by the Russian Orthodox Church and two operated by the Roman Catholic Church in the Baltic region.[90]

Since the Russian Orthodox Church has essentially reconciled itself to functioning at the authorities' pleasure and even to operating as an administrative arm of the regime, it is the religious revival among the sects (Baptists, Adventists, Jehovah's Witnesses) and the organizations associated with non-Russian national groups (Catholicism, Islam, and so forth) that takes on a threatening dimension, so far as the Kremlin is concerned. But even among Orthodox believers, the "True Orthodox Church" has survived for decades on the strength of its repudiation of the patriarchate's accommodation to the regime.

Among non-Russian groups, Estonian priests, for instance, have been deeply involved in resistance to the Russification of Estonia, where political opposition became bolder and more violent after the Gdansk strikes of July–August 1980. Estonia erupted with student demonstrations and workers' demonstrations in Tallinn and other cities in September 1980, and the republic has remained unruly. In summer 1981, Father Vello Salum, a Protestant pastor in Estonia, was locked up by the KGB after publicly declaring that it was the duty of the Evangelical-Lutheran Church in Estonia to function as an opposition political party and to defend the language, territory, and welfare of Estonians.[91] In Latvia, too, the church has grown more active, and Latvian party chief A. Voss complained of the church's "negative influence" and of its support for Latvian "bourgeois nationalism."[92]

Similarly, in the Soviet republic of Georgia, the Georgian Orthodox Church has displayed a marked restiveness and boldness over the past few years, taking it upon itself to defend Georgian interests against Russian encroachment.[93] Belorussia, too, may be affected by the trenchant Catholic protest movement. The religious revival in Belorussia has been characterized by the organization of clandestine religious instruction in Belorussian towns and villages, with groups of young pupils numbering about fifty on the average; in mid-September 1982, the Soviet daily

Sovetskaya Byelorussia sharply attacked four Catholic priests (Frs. C. Kuchinsky, R. Tokovich, K. Shanyavsky, and P. Bartoshevich) and two women (J. Subko and E. Sitko) for organizing such instruction.[94] Earlier, in what was certainly a token of apprehensiveness on the Soviets' part, the Belorussian journal *Polymya* published a long and derogatory attack on the pope by Ales' Bazhko in its March 1981 issue. Describing the pope as schizoid, Bazhko accused him of passive support for the Nazi occupation authorities in Poland during World War Two.[95]

But it is Lithuania and Ukraine that remain the flashpoints of the Soviet religious renaissance and the areas more directly affected by the example of the worker-church alliance in Poland and of the steadfastness of the Polish Church. The symbiosis of Catholicism and nationalism in Lithuania has rendered that republic indigestible by its Russian masters and has reinforced religious devotion there. Since 1972, moreover, the solidarity and self-assurance of Lithuanian Catholics have been strengthened by the regular appearance of the underground periodical, *Chronicle of the Lithuanian Catholic Church*. Lithuanians have also made full use of their right, as guaranteed in the Soviet constitution, to submit petitions and protests to the various Soviet authorities. Scores of petitions have been submitted over the past decade, with more than 1,000 signatures each, while in late 1979, some 148,149 Lithuanians (an unprecedented number) signed a petition addressed to Brezhnev, demanding the return of a church confiscated by the authorities.[96] In Lithuania, understandably, the election of Wojtyla had an effect almost as electric as in Poland. Rumors quickly spread through the republic that the new pope was part Lithuanian—an unfounded fabrication that was nonetheless lent some credence by Wojtyla's declaration, on one occasion, that half his heart was in Lithuania. Within a matter of weeks of Wojtyla's election and, by their own admission, encouraged by John Paul II's public avowal that the Vatican would speak out on behalf of Catholics under communist rule, five Lithuanian priests formed a Lithuanian Catholic Committee for the Defense of Believers' Rights. Three of the committee's founders subsequently held a press conference to list their grievances: the closure of churches and monasteries, restrictions on the number of students allowed to enter Lithuania's only seminary, the lack of catechisms and other religious publications, and the persecution of believers.[97]

Lithuania's youth have been increasingly drawn to Catholicism, and the annual pilgrimage to Šiluva has, in recent years, drawn ever larger crowds—with perhaps 45,000 to 50,000 believers taking part in 1983. The Lithuanian Church itself appeared more confident, continuing to assail the authorities in the *Chronicle of the Lithuanian Catholic Church*. In mid-1978, the *Chronicle* had published a memorandum proposing revision of the articles of the new Soviet Constitution that dealt with religion and the rights of believers and demanding the creation of a separate organ to oversee the execution and interpretation of the Constitution, since, it was argued, the body so authorized, the Presidium of the Supreme Soviet of the Lithuanian SSR, was unfit for the task. More recently, there have been reports of an underground seminary that trains priests whom the authorities keep out of the "official" seminary at Kaunas.[98]

The Lithuanian edition of *Kommunist* signaled a hardening of the regime's already tough religious policy when it printed, in its September 1980 issue, an overt attack on the church by the prominent atheist writer, J. Aničas. The principal thrust of the article was that the Lithuanian Catholic Church was refusing to limit itself to "satisfying the religious needs of believers" (by which Aničas meant conducting religious services), was aiming to convert itself into a political force, and was exploiting Lithuanian "bourgeois nationalism" for that purpose.[99] The commissioner of the Council for Religious Affairs in the Lithuanian SSR, Petras Anilionis, and his deputies organized a series of meetings with Catholic representatives during the early part of 1981 in the attempt to bridle the rebellious religionists.[100] These meetings often turned out to be little more than occasions for mudslinging and name-calling. At a meeting in Radviliškis on March 10, 1981, for instance, Communist officials called the priests "well-fed bloodsuckers" and "exploiters." The Polish peril was specifically raised at an "educational" meeting at the Šilupe kolkhoz in December 1980. The speaker lashed out at allegedly "fanatical" agents of the pope who were engaging in disruptive activity in Poland and complained of the opposition activities of "extremist" clergy in Lithuania, singling out Alfonsas Svarinskas and Sigitas Tamevičius, both members of the Lithuanian Catholic Committee for the Defense of the Rights of Believers, as the "most rabid" of the lot. Another priest, Fr. Bronius Laurinavičius, a member of the Lithuanian Helsinki-Watch group, was killed in a traffic accident in Vilnius in November 1981. Many Lithuanians suspected that the KGB had engineered the accident.[101] In summer 1982, the Moscow newspaper *Literaturnaia gazeta* claimed to have evidence that many Poles resented the church's support of underground Solidarity and wished the church would stay out of politics.[102] The Soviets followed that up by arresting Fr. Svarinskas in spring 1983, sentencing him to seven years in prison for "anticonstitutional and antistate activity."

The January 1985 issue of *Sovetskaia kultura* reported the arrest and trial of five religious activists in Lithuania. Accused of having printed religious material illegally, the five received prison sentences of one to three years.[103] In February 1986, another priest was killed in a traffic accident; as before, KGB engineering was suspected. The victim, Fr.

Juozas Zdebskis, was one of the five founding members of the Catholic Committee for the Defense of the Rights of Believers and had been under close surveillance for more than twenty years. Well known as a defiant champion of the Catholic faith, Zdebskis had been brought to court on two occasions and had been threatened by the authorities. According to Saulius Girnius, he had "had a close brush with death in several other suspicious incidents."[104]

The Soviets terminated the free flow of Polish newspapers and magazines into Lithuania, drastically curtailed traffic between the two areas, obstructed the 1981 pilgrimage to Šiluva, and even tightened the monitoring of correspondence between Poland and Lithuania. In late 1982, a new branch of the Institute of Scientific Atheism was established in Vilnius, under the direction of Serapinas Kraujelis, to coordinate and promote research on questions of religion and atheism in Lithuania, Latvia, Estonia, and Belorussia. The KGB also allegedly stepped up its surveillance of church sermons, wary of signs of political agitation.[105] Nonetheless, the Lithuanians continue to receive Radio Vatican, which beams fifteen minutes of Lithuanian-language broadcasting into the republic every night. In the western part of the republic, they also are able to receive Polish television and radio. With more than half of the Lithuanians counted as practicing Catholics,[106] Moscow grew apprehensive lest the "Polish bacillus" compound the oppositionist infection with which Lithuania has, since its annexation, been "stricken."

RELIGIOUS FERMENT IN UKRAINE

The kernel of Moscow's religious dilemma in Ukraine has been the existence of a well-organized underground Greek Catholic (Uniate) Church claiming some four million faithful, 350 to 500 priests, three or four clandestine bishops, and several clandestine convents.[107] Soviet authorities tried to suppress the Uniate Church in western Ukraine when they annexed the region at the end of World War Two. In the fall and winter of 1944–45, Uniate priests and bishops were forced to attend "reeducation" meetings; poor "learners" were given extra "tutoring" by the NKVD in all-night sessions. Eventually, all the Uniate bishops were imprisoned, the priests were compelled to recognize the authority of the Russian Orthodox Patriarch, and finally, in a pseudo-synod of the Greek Catholic Church organized by the authorities in March 1946, the church's link with Rome was severed and the church was "reunited" with the Russian Orthodox Church.[108] Since then, the Ukrainian Uniates have been one of the most persecuted religious bodies in the USSR, unable to practice openly and victimized by the periodic jailing of their ministers.

Despite repeated attempts to obtain the legalization of the Greek Catholic Church, the regime has remained convinced of the nationalist character of the church and has viewed the prospect of its open reestablishment as anathema. When, in 1968, under the impact of the Prague Spring, the Greek Catholic Church reemerged into the open in Western Ukraine, the regime launched a systematic campaign of new reprisals against the recalcitrant Ukrainians. Typical of the official policy toward the Greek Catholics was the sentencing of Bishop Basil Velychkovsky to a three-year prison term in March 1970 for having performed religious functions in defiance of the ban on the church.[109]

Central to the understanding of Ukrainian Greek Catholicism is the fact that it is concentrated in the western oblasts, where it is the dominant religion. These oblasts have traditionally figured as a vanguard of Ukrainian nationalist thinking and could catalyze a nationalist revival in Ukraine. Because of that and because Greek Catholicism is identified with separatism, its importance is probably greater than a mere numerical tally would suggest. Its adherents, moreover, are devoutly loyal. Legalization of the Ukrainian Uniate Church remains, thus, out of the question—at least as long as the church insists on maintaining its ties with Rome. And after Ukrainian dissident Iosyp Terelya and four others formed an Action Group to press for the church's legalization, Soviet police arrested Terelya in December 1982 and sentenced him on charges of "parasitism" to one year in a strict-regime camp. Released in December 1983, Terelya was approached by the authorities, who broached the idea of legalizing the Uniate Church provided that Terelya take charge of it and agree to break ties with Rome. Terelya refused and was rearrested on February 8, 1985, charged now with the more serious offense of "anti-Soviet agitation and propaganda." In August 1985, Terelya was sentenced to seven years in a labor camp. He was released in February 1987, along with 41 other dissidents.[110] In the meantime, the authorities had succeeded in crushing the Action Group.[111]

Under the papacy of Paul VI, relations between the Vatican and the Ukrainian Uniates had steadily deteriorated. Paul VI was pursuing an Ostpolitik of détente, and the impression was conveyed that the Vatican no longer even recognized the Ukrainian Greek Catholic Church.[112] In particular, the Vatican continued to deny the Ukrainian prelate, Josyf Cardinal Slipyj, the status of patriarch. This denial produced a minor incident in October 1977 when Slipyj walked out of a papal mass in the Sistine Chapel because he was denied the place of honor traditionally reserved for patriarchs.[113]

But with the election of John Paul II, the relationship changed. The Polish pope convoked the first official synod of the Ukrainian Uniate

Catholic Church in fifty-one years, with fifteen of the eighteen Uniate bishops in attendance. The synod, at the Vatican, began on March 24, 1980, and signaled Vatican recognition of the Uniates. The pope also named Archbishop Miroslav I. Lubachivsky, the metropolitan of the Ukrainian Catholic Archeparchy of Philadelphia, to become coadjutor with Slipyj and to succeed the latter, upon his death, as archbishop of Lviv, in western Ukraine.[114] Before the year was out, Slipyj had, with the pope's approval, convoked a second synod of Ukrainian Greek Catholic bishops in Rome, principally to deal with ecclesiastical appointments but also to express support for the ongoing struggle by Catholics in the Ukraine and to underline the importance of the Ukrainian-language programs transmitted to Ukraine by Radio Vatican.[115]

The pope also gave direct encouragement to the Ukrainian Catholics themselves. In October 1979, while on a visit to the United States, the new pontiff told a congregation at the Ukrainian Catholic Cathedral of the Immaculate Conception in Philadelphia:

> For many years, I have highly esteemed the Ukrainian people. I have known of the many sufferings and injustices you have endured. These have been and continue to be matters of great concern to me. I am also mindful of the struggles of the Ukrainian Catholic Church, throughout its history, to remain faithful to the Gospel and to be in union with the successor of Saint Peter.[116]

The pope had, in other ways, shown a readiness to defend the Ukrainian Uniates even at the expense of Ostpolitik. Thus in February 1980, he suggested to Slipyj that the long-vacant Ukrainian bishopric in Peremyshl in Poland be filled and the diocese restored to active status, and in July, he received four prominent lay Ukrainian émigrés, who presented him with a letter concerning problems facing the church in Ukraine.[117] Finally, the Vatican underwrote the establishment of a Ukrainian Catholic University and several Greek Catholic seminaries.

Cardinal Slipyj has been actively urging the Vatican to step up its radio broadcasts to Ukraine—a demand that has not escaped the notice of Soviet polemicists. Apprehensively, the Ukrainian communist press fretted that the Polish pope was proving "more gracious than his predecessor in his response to the groundless claims of the Uniate nationalist extremists,"[118] and spoke of "a new anti-Communist 'crusade' . . . to whitewash the Uniate Church and to 'revive' it in the Ukraine."[119] In a lengthy article for the Ukrainian daily, *Radyans'ka Ukrayina,* Klym Dymtruk hysterically assailed the "Ukrainian-language broadcasts from the Vatican, broadcasts prepared by dyed-in-the-wool anti-Soviets and Nazi remnants garbed in soutanes, of the ilk of I. Hryn'yokh and R. Holovats'kyy." Dymtruk continued:

Alongside religious subject matter which, incidentally, has recently been occupying an increasingly smaller place in Ukrainian-language radio broadcasts [from the Vatican], anti-communism and anti-Soviet propaganda are openly disseminated. . . . In addition, these radio saboteurs praise bourgeois-nationalist ideology, and preach a sinister alliance between the cross and the trident. . . .[120]

In a revealing passage, Dymtruk linked Soviet worries regarding the religious situation in Ukraine with the Polish crisis; that suggests that the Soviets have taken the Polish example most seriously.

Indeed, there has been a tangible Ukrainian response to papal gestures. Ukrainian Catholics have taken heart, and many have sent appeals to the pope for help. In September 1982, a group of Ukrainian Catholics, including several priests, established an Initiative Group for the Defense of the Rights of the Church, emulating a parallel move in Lithuania, and sent a petition to the Kremlin, asking that Uniate churches and monasteries be allowed to reopen.[121] One interesting *samvydav* (Ukrainian for *samizdat*) document written in the wake of Wojtyla's election and trip to Poland was a tract by Mykola Ihnatenko, a worker in Kaniv. Ihnatenko's tract accused the Soviet government of employing Orthodoxy in Ukraine as an instrument of Russification and closed with demands for the reopening of Catholic monasteries and convents in Ukraine, the abrogation of church taxation, and the grant of freedom of religion in Ukraine.[122] The Kremlin, already disconcerted by the attraction that Solidarity had demonstrated for Ukrainian workers,[123] was taken aback by this aggravation of the Uniate problem by the Vatican, and the synod of Ukrainian Uniate bishops convoked by the pope in March 1980 was attacked in two separate articles in the Ukrainian party news organ, *Radyans'ka Ukrayina.*[124]

In April 1981, *Zhurnal Moskovskoi Patriarkhii,* the heavily censored organ of the Russian Orthodox Church, joined the fray with the publication of an exchange of letters between Patriarch Pimen and Pope John Paul II, in which the latter was alleged to have distanced himself from documents released after the March 1980 synod, which had declared the abolition of the Ukrainian Catholic Church in 1946 invalid.[125] Clearly, the Soviets have been worried about the impact that the Slavic pope is having in their western territories.

THE PLOT TO KILL THE POPE

By the time Pope John Paul II made his triumphal visit to Poland in 1979, if not before, the Soviets had concluded that he constituted, both in his policy and in his nationality, a potent threat to the stability of the Soviet

empire. His strong support for Lithuanian Catholics and for the suppressed Greek Catholics of Ukraine soon stimulated Soviet apprehension,
and a leading Lithuanian atheist writer would complain, in spring 1980,
that Wojtyla had "been elected simply because 'most of the cardinals were
dissatisfied with the Eastern policy of Pope Paul VI.' "[126] A Ukrainian
writer charged the pope (in March 1981) with advocacy of the "aggressive
penetration by clerical ideology into the socialist countries,"[127] while an
article appearing in the Vilnius edition of *Kommunist* in August 1982
noted:

> it is also necessary to take into consideration the fact that the Vatican's
> activities are not limited to church or religious confines. The Vatican con-
> tinues to be a major international anticommunist center that still has at its
> disposal large amounts of means for exerting an ideological and policy effect
> upon the broad masses of the faithful.[128]

It was bad enough, the article went on, that Wojtyla had no faith in
dialogue with Marxists and had made clear his conviction that, of the two
superpowers, the Soviet Union was by far the greater threat to peace and
security in the world; far worse were Wojtyla's aspirations to expand the
role of the church in Eastern Europe. The Holy See was said to have
designated the Polish Church to play a kind of vanguard role in the "re-
Christianization" of Eastern Europe, and even Vatican contacts with the
Russian Orthodox Church, let alone with Prague's Cardinal Tomašek or
the Lithuanian Church hierarchy, came to be considered suspect.[129]

The Kremlin, according to Claire Sterling, became obsessed with the
idea that Wojtyla's election had somehow been "engineered by President
Carter's national security adviser, Zbigniew Brzezinski, to destabilize
Poland and dislodge it from the Soviet bloc."[130] At some point in 1979 or
1980—most likely shortly after the papal visit to Poland—the Kremlin
came to the conclusion that the Polish pope had to be eliminated. Such a
decision could only have been taken at the very highest level, and thus we
may be certain that Brezhnev, Andropov, Suslov, and perhaps also
Ponomarev, the Central Committee secretary charged with relations with
Eastern Europe, were involved in the decision. The decision, for that
matter, may have been taken at a regular Politburo session, with all
Politburo members present. The assassination would be "sanitized" by
hiring a Turkish leftist (camouflaged as a right-wing terrorist) to do the job
and by entrusting supervision of the plot to the Bulgarians. The Soviets
hoped the pope's murder would terminate the Vatican's new policy of
activism in Eastern Europe—epitomized by the creation of the Cyril and
Methodius Institute of Slavic Studies in Rome in November 1981. The
Soviets also hoped the assassination would plunge the Poles into a melan-

choly that would facilitate the reestablishment of "normalcy" in Poland, or into a national chaos of sufficient magnitude that a Soviet military invasion would be viewed as "justifiable" in the interests of restoring order. The murder—had it succeeded—would also have removed an important symbol of hope and encouragement to millions of believers throughout Eastern Europe.[131]

CONCLUSION

How significant are these phenomena? In social terms, it is evident that we are witnessing in Eastern Europe a burgeoning of collective solidarity based on religion, which underpins the workers' revolt in Poland and probably has more hold on the people than class loyalty does in Lithuania, western Ukraine, Slovakia, Croatia, and perhaps also Bulgaria and Romania. It is also evident that the communist policy of religious persecution has, if anything, backfired, fueling religious ferment. In political terms, it is evident that the party's organizational monopoly naturally encourages the sole independent institution, the church, to become involved in political and quasi-political questions and that religious revival therefore strengthens this form of opposition to communist rule. Moreover, the symbiosis of religion and nationalism in many of these regions elevates religious questions into ethnonational concerns and creates the possibility that religious revival might catalyze or reinforce a substantial change in consciousness—to Moscow's detriment—that could prove permanent. Such a change in consciousness would involve heightened nationalism, deepening of the hatred of things Russian or Soviet, growing disillusion with the communist party, and a conviction that the church ought to be used as a political weapon against communism and Soviet rule. To a significant extent, just such a change has already taken place as a result of the religious ferment of the past decade.

This religious ferment, which began to affect the Soviet Union and Eastern Europe in the early 1970s, has been greatly intensified by Pope John Paul II's activist orientation toward the Slavic nations and by the example of efficacious resilience set by the Polish Church, in particular. The Polish pope and the "Polish syndrome" have directly or indirectly affected almost all the countries of Eastern Europe. They directly incited religious ferment in Slovakia, Croatia, and Ukraine and provided both reinforcement and model to the Lithuanian Catholic Church and the Evangelical and Catholic Churches in East Germany. They also offer a potential model in Estonia, Latvia, Georgia, Hungary, Romania, and perhaps even Belorussia; and thus they directly threaten the ruling elites in Moscow, Budapest, and Bucharest as well. The pope himself has urged

Catholic prelates in East Germany, Hungary, Czechoslovakia, and elsewhere to stand up to the communist elites and to avoid retreats or agreements that would compromise the interests of the Roman Catholic Church.

From the very beginning of Solidarity, the Catholic Church in Poland gave strong support to the independent trade union. It maintained constant contact with Solidarity leaders, and unequivocally endorsed the Farmers' Free Trade Union's struggle to obtain official recognition.[132] With the imposition of martial law in Poland and the suppression of Solidarity, the Polish Church resumed its posture of opposition to the party, and in his New Year's message at St. Peter's Square (in 1982), the pope gave strong support to Solidarity in its underground struggle against the military government.[133] The Warsaw Episcopate has repeatedly demanded the restoration of Solidarity and Rural Solidarity and an end to military rule, and the pope echoed these demands in October 1982, before a Polish state delegation in Rome.[134]

In mid-February 1982, the Warsaw daily *Trybuna Ludu* published an abrasive article in what proved to be the inception of a press campaign against the Catholic Church. At the same time, "reliable Polish sources" revealed that the Polish security service had drawn up lists of priests viewed as dangerous and was planning its strategy.[135] Among the numerous arrests that followed were those, in late 1982, of Janusz Krupski and Jan Stepek, editors of *Spotkania,* a clandestine Catholic journal.[136] In mid-1984, *BIS,* a Polish *samizdat* bulletin, carried a story about a sharp increase in the number of fires in Polish churches, set by vandals. The implication was that the regime was behind it.[137]

The Warsaw regime's refusal to allow the pope to make a second visit in August 1982, as originally planned, betrayed the evident insecurity of martial law's administrators. Evidently, some members of the Polish regime hoped to block a papal revisit indefinitely. Foreign Minister Stefan Olszowski, well known for his hard-line views, was among those who opposed Jaruzelski's decision to allow the pope back a second time. Olszowski is reported to have tendered his resignation in protest of that decision.[138] The Kremlin also viewed the prospect of a second papal visit with dismay, as did several of the other Warsaw Pact parties, most especially the Czechoslovak party, which vehemently assailed the visit when it finally came about.[139]

Upon returning to Poland, thus, in mid-June 1983, the pope boldly upbraided the Warsaw regime for imposing martial law and detaining political prisoners, requested an amnesty for the latter, and challenged the regime to live up to its 1980 reform agreements. The thousands upon thousands who turned out to greet him included a number who carried

Solidarity banners, and even some whose banners specifically linked the pope with the banned trade union.[140] A dismayed Gromyko, speaking before the Supreme Soviet while the pope was in Poland, reiterated the Kremlin position that it has "legitimate interests" in Poland, that Poland "remains an inalienable part of the socialist community," and that the Kremlin reserves the right to "ensure the reliability" of Poland.[141]

On balance, four points seem clear: first, that the religious revival in Eastern Europe and the Soviet Union has grass-roots strength and is too far developed to be capable of being diminished by repressive action in Poland; second, that, in Poland itself, the authorities need the cooperation of the church if they are to restore political order and revive the economy; third, that in the Slavic world as elsewhere, religious repression has only served to deepen religious conviction and heighten clerical tenacity; and fourth, that the religious ferment, although it is associated with other socioeconomic and political currents, has autonomous roots and ramifications. Because this religious ferment has been associated with ever bolder demands for human rights and, in the case of the captive nationalities of the USSR, national rights, and because waxing religious consciousness derives from an independent center of authority, thus constituting a challenge to the legitimacy of the communist organizational and political monopoly, the religious revival presents the communist authorities with a challenge as trying and as complex, and possibly as politically potent, as the multifaceted economic mire into which the Soviet bloc is gradually sinking.

NINE

Protestants and Catholics after Popieluszko

The 1970s were a period of cautious optimism for many members of the clergy in Eastern Europe. Church and state seemed to reach an understanding in East Germany, Poland, and Hungary. In Czechoslovakia, where pressure on the churches had been a fixture since 1969, Frantisek Cardinal Tomašek, archbishop of Prague, tried for many years to pursue a policy of conciliation rather than confrontation.[1] In Hungary, the Reformed Church and the Lutheran Church had accommodated themselves to the communist authorities at an early juncture, and, after 1974, when László Cardinal Lékai became primate of Hungary, the Roman Catholic Church followed suit. In Poland, the Catholic Church won concessions in education and church construction in 1976, and First Secretary Edvard Gierek's visit to the Holy See in December 1977 and first-ever meeting with Stefan Cardinal Wyszynski the same month signaled a new willingness on Warsaw's part to compromise. And in East Germany, the meeting between Bishop Albrecht Schönherr, chairman of the Federation of Evangelical Churches, and East German President Erich Honecker in March 1978 led to immediate and tangible improvement in the Evangelical-Lutheran Church's circumstances.

The modus vivendi worked out between church and state in the 1970s in these countries is coming apart in the 1980s. In fact, across much of Eastern Europe, church officials are being confronted with new pressures—whether from the regime or from their own ranks—and are being forced to choose between accommodation to the rank and file and the atrophy of these ranks. In Romania, where the Orthodox Church made peace with the regime in the 1950s, unrest among believers is straining the continued viability of this "peace."

The upshot is that the preconditions for the sundry solutions worked out in the countries of Eastern Europe are changing, and the solutions are proving fragile. Seen in this light, the murder of Polish priest Jerzy Popieluszko in October 1984 is not an aberration but a symptom of a broader change in the climate of church-state relations in Poland and elsewhere. Indeed, Popieluszko's accused murderers based their defense in part on their claim that orders to rough up the prolabor priest came "from above."

Only in East Germany has a major Christian church—in this case, the Evangelical-Lutheran Church—been able to adopt an assertive posture and engage in pointed criticism of the regime, without either endangering its position and prerogatives or evoking a virulent antichurch press campaign. Elsewhere, the churches have been forced to choose. In Hungary and Bulgaria, the Christian churches have chosen to reach accommodation with the authorities. In this they have followed the model of the main part of the hierarchy of the Russian Orthodox Church, which praises atheistic communism as more compatible with Christianity than Western liberalism, speaks out against NATO armaments, and follows the Kremlin foreign policy line in other respects.

There has been some pressure in East Germany for the Evangelical Church to follow this course. The proregime Christians of the Christian Democratic Union-East wing have been the leading advocates of this approach. For instance, in a recent book published in East Berlin, Günter Wirth, chief editor of the proregime Protestant journal *Standpunkt,* wrote: "The path for an evangelical Church in socialist society in the first place simply means the path for an evangelical Church into socialism."[2] Yet, instead of meekly following the Russian Orthodox example, the Evangelical Church of East Germany has carved out a rather unique role for itself as a champion of pacifism and conscientious objection and an advocate of environmental concerns. Finally, in Poland, Czechoslovakia, and Romania, there is little prospect that pressures will ease in the foreseeable future.

What accounts for the new tension in church-state relations? Part of the answer is supplied in noting that the churches concerned are Catholic and Protestant—not Orthodox. Both Catholic and Protestant churches in Eastern Europe have strong ties with sister organizations in the West. Hence, the end of détente and the renewal of East-West tensions revived fears among some communist officials that these churches could function as Trojan horses for Western values. A second source of tension, at least where Catholicism is concerned, is the activist policy adopted by Pope

John Paul II. A third source is the tangible renewal taking place among the Catholic and Protestant churches of Eastern Europe. Young people are being drawn back to the churches, and church services are, in many places, better attended today than in many years.

EROSION AND CHANGE IN ROMANIA

Religious ferment in the area is not confined to the older, more established churches (the Roman Catholic Church and the Evangelical-Lutheran Church). It has also been carried forward by newer Protestant sects, chiefly Baptists and Pentecostals but also Seventh-Day Adventists, Jehovah's Witnesses, and others. In Romania, where the Orthodox Church's cooperation with the regime has alienated large numbers of Christians, this development is especially significant. And today, there are some 450,000 new Protestants in Romania, almost half of them Baptists. That is more than in all other East European countries combined.

The Romanian regime has, of course, long been known for its hostility toward organized religion.[3] But an important distinction must be drawn between the regime's relations with the Orthodox Church and its relations with other Christian denominations. The Romanian Orthodox Church enjoys uniquely favorable opportunities to train clergy, operates six theological seminaries and two theological institutes, sends theological students to the West from time to time, and publishes a number of informational and theological periodicals, some of them of high professional quality.[4] The church has more than 10,000 priests and some 12,000 churches, most in good repair, and its Sunday services are well attended. Early in the decade, moreover, the regime approved plans to build an International Ecumenical Center in the Bucharest suburbs for inter-Orthodox, interconfessional, and perhaps also Christian-Marxist dialogue.[5] In part, these facts reflect a unity of purpose between the church and the regime, best seen in the former's deep-seated aversion to any talk of relegalization of the Eastern-rite Catholic (Uniate) Church.[6] In part, however, it reflects a kind of "bargain," whereby the Romanian Orthodox Church finds itself having to shower Romanian President Nicolae Ceauşescu with praise, on a routine basis, for his policy achievements.

It should be kept in mind, though, that the regime's attitude toward the Orthodox Church is not a sign of favor as such but is rather a factor of the subservience of the church to the regime. When Romanian Orthodox priests dare to speak up to criticize the church's subservience to the state and, still worse, to call for reforms, they are apt to be moved to remote parishes and threatened with defrocking. One such priest, Fr. Radu Pamfil, whose problems with hierarchy and state alike date back to April 1981, was summoned to an ecclesiastical court in 1985 and charged with having performed "occult practices." A few months later, he was transferred from his parish in Timiş county.[7]

At the same time, the Orthodox Church's unmistakable subservience to the regime is part of the explanation of the growth of neo-Protestant groups in Romania. Pressures produced by regime-sponsored atheization on the one hand and the appurtenances of social modernization on the other hand are also relevant. The regime is well aware of the connection. At a round-table discussion by Romanian academics concerned with atheist work, Georgeta Florea drew a direct connection between the regime-promoted "reversal of religious belief" and the nurturing of smaller sects. In some cases, as she put it,

> this reversal of religious belief has created a paradoxical situation. It has only meant loss of confidence in the traditional religions and preservation of the illusion that there must be a better faith. In one way or another, this has brought them under the influence of the neo-Protestant sects, which are becoming increasingly militant.[8]

By early 1986, there were some 200,000 baptized Baptists, 200,000 Pentecostals, and 45,000 Plymouth Brethren in Romania. The current growth rate for these three denominations collectively has been estimated at 15,000 to 20,000 new converts a year.[9] In 1978, an independent Christian Committee to Defend Freedoms of Religion and Conscience was established, with heavy Baptist and Seventh-Day Adventist involvement. This committee aspired to monitor cases of religious persecution and to pressure the authorities to honor constitutional and legal guarantees. Instead, many Baptist and Adventists ministers and laymen were imprisoned.[10]

In the past few years, the Bucharest regime has brought a number of clergymen to trial, almost all of them Protestants. They include Ioan Ştef and Beniamin Cocar, two unregistered Baptist pastors; Petre Popescu, a lay Baptist pastor arrested in April 1985; and Dorel Cataramă, a Seventh-Day Adventist. Two other clergymen, Baptist pastors Nicolae Gheorghita and Paul Negrut, have been stripped of their pastoral licenses, while Constantin Sfatcu, a Baptist pastor from Iaşi, was sentenced to seven-and-a-half years in prison in July 1985 on charges of having attempted to kill a police officer.[11] Still another Baptist pastor, Rev. Petre Dugulescu of the Hateg Baptist Church in western Romania, suffered multiple fractures when a bus careened into his car in Timişoara in September 1985. Dugulescu had been threatened with an "accident" by security police on two occasions the preceding month. Keston College, the prestigious British center for the study of religion under communism, suggested that since the bus was a battered one, had no license number, and was carrying no passengers, one would be inclined to conclude that the mishap was arranged.[12]

Since late 1983, the regime has closed or demolished several Baptist and Pentecostal churches—in Tîrgu Mureş, Aiud, Bistrita-Năsăud, and Bucharest. In one case, the building was just over a year old when it was demolished.[13] While in at least two of these cases the regime cited the need to use the property to build new apartment complexes, it is clearly no coincidence that the Protestant churches have been the hardest hit by the government's "housing" program. In September 1984, moreover, the government ordered the Second Baptist Church of Oradea demolished—again, allegedly to provide space for the construction of new apartments. With 2,000 members, this church is the largest Baptist community in Europe.[14] Some Orthodox churches and monastery buildings have also been destroyed or sealed,[15] but most church buildings targeted seem to belong to Protestant sects.

Among the Protestant denominations in Romania, the Hungarian Reformed Church comes closest to the Orthodox model. With 800,000 registered members, the Reformed Church is administered by two bishops, Gyula Nágy and László Papp, who were both appointed by and are subservient to the regime. Meetings of the church's Executive Council reflect this subordination in that its agenda is set by representatives of the regime's Department of Cults, who participate in all its meetings. The result is that it may take no decisions without the approval of department representatives. The church's lack of autonomy is further shown in the fact that it is legally barred from operating its own seminary and, since 1949, has had to share a common Protestant Theological Institute in Cluj-Napoca with the Evangelical and Unitarian congregations. In a poignant humiliation, the two bishops were compelled to acquiesce in the seizure by communist authorities of some 10,000 Bibles sent to the church from the West in 1981. The Bibles were sent to the pulp mill and reappeared later in the form of toilet paper, with some passages from the scriptures still clearly visible.[16]

The Roman Catholic Church's situation is a rough mixture of these extremes. Like the smaller Protestant groups, the Catholic Church is treated with suspicion. It is unable to publish any periodicals or religious books, or to import religious works, and does not operate schools or monastic orders. And unlike the other recognized churches in Romania, the Catholic Church lacks a legal charter guaranteeing its position in society. Yet like the Orthodox Church, it is dependent on the state for financial subsidies, and its appointments require approval by the Department of Cults. Moreover, even the ordination of priests requires specific approval from the department.[17] Like the Orthodox Church, too, the

Catholic Church finds its support eroding. From 1977 to 1982, the number of Roman Catholics in Romania declined from 1.3 million to 1.2 million. The decline cannot be accounted for merely by emigration, since the Catholic birthrate exceeds the emigration rate.[18]

With the grant of permission by Bucharest for a group of Roman Catholics to make a pilgrimage to Rome in October 1983 and the announcement a year later that the Vatican had appointed Msgr. Ioann Robu apostolic administrator of the archdiocese of Bucharest and titular bishop of Celle di Proconsolare, Western observers speculated that Bucharest might agree to a "concordat" with the Vatican. Still unclear was what concessions the church would be expected to make.

BACKLASH IN CZECHOSLOVAKIA

Whereas Romanian Orthodox docility has driven some believers into Protestant sects, in Czechoslovakia there have been some signs of a backlash to persecution, especially in Slovakia, where Catholicism has traditionally been strong. Despite the pressures of a tough antireligious campaign, under way since 1980,[19] as much as 50 percent of the population of Czechoslovakia may still be religious,[20] and some reports hint at growth in church congregations recently.

Pressure has been worst for the Catholic Church, whose primate, Cardinal Tomašek, eventually felt constrained to anathematize both the Pacem in Terris priests' association and the supposedly Catholic newspaper, *Katoličke Noviný*. Both are decidedly proregime. As early as March 1982, Pope John Paul II had ordered Catholic clergy to leave Pacem in Terris, and in the months following that order, the organization's membership fell steadily. Early in January 1985, Cardinal Tomašek wrote a pastoral letter to all Czechoslovak dioceses, underlining the strictness of the church's ban on membership in Pacem in Terris. To that, Deputy Prime Minister Matej Lucan replied that "any attack on Pacem in Terris is an indirect attack on the socialist system"[21]—a statement that makes quite explicit how Pacem in Terris fits into the regime's program.

The Czechoslovak regime follows the classic communist paradigm of supporting clergy who allow themselves to be manipulated, while applying steady and often coercive pressure on those who do not. Hence, according to the Slovak daily newspaper, *Pravda,* Pacem in Terris's "activity is contributing toward establishing good relations and mutual cooperation between the socialist state and the church in fulfilling the construction program of the National Front and in the common battle for achieving peace in the world."[22] At the same time, the regime has refused to approve the appointment of new bishops to vacant sees, and as of mid-1985, ten of the thirteen episcopal sees were vacant. In addition, regime control of admissions to seminaries has contributed to a shortage of priests, and 1,161 of the 4,336 Catholic parishes in Czechoslovakia lack a parish priest.[23]

In early 1986, the pedagogical organ *Učitelske noviný* called for a toughening of the atheization campaign, and there have been reports suggesting that the regime hopes to suppress the Basic Communities of the Oasis Movement, which may number as many as 5,000 adherents as of 1986.[24]

In mid-1983, a group of Slovak Catholic clergymen and laymen addressed an open letter to Czechoslovak President Gustav Husak. This letter protested, in particular, a raid carried out by state security police on March 27, 1983, of houses and apartments of Catholics throughout Slovakia. The letter also charged that house searches and arrests were executed simultaneously in certain locations in Bohemia and Moravia.[25] Another letter of protest was filed in September 1984 by the mothers of fifteen Slovak theology students who had been expelled from the Bratislava Theological College on regime orders. The expulsion, in 1980, was in reprisal for a hunger strike staged by some 122 students at the college to protest Pacem in Terris's interference in college affairs.[26]

Nonetheless, the harassment and arrest of clergymen in Czechoslovakia have continued.[27] Teachers have been encouraged to take it upon themselves to dissuade their young pupils from attending religious instruction, and in Slovakia, the militia has been active in recruiting informants to report the religious activities of priests and laity.[28] In early 1984, the Prague government seemed to hold out an olive branch to the Vatican, and the two sides opened talks regarding vacant bishoprics and a "normalization" of relations. By mid-year, after these talks ran aground, reports surfaced that what the Husak regime hoped for was to detach the Czechoslovak Catholic Church from the Vatican and to integrate it into the bureaucratic structure.[29] The regime-controlled newspaper *KatolIčke Noviný* even noted:

> Of all the separate Churches, the one we are closest to is the Orthodox Church. That is why we associate most frequently with the largest [of the Orthodox Churches], the Russian Orthodox Church.[30]

Strikingly, a high-ranking Pacem in Terris delegation paid a visit to the USSR in March 1984 to hold discussions with the Russian Orthodox hierarchy. Moreover, in June, *KatolIčke Noviný* chose to honor Tomašek's eighty-fifth birthday with an article largely devoted to praising his efforts at promoting relations with the Moscow patriarchate. The article highlighted

Tomašek's 1978 visit to Moscow Patriarch Pimen and quoted the cardinal as having called upon Catholic and Russian Orthodox bishops to convene a joint meeting to unite their churches.[31] There were also reports that Vasil Bilak, first secretary of the Slovakian party organization, had told a meeting of Pacem in Terris activists that the Czechoslovak Catholic Church should be placed under the jurisdiction of the Moscow patriarchate.[32]

If these reports are reliable—and the circumstantial evidence cited suggests they are—then the Catholic Church is being presented with a clear and explicit choice between accommodation on the regime's terms and persecution. Nor are these difficulties the exclusive preserve of the Catholic Church. Both pastors and laity of the Czech Brethren Church have been under pressure lately, while three Jehovah's Witnesses, whose sect is outlawed, were tried in July 1983.[33] In the former instance, the case of Rev. Jan Keller, a Czech Brethren minister, aroused particular attention. In 1983, he lost his license to work as a minister, for allegedly "obstructing state supervision of the church." In 1985, after organizing meetings with young people, he was brought to court for doing evangelistic work without a license.[34] The authorities have also felt at liberty to raid the homes of both Catholics and Czech Brethren to confiscate religious literature, *samizdat* material, and foreign publications.[35]

THE HUNGARIAN MODEL

But it is Hungary and Poland that in some ways best exemplify the two extremes of accommodation and advocacy in the face of harassment. In Hungary, both Catholic and Protestant churches have adopted a cautious strategy. Both the late Catholic Cardinal Lékai and the Catholic Bishop of Pecs, József Cserháti, have been proponents of the idea that the church must "accept the social targets and structure of the socialist people's society," as Cserháti put it.[36] The state has also been given a veto over church hierarchical appointments, and the tone of the church press has been tailored to suit regime tastes. In exchange, the church has hoped for a modicum of religious freedom and the possibility of continuing its operations unobstructed. A curious by-product of this modus vivendi, mentioned in chapter 4, is the proliferation of state decorations, sashes, and medals among Catholic clergy—tokens of the regime's appreciation. But the church has also benefited concretely from accommodation. Specifically, since 1974, catechism classes may be conducted for children in the churches themselves, and since 1982, religion classes may also be held in parish halls. In addition, the regime has granted military exemption to certain Protestant groups, and at the request of the Hungarian Catholic episcopate considered extending the legal right of conscientious objection to Roman Catholics as well.[37] In 1985, the regime gave permission for the establishment of a new female religious order, the Sisters of Our Lady of Hungary. The order has been granted authorization to engage in charity and social work, thus restoring to the Catholic Church an activity it had pursued prior to the communist takeover. The regime has also allowed the primate to set up a three-year correspondence course for lay persons at the Budapest Theological Academy, enrolling 450 students annually.[38]

Similarly, Hungary's Lutheran Church, under Bishop Zoltan Káldy, has opted for dialogue complemented by "practical political cooperation with the government," as one observer phrased it.[39] Káldy spelled out his views on accommodation as early as 1955, when he told a national conference of pastors:

> The contemporary Hungarian Lutheran regards the present-day Hungarian state authority as a servant of God, and accepts that authority as coming from the hand of God. If, however, he accepts it as coming from the hand of God, he will honor and help it in all good things that promote a more beautiful and happier life for its subjects.[40]

Like Cserháti,[41] Káldy has offered to promote the development of socialist patriotism. He has gone further yet, and declared that the church and the state can cooperate on the basis of an official doctrine of materialism. In 1973, Káldy addressed the Eighth Hungary Peace Congress in these words:

> Our Protestant Churches are not neutral. There is no "third way for travellers" between socialism and capitalism. They cannot look at the conflict of world dimensions between socialism and capitalism with the cool wisdom of "those who know everything." We stand unambiguously on the side of socialism.[42]

Káldy, a long-time member of the Hungarian Parliament, has repeatedly endorsed the program of the regime's umbrella organization, the Patriotic People's Front.[43] The Lutheran Church has been rewarded for this fidelity; in spring 1985, for instance, it was announced that the church would establish a new Academic Theological Society.[44]

The results of these policies have been similar. Among Catholics, there has been a mushrooming of the grass-roots Basic Communities,[45] which involve members in reading and discussing the Bible and seek to restore "authentic" Christianity, in defiance of the Hungarian hierarchy. Within the Lutheran Church, opposition to Bishop Káldy's proregime "Diakonia theology" has grown, and in April 1986, nineteen reform-minded pastors and laymen sent a letter to Bishop Gyula Nágy and to all of Hungary's

Lutheran parishes, urging radical reform, including the election of church leaders not under "alien," i.e., communist, influence. At the same time, traditional Hungarian Protestantism is in decline. Hungarian youth are in fact drifting away from both the traditional Protestant churches in the country (Lutheran and Calvinist-Reformed). The newer Baptist and Pentecostal churches seem to be the beneficiaries of this drift.[46]

NEW UNCERTAINTIES IN POLAND

It used to be said that Poland's Catholic Church enjoyed a uniquely privileged position in Eastern Europe. The picture was never that simple, and in any event, it was only in the late Gierek period and during the brief secretaryship of Stanislaw Kania that the pressures on the church eased significantly. Indeed, in the late 1970s, and even until the proclamation of martial law in December 1981, it had seemed that the Polish communist regime was willing to accept the church as a kind of partner. Particularly during 1981, the spectacle of Cardinal Glemp meeting with the general secretary of the Polish party invited speculation that the church's counsel was actively sought by the communist government. But the launching of Operation Raven in February 1982[47] brought an end to notions that the party was ready to accept the church as a legitimate social actor. The draft charter granting the church formal legal status has been held up, as has official approval for the Western-financed church agricultural fund, first proposed by Archbishop Glemp in 1982.[48]

In July 1983, the Polish Parliament stiffened penalties to prevent opposition protests, approving a maximum three-year prison term for participation in activities of illegal organizations like Solidarity. The church objected to the measure, but it passed anyway. By September 1983, church and state leaders were exchanging salvos over the regime's treatment of opposition groups.

Beginning in 1984, the regime adopted a practice of singling out individual priests for criticism. Heading the list was Fr. Jerzy Popieluszko, who had been holding monthly "masses for Poland." Popieluszko's highly political sermons quickly won him a national following. In an August 1982 sermon, for instance, Popieluszko had declared:

> Any government which has no other means of implementing its policies than the use of force is not a government but a blasphemous usurper, and the people are as defenseless as an unarmed man who is confronted by a highway robber.[49]

In a later sermon, commemorating the third anniversary of the Gdansk agreement of 1980, Popieluszko declared that "Solidarity has a right to a free existence," and amplified this statement by urging that "justice is pluralism . . . pluralism for trade unions, for creative organizations without the aegis of a single patronage."[50] Critical of the government, he was unreserved in his praise of Solidarity:

> Solidarity helped us to see evil and its mechanisms clearly; it brought to the surface many historical events which had previously been passed over in silence. Solidarity wanted to work for God and for the benefits of the people, it wanted to build God's kingdom on earth.[51]

As a result, Popieluszko was vilified in the press and subjected to legal harassment. Entries in Popieluszko's diary indicate that he was aware of being under police surveillance as early as November 1982 and that a bomb was set off at his apartment the night of December 13–14, 1982.[52]

In summer 1984, the Polish weekly *Tu i Teraz* published an attack on Popieluszko for "fanaticism and hatred toward communist Poland."[53] The article was signed "Jan Rem," the pseudonym of Jerzy Urban, the government press spokesman.

The government repeatedly tried to persuade Cardinal Glemp to transfer the popular Popieluszko to an obscure parish. His abduction and murder by Polish secret police in October 1984 was therefore fully consistent with the government's previously expressed attitude. High-ranking government officials were implicated in the abduction, including Deputy Interior Minister Gen. Wladyslaw Ciaston; the head of the Church Monitoring Department, Gen. Zenon Platek; and Col. Zbigniew Jablonski of the Polish Security Police. In addition, Lt. Gen. Miroslaw Milewski, a hard-liner and member of the Politburo, was widely suspected of complicity in the plot.[54]

Embarrassed by the outcry in response to Popieluszko's murder, the Polish government put the four police officers directly involved on trial. However, even the trial became a vehicle for assaulting the church: One of the accused, Grzegorz Piotrowski, was allowed to accuse Bishop Ignacy Tokarczuk (well known for his championing of human rights) of having collaborated with the Gestapo during World War Two, to charge a Wroclaw bishop with having hidden money for Solidarity, and to describe unnamed clergymen as "dissolute."[55] Tokarczuk had been under pressure from the authorities for several months.

Although the four police officers ultimately received sentences of fourteen to twenty-five years in prison, their trial dwelled less on their crime than on the church's "provocations." In fact, the trial seemed orchestrated to sully the church. The strategy had several dimensions. First, Popieluszko was described as a ringleader for a "counterrevolutionary organization," motivated by "hatred for the Polish socialist state, its institutions, [and] its political system."[56] And he was said to have been influenced by foreign "espionage centers." Second, besides Popieluszko and Tokarczuk, several other Catholic clergymen (notably Jankowski, Malkowski, and Archbishop Henryk Gulbinowicz of Wroclaw) were singled out for attack, even though none of this testimony had anything to do with the case before the court. Third, testimony by Platek, in particular, repeatedly intimated that there had long been close collaboration between the secret police and the church hierarchy—often, allegedly, at the expense of the lower clergy. Platek, a former head of the Security Service's Fourth Department (in charge of supervision of the Catholic Church), implied that he had had regular confidential meetings with Archbishop Bronislaw Dabrowski, the episcopal secretary, and other members of the hierarchy. He claimed that the church had planned to send Popieluszko abroad, as a concession to the regime. He also asserted that the secret police kept tabs on the clergy and shared their files on lower clergy with the bishops.[57] Fourth, the regime chose this moment to open long-delayed legal proceedings against Catholic Frs. Eugeniusz Kubowicz of Tarnow and Wladyslaw Siennicki of Warsaw on charges of attempted murder, even though medical experts had testified that both priests were mentally ill.[58]

There have been other pressures. In the wake of Popieluszko's murder, two other Roman Catholic priests from Lublin, Frs. Eugeniusz Kosciolko and Zenon Ziomek, were beaten, tortured, and robbed, allegedly by Polish secret police. Fr. Rufin Abramek, a Pauline monk from the monastery of Jasna Gora, was seriously injured in a suspicious car accident in November 1984, while Fr. Tadeusz Zaleski-Isakowicz, well known for his pro-Solidarity sympathies, was assaulted and burned by masked assailants in April 1985 and attacked again by persons disguised as medical personnel in December 1985.[59] The regime also began criticizing Fr. Stanislaw Malkowski, and, after an article vilifying him appeared in the party weekly in 1984, Cardinal Glemp suspended him from preaching in Warsaw churches—perhaps to protect him.[60] At the same time, the authorities have used the bureaucracy to wear down outspoken clergy with petty harassments ranging from Fr. Jankowski's repeated difficulties with his car registration to the embranglement of other clergymen in tax problems or other red tape.[61]

The regime has also used its censorship mechanisms against the church. For example, in reporting sermons by Cardinal Glemp, the official press routinely deletes parts it does not like and plays up those it finds useful. The result is the perpetration of an image of Glemp as submissive to and cooperative with the regime.[62] At the same time, the authorities obstruct the church in its effort to get its message across. Thus, in summer 1984, authorities prevented a local parish in Warsaw from putting on a festival to commemorate the second anniversary of the pope's second visit to Poland. And in February 1985, authorities confiscated copies of the Polish edition of *L'Osservatore Romano* because it carried the text of a papal speech declaring Catholicism incompatible with any ideology preaching class hatred and class struggle.[63] When protests were lodged in connection with the aborted festival, a government official explained that "it is in the Church that the main ideological battlefront lies."[64]

The authorities have systematically monitored sermons throughout the country. In spring 1986, Jerzy Urban, the government's press spokesman, presented a compilation of politically charged excerpts from priestly sermons. According to Urban's examples, a priest in the Silesian city of Wroclaw compared communism to Nazism, while a priest from the port city of Szczecin described communism as "collective madness." In a departure from usual practice, Urban's article, which was published in the communist press, included the names and addresses of "hostile" priests.[65] About the same time, the Warsaw daily, *Polityka*, published an inflammatory article by Jerzy Jarzeniec, alleging that there were enough churches in Poland for the time being and that the current need was for apartments. Catholic journalist Slawomir Siwek shot back in the church press, accusing Jarzeniec of using misleading statistics and pointing out that church construction is financed out of church funds—thus "invalidat[ing] the journalist's implied assumption that fewer churches would somehow mean more apartments."[66]

The regime had been perturbed by the results of a 1983 poll showing that the Catholic Church commanded greater trust among the Polish people than any other institution, including the military, the judiciary, and the parliament (the Sejm), and far ahead of the party and the police, which placed last among those institutions mentioned. Between 1983 and 1986, the authorities concentrated their energies on undermining the authority of the church. "The churches," said *Polityka* in April 1985,

> are becoming the fronts for political opposition and priests continue to use the pulpits for attacks against the socialist system. . . . The churches continue to be used as places for clearly antigovernment hunger strikes. Some churches have already become symbols of opposition and have been plastered by banners, badges, and slogans whose eloquence is obvious to anyone who is able to think a little.[67]

Atheist education was given a new emphasis in schools, and teachers were required to fill out questionnaires on their religious and political attitudes.[68] The campaign seems to have had some success, judging from the fact that a 1985 poll showed that the church had dropped to third place

(65.7 percent) among school-age children, behind the Sejm (78.1 percent) and the armed forces (77.7 percent).[69]

Glemp is scarcely the submissive prelate he is sometimes painted. He seems to see himself as a cautious realist and to think in terms of small gains rather than grand confrontations. In March 1984, he revealed some of his thinking when he told interviewer Andrzej Micewski[70]:

> Personally, I see enormous difficulties with the attainment of reconciliation based on the conscious agreement to mutual concessions. This is why I do not talk about reconciliation so as to avoid being misunderstood. In the present phase of our moral and social crisis it would perhaps be better to speak of the need for coexistence in the midst of conflict.[71]

Hence, when the primate met with Jaruzelski in summer 1985, the result was essentially a stand-off, with no concessions on either side.[72]

Meanwhile, Glemp proceeded with the opening of an Archdiocesan Publishing House in Warsaw in 1983 and with plans to unveil a ten-foot-tall monument to his predecessor, Cardinal Wyszynski, in May 1986.[73] In October 1985, thousands of Poles gathered at Popieluszko's grave to mark the first anniversary of his murder. The regime newspaper, *Zycie Warszawy,* responded by accusing the church of interfering in politics.[74]

But according to Cardinal Glemp, the church has every business addressing itself to social and political concerns, and he has promised that the Polish Church will not allow itself to be confined to the passive role of being no more than a locus for liturgy and ritual worship.[75] In August 1985, before a receptive crowd of 200,000 faithful, Glemp criticized the regime for excluding believers from full participation in the political life of the country, assailed atheist education in schools, and—amid tumultuous applause—declared that in communist Poland, religious toleration means only "the right to defend atheism."[76] Later, in March 1986, the Episcopal Council issued a statement challenging the regime on several issues, including atheization in the schools, restrictions on church construction, and the number of political prisoners still behind bars.[77]

In spring 1985, the State Office for Religious Affairs issued a series of directives to its regional branches. In specific, according to Keston College, the directives called for promulgation of the idea that the Polish primate and the pope were often at odds and of the notion that some priests were "extremists," for a moratorium on permission to build further churches, for the manipulation of newsprint supplies to curtail print runs of Catholic periodicals, and for the eventual suppression of the Catholic periodicals *Znak, Wiez,* and *Powsciagliwosc Praca.*[78] At the same time, importation of the Polish edition of *L'Osservatore Romano* has been variously embargoed or held up—on one occasion for five months.[79]

The other churches of Poland have not found their situation changed, on the whole. Adam Lopatka, the minister for religious affairs, even commended the 500,000-member Polish Autocephalous Orthodox Church in March 1985 for having "introduced a special prayer for the Polish Army during the period of martial law."[80] The ultimate litmus test, though, is not the size of the church but its quiescence. And thus, after a Polish Orthodox clergyman, Fr. Piotr Poplawski, began discussing Solidarity favorably in his sermons and warning his congregation that underground Solidarity was vulnerable to infiltration by secret police, he was stabbed to death and strung up from a tree.[81]

THE EAST GERMAN EXCEPTION

With reports surfacing of a souring of church-state relations also in Yugoslavia,[82] it may seem all the more remarkable that the Evangelical-Lutheran Church in East Germany has been able to retain both its critical posture and the benign toleration of the government. Yet despite its outspoken activism in defense of conscientious objectors, its role in fostering an independent peace movement in East Germany, and its criticism of the "militarization" of East German society, the church enjoys better relations with the ruling party than ever. Indeed, Bishop Johannes Hempel, then chairman of the Evangelical Church Federation in the German Democratic Republic, recently commented, accurately, that there is "something like a basic trust" between the church and the ruling party in the GDR.[83] An important recent expression of this trust was the very considerable collaboration between the church and the state in celebrating Martin Luther's quincentenary in 1983. And while church synods held in Greifswald in September 1984 and Berlin in April 1986 reiterated church dissatisfaction in a number of areas,[84] church-state relations on the whole display a cordiality unusual in the region.

If the Evangelical Church's social activism has not cost it the cordiality of the regime, it has at the same time given it a new resilience. Enrollments in the church's six theological faculties are at an all-time high, to the extent that the church expects to have enough pastors to meet its institutional needs in the foreseeable future.[85] Its peace workshops and ecological forums are attended by Catholics as well as Lutherans, and even by nonbelievers. And attendance at its services has strengthened, especially among the young.

East Germany will probably remain an exception in the region. Various factors unique to this country permit a unique church-state relationship, including the country's susceptibility to West German television and radio, the strong ties between the Evangelical-Lutheran Churches of East and

West Germany, the stronger material resources of the Evangelical-Lutheran Church in comparison with the other churches of Eastern Europe, and the basic fact of the country's prevailing Protestantism.

CONCLUSION

Neither in Poland nor in the other countries discussed in this chapter is the situation reducible purely to a question of stiffening regime policy toward the churches. On the contrary, both church and state face opposing pressures in each of these countries, and both respond according to the nuances of the particular context.

But in all of these countries, the combination of countervailing pressures is producing a breakdown of earlier patterns of modus vivendi and resulting in important religious and policy shifts. There are strong pressures from below, within the ranks of both the Evangelical-Lutheran and Catholic Churches in the GDR and the Catholic Church in Czechoslovakia, Poland, and (via the Basic Communities) in Hungary. In Romania, discontent with the Orthodox Church is reinforcing a growth among neo-Protestant groups, much to the regime's consternation.

But while signs of religious ferment are evident in all these countries, the regimes and the churches respond to the ferment in different ways. As a result, the climate of church-state relations varies considerably from country to country. In East Germany and Hungary, as in Bulgaria, church and state remain on good terms. Officials in these countries even talk of long-term cooperation between Marxists and Christians in the building of socialism.[86]

In Poland, Czechoslovakia, and Romania, on the other hand, signs have appeared of deepening distrust on both sides. In Poland and Czechoslovakia, the regimes appear to want to "tame" the churches. In Romania, where the regime long ago succeeded in taming its Orthodox Church, there is considerable animosity, on the regime's part, toward Baptists and other Protestant groups, and hence the instances of Romanian police demolishing Baptist churches.

Because of the diversity of factors and conditions, it is extremely unlikely that church-state relations will evolve in a uniform direction in these countries. But both internal and external pressures for change are present, and the climate is already tangibly different from what it was only a decade ago.

At a somewhat higher level of generalization, three conclusions seem warranted. First, important commonalities exist among the religious policies of the communist systems of Eastern Europe, some of which reflect Soviet influence. Second, the change in church-state climate reflects the regimes' assessment of what is possible. Church-state relations are stable in the GDR partly because, for the time being, no other formula for coexistence seems possible. At the same time, the authorities in some of the other countries are becoming aware that the taming of established churches often leads to the sprouting of new, defiant religious organizations. And third, because of the communist aspiration to tame the churches, one is entitled to distinguish between church organizations that have been incorporated into the political apparatus (the Russian, Bulgarian, and Romanian Orthodox Churches and, I would argue, the Catholic and Lutheran Churches in Hungary), and those that remain independent.

PART IV

Theoretical Considerations

TEN

Pitfalls in the Study of Church-State Relations

This book has examined the possibilities of theory-building in the study of church-state relations. It has two basic premises: that this subject can benefit from the judicious application of social science principles, and that alternative theoretical approaches can for the most part be seen as complementary rather than rival approaches, in which differences of viewpoint reflect differences in the questions being asked and hence in the evidence that will prove relevant.

The four parts into which this book is divided represent analytically distinct approaches to theory—or, to put it another way, they are meta-theoretically different. Taking them in ascending order of generality, Part III represents lower-range theory in the form of simple hypotheses. Chapter 8 hypothesizes that the election of Karol Cardinal Wojtyla to the papacy contributed to a religious awakening among Catholics in Eastern Europe and the Soviet West, and that religious ferment presents the Kremlin and its cohort parties with a long-term, complex challenge. Chapter 9 hypothesizes that forces leading to a redefinition of the church-state relationship are present in several countries of Eastern Europe, and that several churches are confronted with a choice between accommodation on the regime's terms and prolonged harassment. These hypotheses endeavor to identify patterns in present trends, without explicit regard to broader theoretical concerns.

Part II presents alternative theoretical approaches to the study of church-state interaction and applies these approaches to different religious organizations. Because the focus in this section is on theoretical

176

approaches per se, in each of which a network of implicit and explicit hypotheses is subsumed, one may speak here of middle-range theory. This term may be defined as an interrelated set of hypotheses that interprets specific aspects of social reality or is interested in questions pertaining to specific spheres of social reality. Chapter 3 applies functional analysis to the Soviet religious context, paying attention to the dynamics of the policy context. The other chapters in this section apply geneticism-monism (chapter 4), the political culture approach (chapter 5), factional analysis (chapter 6), and organization theory (chapter 7). These theories ask somewhat different questions and look for explanations in very different quarters. In some ways, the two approaches that are most similar are geneticism-monism and political culture, since they both see communally shared attitudes as an intervening variable between past experience and present behavior.

Parts I and IV present the outline of a general theory of church-state interaction and thus, from the standpoint of theory, represent the highest level of generalization. Chapter 2 presents a theory of the interplay of religious policy and nationalities policy in the area, as well as of the political role of religious organizations more generally. Chapter 11 combines a theory of church-state interaction under communism with metatheoretical observations on theorizing about church-state relations.

Social science, despite its important strides in the past two-and-a-half decades, still seems condemned to persist in the quest for what is ultimately seriously constricted scientific rigor.[1] But the ideals of purposive focus, parsimony, internal consistency, external fidelity, logical rigor, and theoretical importance may serve, all the same, as lodestars in this quest.

Theory is ultimately about questions. Theory is interesting when the questions it raises are interesting and when the evidence summoned and the answers tendered seem useful. When it comes to the study of church-state interaction, the following clusters of questions suggest themselves:

Structural. What parts of the state apparatus interact with what parts of the church apparatus? Under what conditions? For what reasons? With what effects? Does the state have an interest in a particular structural order on the part of the church? And does the church adapt its structure to the particular (political) environment in which it finds itself? In many ways, organization theory may be the approach that is most at home with these questions.

Procedural. How is regime policy toward churches formulated and executed? How is church policy toward the regime formulated and executed? What are the factional elements in these policies and in the resultant interactions? What elements are unstable? And are different people or agencies involved in formulating regime policy toward different religious organizations? Both organization theory and factional analysis suggest themselves as natural avenues by which to approach these questions.

Legal. What is the relationship between civic and ecclesiastical regulations and actual practice? What purposes are served by the laws? How often and under what circumstances have the laws affecting religious organizations been changed? What traditions underlie the laws? Of the approaches surveyed in this book, geneticism-monism would seem the best suited to this cluster of questions. Functional analysis may also be useful here.[2]

Cultural. What is the relationship of religion to nationalism in a specific country context? What explains differences in this relationship from one country to another, or from one religious organization to another? How is one to explain differences among religious organizations in attitudes to secular authority, rebellion, law, progress, social protest, pacifism, and other issues? Here, the political culture approach is in its element.

I make no pretense that these chapters contain a complete cookbook of theoretical approaches. Class analysis, for example, is not represented here. The purpose of this book is not to exhaust the topic but to challenge the student of church-state relations to think theoretically.

In the remainder of this chapter, I wish to consider certain analytical pitfalls or fallacies to which studies of church-state relations are vulnerable. Some of these pitfalls are specific to the subject matter. Most are reflections of more or less universal dangers to be avoided.

FALLACIES OF INTERPRETATION

Most of the pitfalls I wish to highlight are fallacies of interpretation. They involve misplaced emphasis, or the overestimation or underestimation of the importance of certain factors.

The incipient fallacy is apt to be the preserve of historians and of church writers with expertise in early Christianity. It is the belief that the spiritual, social, and political tradition of a church is to be understood *exclusively* in terms of its origins and earliest years, and that all subsequent events and developments are merely "environmental" factors. Accordingly, "true" Christianity may be described as a nonhierarchical, communal phenomenon in which the role of the clergy is that of participant rather than leader—thus harking back to certain currents in the earliest days of Christianity. Or again, the "Orthodox tradition" has been described by one scholar strictly in terms of Byzantium, thus excluding the accommodations made in the Ottoman Empire and tsarist Russia. The attitudes and behavior of contemporary churchmen are then traced to this early tradition, and the patterns of thinking imposed by recent decades and even recent centuries are ignored. It represents, thus, an exaggeration of the genetic-monist method.

The ahistorical fallacy, the reverse of the incipient fallacy, is a pitfall into which political scientists and journalists are prone to slip. This fallacy entails treating the present configuration of church-state relations in abstraction from its historical roots and thus ignores factors anchoring relations to a general configuration. Since those who ignore the sources of present problems and issues cannot understand the evolution of debates over time, they cannot assess the interests vested in advancing specific outcomes and therefore have no reasonable basis for predicting future development.

The dynamic fallacy is the tendency to overemphasize change in religious currents or church-state relations. It is the great temptation in journalism, which places a premium on reporting what is new and different and thus encourages its practitioners to dramatize elements that appear to show change. The frequency of reports of religious revival or crackdowns on religion and so forth over the years, many of which presented revival as a completely new phenomenon, is an unmistakable symptom of this fallacy. There have, to be sure, been instances of genuine religious revival, as discussed in chapter 8, but they cannot be reported as new phenomena for the same country year after year (which happened throughout the 1970s and early 1980s in reportage of the Soviet scene).

The static fallacy is the reverse of the dynamic fallacy; it involves the understatement of change and the overemphasis of constancies in church-state relations. Some churchmen and some politically engaged writers have been particularly tempted on this score. It may be a fact, for instance, that in the early years of Bolshevik rule in Russia the regime targeted clergymen primarily out of hostility toward all forms of theism and because of the Orthodox Church's links with the overthrown political establishment. It does not follow that present-day Soviet hostility toward any specific religious organization is motivated primarily by these considerations.

The monolithic fallacy is one of the most common distortions in writings on church-state relations. It is easy to treat both church and state as monoliths and to homogenize their interests and interactions in such a way as to gloss over the complexities of intrachurch and intrastate factionalism. But factionalism is the very lifeblood of politics, and church-state relations are not exempt from the entanglements of rival factions and competing viewpoints. Not only does this fallacy produce considerable oversimplification of the situation; it also has ramifications for analytical hypotheses being tested or advanced. If, for example, a study devoted to

the impact of modernization on the church ignores the presence of reformist and modernizing currents within the church in question, the result may
be a study with only limited and partial validity.

The factional fallacy is relatively rare in writings on church-state relations. The reverse of the monolithic fallacy, it is characterized by overestimation of the importance of intrachurch or intraelite differences. While
a number of communist countries have succeeded in drawing clergy into
proregime organizations—which is only one instance of intrachurch factionalism, of course—on the whole, clergy are apt to feel greater solidarity
with other clergy of the same church than with the regime, since each
church has a relatively clearly defined mission: to sustain and propagate
its set of beliefs and practices.

A related fallacy is the tendency to treat church press organs as representing the viewpoint of the church as a whole. On the one hand, some
organs, like the Russian Orthodox publication, *Zhurnal Moskovskoi Patriarkhii,* and the Czechoslovak Catholic newspaper, *Katoličke Noviný,*
may be either so heavily censored or in fact controlled by regime agencies
as to have little in common with the viewpoints of any important segment
of the church. On the other hand, an organ such as the Slovenian Catholic
newspaper, *Družina,* while clearly the mouthpiece of its archbishopric,
cannot be thought to speak on behalf of the ecclesiastical organization in
the country as a whole.

A more perturbing pitfall is the apolitical fallacy, which consists in
believing that churches are not necessarily or not intrinsically political
actors. In the Orthodox case, for instance, this fallacy is manifested in the
belief that the intense spirituality of Eastern Christianity, with its con-
templative bent, implies disinterest in the temporal order. On the contrary,
religious leaders among the Orthodox, Catholic, Calvinist, Puritan, and
other Christian denominations, as well as among Muslim and Jewish
communities, have, over the centuries, been eager for the opportunity to
establish their own denominations as the "state religion" and to mold the
laws of the country and the moral-behavioral codes of the people in
accordance with church tenets. A truly apolitical church is virtually incon-
ceivable, since as soon as one moves from liturgical rites to religious
teaching, one is in the domain of social interests.

Analytically related to the apolitical fallacy is the pragmatic fallacy,
which shifts the emphasis in the opposite direction. To be pragmatic in this
sense is to ignore the doctrinal content of the church in question and the
goals of the regime and to treat church-state relations as if the two parties
differed only in certain specific beliefs, rather than in attitudes and
broader assumptions. Certainly, in any country in which church-state
relations are troubled or uncertain, church and state will be apt to view
each other with suspicion. But the kinds of behavior that each takes as the

norm may differ, and the expectations with which each approaches the other will be colored by a host of variables, including past contacts and sociopolitical assumptions rooted in institutional teachings.

The isolationist fallacy is the belief that the religious policy of a regime exists in isolation from its other policies. The consequence, if this were true, would be that the goals being pursued in the religious sphere would be specific to that sphere, i.e., that they would be irrelevant to other spheres. That is patently false, as I have shown in chapters 2, 3, and 7. On the contrary, the religious policy of a state is guided by a host of considerations, including questions of socialization, the aspiration (in some cases) to curtail the independence of any and all institutions, foreign policy issues (as in the Bulgarian Orthodox Church's role vis-à-vis Macedonia), nationalism, military conscription, and demographic factors.

The last fallacy of interpretation involves overestimation of the importance of Christian-Marxist dialogue and of the Marxists who are engaged in the dialogue. If dialogue is entrusted by the regime to sociologists or second-rank officials concerned with religion, one may conclude that only small questions—if any—will be resolved through such dialogue. The rest will be only talk. A further problem is that the motivations of church and state in promoting dialogue may differ from one another and from the motivation that might seem, superficially, to be implicit in seeking dialogue: to further understanding.[3] Church-state dialogue has of course led to improvements in the climate of church-state relations in some countries; the German Democratic Republic is an example.[4] In other countries, like Yugoslavia, Christian-Marxist dialogue has made less of an impact on church-state relations because of factionalism on both sides.

OTHER FALLACIES

The Baconian fallacy involves question-framing. As David Hackett Fischer has noted, it

> consists in the idea that a historian can operate without the aid of preconceived questions, hypotheses, ideas, assumptions, theories, paradigms, postulates, prejudices, presumptions, or general presuppositions of any kind. He is supposed to go a-wandering in the dark forest of the past, gathering facts like nuts and berries, until he has enough to make a general truth. Then he is to store up his general truths until he has the whole truth. This idea is doubly deficient, for it commits a historian to the pursuit of an impossible object by an impracticable method.[5]

Fact-gathering in the absence of a theory is condemned to remaining random, disjointed, haphazard, and void of meaning. At some point, a researcher must make a leap into the realm of hypotheses or relinquish any hope of producing a purposive and well-constructed study. If the researcher waits until he has gathered his berries before framing his hypotheses, it will be impossible for his research to be informed by his theory, and he will lose the opportunity of being alert, in the earlier stage, both to confirming and to disconfirming evidence.

The motivational fallacy consists in the endorsement of one position or another in such a way as to compromise scientific objectivity. When, for instance, Timothy Ware describes early Slavic Christianity as "a popular religion *in the best sense,*"[6] he betrays the fact that his study is intended, in part, as an apologia for Christian belief. When other writers refer to the status of Christian organizations under communism as unhealthy, they are verging on the motivational fallacy by assuming certain values on the part of the reader. Not everyone would agree that this assumption is a pitfall. But I think it should be so considered, at least potentially, because it threatens to beg all sorts of questions. For example, if religion is good in and of itself, are all religions equally good? If not, who is entitled to judge among them? Is a religious revival always good in all its aspects and effects? Is atheistic socialization always bad (or good) in all its aspects and effects? Is ecclesiastical independence of secular authority necessarily to be praised, or ecclesiastical subordination to secular authority necessarily to be condemned? Should a worsening of church-state relations in a communist state necessarily be assumed to be welcome to state authorities or inimical to the faith itself? This fallacy is the more dangerous when combined with excessive pessimism, in that this combination could dispose the writer to believe that his central values are massively threatened by certain regimes; with such an attitude, cool objectivity could be difficult to attain.

Hyperbole is a fallacy of factual significance. It consists in over-dramatizing the subject matter by reading too much into small things. An instance of it would be the transforming of a few antireligious newspaper articles into "a tough new line" or even "a new antireligious campaign." The best remedy for this fallacy is to carefully assess the sufficiency of the evidence and to consider what facts may seem to be inconsistent with the proposed inference.

And finally, there is the fallacy of transference—the tendency to transfer conclusions established in one context to another, seemingly similar context, in which the applicability of the conclusions is not actually proven. In the study of church-state relations under communism, this fallacy has two common forms. First, there is the occasional temptation to characterize the entire church-state climate on the basis of evidence drawn from one or two religious groups. In societies in which a single church is clearly predominant (as in Poland, Lithuania, and Bulgaria), this temptation is much less of a problem than it is in multiconfessional societies, where it may lead the observer to ignore important exceptions and, with them, clues to the variables affecting church-state relations. Second, among observers of the communist world, there is sometimes (most often among casual observers) a tendency to treat domestic developments in Eastern Europe as necessarily parallel to developments in the USSR, and to construct uniform periodization schemes. More common is the tendency to see the church-state relationship in Poland as a paradigm of church-state relations throughout the region—which it is not.

CONCLUSION

Political relationships are defined by institutional forms and resources, external pressures, contextual factors, and the content of the political actors. Insofar as religious organizations are treated as political actors, they are distinguished by a particular content—religious belief. What religious belief adds to the organization as such is membership fluidity and doctrinal conviction: New members, who were "outside" the community, become "part" of the community through conversion—that is, by accepting the religious beliefs of the community—while current members may divorce themselves from the community merely by ceasing to accept the beliefs of the organization. Few other organizations have so fluid a criterion for membership. Ethnic groups, for instance, are fixed; one is either born into a given ethnic group or one is not. Political parties accept new members, but in many countries they impose rigorous criteria for admission and expect the performance of prescribed duties for the party. Bureaucracies hire and fire personnel on the basis of standardized tests, nepotism and corruption, talent, cronyism, and a host of other factors, but rarely on the basis of one's world view. And the canons of Marxism-Leninism notwithstanding, the Polish United Workers' Party and its associated bureaucracy have long made an open practice of allowing religious believers into their ranks.[7]

The combination of membership fluidity and doctrinal conviction makes religious organizations especially resilient political actors, at least as long as membership fluidity does not work against them. The reason is self-evident: When the ruling party in a communist state alienates an important sector of the population and members of this sector become disillusioned with communist promises, they are apt to look to alternative institutions for affiliation. The openness of ecclesiastical membership helps make the churches an obvious recourse for alienated youth under communism. Religious organizations are therefore, in political terms, unlike any other organizations.

ELEVEN

Conclusion: Toward a Theory of Church-State Interaction under European Communism

The preceding chapters have treated specific country contexts, applying different theoretical tools in each case. In this chapter, I will summarize the more salient propositions I have developed, and indicate how these different theoretical tools fit together in an overall theory of church-state interaction. This theory is summarized graphically in the model of church-state interaction on the following page.

In this model, church (left) and state (right) are presented as institutional actors and are described in terms of common analytical categories. Previous experience and precedents (above), whether of historical or recent vintage, are seen as factors affecting perceptions, while environmental factors (below)—which, for most East European countries, include Soviet wishes and pressures—have more direct impacts. Factional and subinstitutional groupings (center) interact both with each other and with the institution as a whole.

The general theory consists of seven organically related partial theories—the middle-range theories mentioned in the previous chapter. These theories in turn may be described as proposition clusters, which are identified by numbers 1 to 7 on the model.

184

A Model of Church-State Interaction

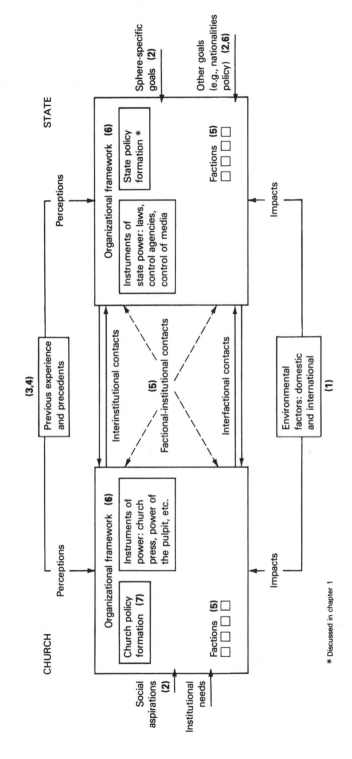

* Discussed in chapter 1

CLUSTER 1: RELIGION AND MODERNIZATION

Cluster 1 is developed in chapter 1, which explores the different kinds and sources of modernization. These environmental factors include social modernization of the kind that produces a cultural identity crisis and role confusion among individuals; political "modernization," which compels churches to adapt to new realities in order to survive; religious modernization, or the adaptation by a church of its doctrine, rites, mores, attitude toward authority, and activities to "modernizing" society (as the Bulányists in Hungary and some Catholic theologians and clergymen influenced by the Vatican II Council have tried to do); and cultural modernization, or the unceasing process of forgetting and remembering history and of reconceiving the meaning of one's history. These species of modernization create stress in a society and have direct impact on the social presence of religious organizations. Or, to put it another way, social modernization exerts pressure on religious organizations to "modernize." The result is a crisis for traditional religions, like Catholicism, which must choose between losing touch with "modernizing" communities and alienating some traditional believers. Insofar as doctrine typically constitutes the basis of a religious organization's claim to legitimacy—at least where the Christian churches are concerned—any overt alteration in doctrine risks evoking doubts in the minds of adherents. But if the organization is to adapt to social and cultural modernization, doctrine cannot be presented the same way century after century. Hence, under the pressure of modernization, religious organizations will preserve formal doctrine but modify the interpretation of doctrine. Religious rites may also be modernized—as the Roman Catholic Church did, for instance, in the wake of the Vatican II Council.

Max Weber suggested, in his study of Protestantism, that one great advantage it enjoyed was that it was better suited to the emergent free enterprise society than was Catholicism. Economic modernization, in short, was making ecclesiastical and theological notions of stability and unchanging verity a handicap. That suggests that under the pressures of modernization, religious organizations may tend to assimilate ideas of progress, displacing earlier ideas of stability. Confessional fragmentation, theological heterogeneity, and pressures for grass-roots participation can be dated to the very origins of Christianity. Modernization has, however, provided an additional stimulus to these trends, and thus has further complicated the religious picture.

CLUSTER 2: RELIGION AND NATIONALISM

Both religion and nationalism provide individuals with collective identities and codes for personal conduct; they are both, in short, social phenomena.[1] They are also capable of symbiotic mutual reinforcement, to the extent that it becomes possible to speak of religio-national identity in certain contexts.

We may begin with the observation that present communist religious policy in Eastern Europe and the Soviet Union is conditioned by at least six central factors: (1) the size of a religious organization, (2) its amenability to infiltration and control by the secret police, (3) its allegiance to any foreign authority, (4) its behavior during World War Two, (5) the ethnic configuration of the country in question, and (6) the dominant political culture of the country. The nationalist issue is expressed explicitly in factor 5 and contingently in factors 3, 4, and 6. It follows that whether a religious organization is suppressed, tolerated, or coopted depends in part on its nationalist demeanor and the significance of this demeanor in the context of the country (specifically, is the country ethnically homogeneous or multiethnic?). Thus, in ethnically homogeneous Hungary, the Catholic and Calvinist churches' low-keyed nationalism is fully compatible with their generally cooperative bearing, which Hungarian Party First Secretary János Kádár acknowledged in 1980 in characterizing the churches as "without exception loyal to our regime."[2]

A religious organization may be nationalist regardless of whether it is a worldwide organization or a regionally restricted one. Far more important is its linkage, or association, with the nation over the course of history. And hence, nationally linked religious organizations tend to figure as nationalist institutions, especially when the nation's self-rule is threatened, constricted, or suppressed. And the greater the ethnic heterogeneity of a society, the more threatening nationally linked religious organizations of minority groups will be to illegitimate regimes. The foregoing ideas were developed in chapter 2, in the context of an examination of the relationship between religious policy and considerations of nationalities policy in the communist world. The overt nationalism of the Greek-Rite Catholic Church in Ukraine, Romania, and Slovakia, for example, led to its suppression in these areas in the late 1940s.

With some 100 ethnic/national groups inhabiting fifteen ethnically defined union republics, the USSR is a particularly apt test case for theories about religio-national symbiosis. Members of these groups tend, as a general rule, to affiliate with a single religion, seen as the group religion (unless, of course, they are atheists). Within this context, religious policy and nationalities policy cannot be seen in isolation from each other.

During the Brezhnev era, in particular, Soviet authorities gave high priority to eroding the symbiosis of religious and national loyalties, which they saw as a chief obstacle to successful political socialization among non-Russians.[3]

CLUSTER 3: GENETICISM-MONISM

Present policies have their origin and history. The historical method ("geneticism") seeks insight into present policies by probing their origins in previous experience and precedents, and tracing their evolution over time. Monism is the belief that policy spheres do not exist in isolation from each other. One may tentatively infer that trauma concentrated in one sphere of society necessarily affects other spheres. Insofar as trauma necessitates policy reappraisal, its effects will penetrate through several issue areas. National trauma with religious dimensions will tend to reinforce the identification of religion and nationalism. Nationalism constitutes a specific confessional resource, and hence, the closer the religio-national symbiosis, the more difficult it is for the state to maintain a purely confrontational attitude toward religion.

If present policies must be traced back in time, so too must currents of opinion. And in this vein, the experience of the Counter-Reformation undoubtedly created a tradition of anticlericalism that makes the Roman Catholic Church especially vulnerable. At the same time, a history of advocacy by the church's lower clergy of national independence and defense of national culture produces a legacy of identification with the people. And hence, confessional strength is positively correlated with national symbiosis and resistance to foreign oppression, while it is negatively correlated with antinational demeanor and cooptation by or alliance with foreign rulers. And the symbiosis of religion and nationalism presumes a compatibility in their relationship to the secular power. More precisely, if nationalism is oppositionist in orientation, church posture must also be oppositionist if religion and nationalism are to be symbiotic. Otherwise, the identification of religion and nationalism in the specific context will tend to wane.

These ideas were explored more fully in chapter 4, in the context of examining the comparative evolution of the Catholic Church in Poland, Czechoslovakia, and Hungary.

CLUSTER 4: RELIGIOUS CULTURE AND POLITICAL CULTURE

Religious culture and political culture may be viewed as intersecting sets of value orientations, attitudes regarding appropriate social behavior, and beliefs. Their intersection may be congruous, if the content of the dominant religious culture is in harmony with the prevailing political culture. Or it may be incoherent and produce conflict, if the dominant religious culture is inharmonious with the political culture. Here the distinction between official political culture and dominant political culture[4] is of the essence, for dominant religious and political cultures are unlikely to remain long at odds, while the official political culture propounded by the ruling elite may remain at odds with the religious culture almost indefinitely. Intracultural strain provokes uncertainty in social mores, however, leading to anomie, anxiety, and a search for reintegrative groups capable of restoring cognitive consistency in cultural norms.[5]

In this context, the religious culture of Protestantism appears more disposed to social dissent and protest than does that of Catholicism. Protestantism arose in the spirit of reformist defiance. Catholicism has traditionally based its teachings on the assumption that adherents should trust to authorities (both pastoral and secular) to represent their interests. The advent of communism threw most Catholic Churches of Eastern Europe into postures of resistance and defiance by 1948.[6] But for the small Catholic Church of East Germany, which has shared the benefits of concessions won by the Evangelical Church, defiance has seemed fraught with risk, and the traditional posture has been retained.

Under communism, religious organizations are usually the only institutions free of party control. Accordingly, the churches of Eastern Europe (and in the USSR, in some instances) have naturally been cast into this dissenting role. In Poland, for example, the 1970s saw increased remonstration against party-enforced constriction of scientific research, among other species of dissent. Responding to pressures from various circles and to the obvious discontent among intellectuals, the Catholic Church came down firmly in defense of scientific and artistic freedom.[7] The Evangelical Church's receptivity to waxing pacifist sentiment in the GDR—explored in chapter 5—similarly reflects the church's response to pressure from below.

CLUSTER 5: FACTIONALISM IN CHURCH-STATE INTERACTION

Stable, distinct opinion-groupings—or factions—can be found in several of the church organizations and several of the regimes in the area. The Yugoslav case is examined in chapter 6; other countries in which factionalism has played a role in church-state relations include the GDR, Poland, Hungary, and the Soviet Union. The Yugoslav case study suggested that where factions or subgroupings exist, they may affect the policies of the institution of which they are a part. In the Soviet policymaking elite, for example, there have long been at least two important groupings: a doctrinaire "fundamentalist" grouping, with strength in the Agitprop organization and in Komsomol, and a more "pragmatic" grouping, with strength in the party apparatus and the police ranks. While the former group has opposed any and all cooperation between church and state, the latter has sought to distinguish between religious groups that are prepared to support regime objectives and those that are not.[8]

On the other side, ecclesiastical factionalism became evident at an early date in the GDR. As early as summer 1958, Evangelical Bishop Moritz Mitzenheim of Thuringia led a church delegation in talks with GDR authorities. Mitzenheim advocated a cooperative posture toward the regime and was, accordingly, decorated on his seventieth birthday (in 1961) with the Fatherland Order of Merit in Gold. But despite Mitzenheim's leadership position, other Protestant bishops repudiated his approach and disavowed the eastern wing of the CDU.[9]

More recently, the regional hierarchs of East Germany's Evangelical Church have displayed some differences in their attitudes toward the militarization of GDR society and in what is the appropriate church response.[10] It seems that when there are several factions or subgroupings in an institution, with no faction clearly dominant, the resultant policy output will be fragmented and disjointed. The religious policy of the Jaruzelski regime in Poland seems at times disjointed; most certainly, it is being executed under the strains of an elite factionalism that goes back to the fall of Gierek in summer 1980. Since then, there have been at various times as many as four opinion groupings within the Polish party: pro-pluralist elements (vocal only up to late 1981); "Kádárites," who have sought to emulate the Hungarian solution; "Husakites" or hard-liners, looking to Gustav Husak's Czechoslovakia, with its mixture of consumerism and repression,[11] for a model; and antipluralist Polish chauvinists, gathered around the regime-sponsored organization PRON and the Gruenwald Union. Evidence of this factionalism appeared in the trial of Fr. Popieluszko's murderers, in the guise of a rivalry between Gens. Miroslaw Milewski (a "Husakite") and Czeslaw Kiszczak (probably a "Kádárite") for control of the Ministry of the Interior.[12] Obviously, the greater the factionalization of a policymaking institution, the greater the fragmentation of resultant policy. Given the institutional vulnerability produced by factionalization, it is clear why communist authorities in most, if not all, of these countries have persistently sought to encourage, incite, exaggerate, and politicize intrachurch differences of opinion.[13]

Factionalism has other effects. In particular, when factionalized institutions interact, factions on either side will tend to adopt different postures toward the respective factions of the other institution. That was borne out by the discussion in chapter 6, which outlined the existence of three factional groupings within Yugoslavia's political establishment (orthodox Marxists, passive contract Marxists, and liberal Marxist sociologists) and three factional splits within the Catholic Church (Zagreb versus Split, Sarajevo and Mostar versus the Franciscans, and Christianity Today versus most bishops). Because of these differences within each side, church-state interactions necessarily differ according to who is interacting with whom.

There is a further dimension, which has to do with constituencies: Insofar as different factions may be appealing to different constituencies, they may give priority to different areas of policy. That is to say, not all elite factions may be equally concerned, for example, about whether church reconstruction permits are issued or withheld. Again, factionalism among clergy may or may not be accompanied by the formation of rival constituencies among believers. In the Yugoslav case, the rivalry between the Bosnian Franciscans and the diocesan apparatus has politicized parishioners in Franciscan parishes, so that the effects of ecclesiastical factionalization reach to lay adherents. Similarly, in Hungary, discontent among the lower clergy with the policies of the hierarchy vis-à-vis the state has been converted into lay support for Basic Community groups free of hierarchical control. On the other hand, the interepiscopal personal rivalries in the Catholic Churches of Poland and Yugoslavia, like the debate over the Croatian organization Christianity Today, have failed to be transmuted into lay opinion factions.

CLUSTER 6: ORGANIZATION THEORY

Organization theory traces policy outcomes to formal and informal rules of the organization, as well as to group formation and group loyalties. As such, organization theory is organically related to, though distinct from, theories of factionalism. Chapter 7 found that in every organization, the formal goals of the organization are scuttled, deflected, garnished, or in some other fashion modified by the informal structure. This finding applies equally to the churches and to the state apparatuses for relations with religious organizations.

A second conclusion developed in chapter 7 was that formal structures exhibit regularities that can be studied in their own right without investigating the motives of the individuals in organizations. Given the Soviet role in shaping the institutional structures of Eastern Europe and in sustaining acceptable patterns of behavior, this proposition makes considerable sense. Moreover, within the Soviet bloc at any rate, the authorities endeavor to set up the administrative infrastructure in such a way as to minimize the impact that specific individuals may have. Hence, even the details of ostensibly casual conversations may turn out to be matters of operational routine. Van der Voort described the routine for recruiting informers among seminarians in the USSR, for example. After entering the seminary, an entrant is

> sent to a room where a nice, friendly, fatherly person starts a talk with him, and asks how he likes the city, the museums and the academy, and how the study is going. When the student feels at ease, suddenly the question is put: "Are you a citizen of the Soviet Union?" As answering "No" cannot be recommended in these cases, the answer, "Yes, of course" is given. The friendly person continues by saying that therefore it is his duty to help his country. As he may know, the Soviet State has many enemies. Of course, the State is not against the Church, the academy and so forth, but there are unfortunately some elements in the academy who are against the Soviet State. Don't forget there are foreign students as well! If he happens to hear something, he should phone or write a report about it. If the student is not very careful, he'll leave that room with a phone number or address, and he is told that a report is expected in a couple of weeks. Sometimes pressure is used, or promises made to get the student's cooperation. There are even cases when a career is started. [14]

The motives and mood of the "friendly person" are irrelevant to understanding the dynamics of this tactic. And the motives of seminarians may be quite different even when the result is the same.

Organizational structures also make a difference by bringing the expected clients or targets of policy into contact with specific agents whose training and background may color the resultant relationship. Or, to put it another way, the subdivision of activities in an organization creates psychological predispositions that affect decision-making and policy-execution behavior. The fact that supervision of religious communities is often entrusted to the security police (as in Poland) is certainly apt to be associated with psychological predispositions on the part of both the agents of regime policy and the church.

Decentralization is also an important facet in organization theory. In this context, it was noted that the more decentralized an organization is, the less coherent its policy will be, and in highly decentralized environments, the policies of individual subunits may be in conflict with each other. It was also noted that in decentralized organizational environments, policy formation will reflect the needs, interests, perceptions, and experiences of subunit actors rather than those of the central authorities. These ideas were developed in chapter 7, in the context of a comparison of the formation of religious policies in Yugoslavia and Bulgaria.

CLUSTER 7: INSTITUTIONAL NEEDS OF RELIGIOUS ORGANIZATIONS

Communist elites adopt conscious policies toward religious organizations. These policies may be coherent or incoherent, consistent or inconsistent, cohesive or fragmented. The same is true of religious organizations in communist societies.

In this context, churches strive to fashion policies that respond to their perceived institutional needs. These needs differ from organization to organization. Hence, the institutional needs of a religious organization are determined by its size, dispersion, existing resources, and operational ideology. The last factor highlights the differences in behavior and orientation between more traditional groups and evangelical neo-Protestant groups. More particularly, when a religious organization's ideology dictates energetic proselytization, the institutional needs of the organization become skewed to this overriding imperative.

The relationship between institution size and pressures for accommodation may remain open to question. But it seems likely, in general, that the larger a religious organization, the greater the need to reach some accommodation with secular authority. Accommodation may, of course, cost a hierarchy some credibility with adherents; but at the same time, a policy of prolonged confrontation has its costs—which are less affordable when an ecclesiastical institution has more to lose. Along these lines, it appears that the overall weakness of a religious organization and the diminution of its educational autonomy are correlated and mutually reinforcing.

While the foregoing has emphasized local resources, various chapters have highlighted affiliation with an external ecclesiastical center, such as the Vatican, and activities and contacts that link a religious organization with believers in other regions. It appears that religious organizations whose cultural and institutional focus is external to the cultural-political region (e.g., the Vatican or Mecca, being external to Eastern Europe) will tend to interact with sister organizations in the respective focal region (i.e., Western Europe or the Arab world). It follows that the greater a religious organization's interaction with organizations external to the political region, the greater the number of interactions that will fall beyond the regime's reach and ability to control. And religious organizations with different focal (culture) regions will be less likely to engage in interconfessional dialogue and cooperation than those with the same focal culture region. This hypothesis should not be understood in narrowly geographic terms but in broader religiocultural terms. Catholics and Protestants, or Catholics and Orthodox, are more likely to engage in interconfessional dialogue than are Christians of any derivation and Muslims, or, for that matter, Protestants and Orthodox. Recent history in Eastern Europe and the Soviet Union bears this out.

The surge in church-state frictions in the late 1970s and early 1980s was traced to a change in the available resources of religious organizations—more specifically, of the Catholic Church. The reason is that when the symbolic resources of a particular religious organization increase suddenly (as in the election of Karol Wojtyla to the papacy in 1978), organization adherents are apt to become more defiant of constrictive legislation and to gain in solidarity. As I argued in chapter 8, Wojtyla's election contributed to a general religious awakening among East European Catholics.

Reversing the direction of change allows one to say that when the symbolic resources of a particular religious organization decline, solidarity among organization adherents is also apt to decline, with the result that incidents of defiance will likewise decline. And, in a similar line, a new religious organization that experiences rapid growth gains symbolic resources insofar as it comes to be seen as an emergent alternative; it therefore is more and more competitive with previously existing religious organizations. Rapid growth reinforces the policies originally adopted by the religious organization. The Baptist Church in Romania is an apt example of this. The most militant among the neo-Protestant groups in that country, it has grown from a membership of 80,000 in 1960 to more than 200,000 in 1985.[15] This dramatic growth has encouraged the Baptists to retain their militant posture.

Repression has long been known to be potentially counterproductive. One reason is that repression increases the symbolic resources of the organization targeted. The success of the Counter-Reformation proves, of course, that repression can work. But the stimulation given by the abolition of religious instruction in Poland to the development of catechetical networks and to the strengthening of the Catholic Church's links with the nation show that below a critical threshold repression is apt to be counterproductive. Moreover, even where the Counter-Reformation is concerned, the fate of Catholicism among the Czechs suggests that a repressive victory may be a Pyrrhic one.

Along the same lines, policy unevenness may stimulate resistance, in part by stirring awareness of the possibility of change and improvement. These themes and issues were, in part, developed in chapters 8 and 9. Chapter 8 focused on the impact of the election of Karol Wojtyla to the papacy and the ensuing religious ferment. Chapter 9 examined the situations of Protestants and Catholics in the wake of the murder of Fr. Popieluszko by the Polish secret police.

CONCLUSION

Any general theory consists of organically related but separable parts: middle-range theories that deal with specific issues and aspects of the general subject. A general theory is thus a kind of map of the theoretical universe. It identifies which middle-range theories address which questions, where they are, and how they relate to each other. It should be clear that I conceive of alternative middle-range theories as potentially complementary tools designed to accomplish different tasks.

This book has not applied the entire general theory to each country of the region. To carry that out, a multivolume study would have been necessary. What I have done, rather, is to apply each hypothesis cluster in succession to a different country or topic, illustrating the various methodologies and, at the same time, endeavoring to illuminate the religious scene in Eastern Europe and the Soviet Union.

To theorize about church-state relations is to attempt to set these relations in their political, social, and analytical context, and to reveal the political content of their reciprocal policies. The purpose of theory is not to constrain the subject matter into a conceptual straitjacket, but rather to open new avenues for understanding the specificities of each situation and each context, even while probing the underlying patterns and meanings embedded in them. This book has approached theory in this spirit.

Notes

I. HOW CHURCH AND STATE COEXIST UNDER COMMUNISM

1. An exception is Bohdan R. Bociurkiw, "The Shaping of Soviet Religious Policy," in *Problems of Communism*, Vol. 22, No. 3 (May–June 1973).

2. That has in fact been the case in Yugoslavia recently.

3. Jane Ellis, *The Russian Orthodox Church: A Contemporary History* (Bloomington: Indiana University Press, 1986), pp. 269–270.

4. Quoted in Walter Sawatsky, "Religious Administration and Modernization," in Dennis J. Dunn (ed.), *Religion and Modernization in the Soviet Union* (Boulder, Colo.: Westview Press, 1977), p. 84.

5. Ellis, *Russian Orthodox Church*, p. 273.

6. *Izvestiia* (November 7, 1985), p. 6, trans. in *Current Digest of the Soviet Press*, Vol. 37, No. 45 (December 4, 1985), p. 25.

7. In the East German context, see *Neues Deutschland* (February 7, 1986), p. 2, (February 8–9, 1986), p. 2, (February 14, 1986), p. 5, and (March 14, 1986), p. 2.

8. Radio Prague (February 4, 1985), trans. in Joint Publications Research Service (JPRS), *East Europe Report* No. EPS–85–026 (February 26, 1985), p. 58.

9. Ivan Cvitković, "Stavovi suvremenih teologa o odnosu religije i religijskih zajednica prema politici u socijalizmu," in *Politička misao*, Vol. 15, No. 4 (1978), p. 653; and *Tribuna* (Prague, November 14, 1984), trans. in JPRS, *East Europe Report* No. EPS–85–010 (January 18, 1985), p. 25.

10. *Rude pravo* (Prague, September 8, 1984), p. 3, trans. in JPRS, *East Europe Report* No. EPS–84–129 (October 19, 1984), p. 12.

11. *Era Socialista* (Bucharest, April 10, 1984), trans. in JPRS, *East Europe Report* No. EPS–84–063 (May 17, 1984), p. 45.

12. Antoni Nowicki, *Wyklady o krytyce religii w Polsce* (1965), as summarized in Karol H. Borowski, "The Sociology of Religion in Modern Poland: A Critical Review," in *Sociological Analysis*, Vol. 46, No. 4 (Winter 1985), p. 394.

13. *Gazeta wspolczesna* (Bialystok, March 1, 1985), p. 3, trans. in Foreign Broadcast Information Service (FBIS), *Daily Report* (Eastern Europe), April 8, 1985, p. G2.

14. Innumerable examples can be found be consulting *Keston News Service*.

15. Dimitry Pospielovsky, "Church and State under Gorbachev: What to Expect?" in Larry Lerner and Donald W. Treadgold (eds.), *Gorbachev and the Soviet Future* (manuscript in progress).

16. Donald Eugene Smith, *Religion and Political Development* (Boston: Little, Brown, 1970), p. 126.

17. See Richard K. Fenn, "Religion, Identity and Authority in the Secular Society," in Roland Robertson and Burkart Holzner (eds.), *Identity and Authority: Explorations in the Theory of Society* (Oxford: Basil Blackwell, 1980).

18. Angela A. Aidala, "Social Change, Gender Roles, and New Religious Movements," in *Sociological Analysis,* Vol. 46, No. 3 (Fall 1985), p. 287.

19. See Oxana Antić, "Persecution of Jehovah's Witnesses Continues," *Radio Liberty Research* (July 9, 1985); "Jehovah's Witnesses in Czechoslovakia," in *Religion in Communist Lands,* Vol. 14, No. 1 (Spring 1986), pp. 102–103; and "Adventism—One of the Major Protestant Confessions in the USSR," *Radio Liberty Research* (August 23, 1985).

20. See " 'The Path of Krishna' in the USSR," in *Keston News Service* No. 243 (February 6, 1986), pp. 17–20; and Julia Wishnevsky, "Persecution of the Hare Krishna Movement in the Soviet Union," *Radio Liberty Research* (November 14, 1985).

21. As cited in Baltic Area/Situation Report, *Radio Free Europe Research* (July 18, 1986), pp. 29–30.

22. V. D. Kobetskii, *Sotsiologicheskoe izuchenie religioznosti i ateizma* (Leningrad, 1978), trans. under the title "Study of the Processes of Overcoming Religiosity and of the Dissemination of Atheism," Part 3, in *Soviet Sociology,* Vol. 19, No. 2 (Fall 1980), p. 78.

23. *Etudes* (January 1979), p. 87, as quoted in M. A. Gol'denberg, "Printsip svobody sovesti i ego klerikal'nye interpretatory," in *Voprosy nauchnogo ateizma* (1981), No. 27, trans. under the title "The Principle of Freedom of Conscience and its Clerical Interpreters," in *Soviet Sociology,* Vol. 23, No. 1 (Summer 1984), p. 12.

24. See S. N. Eisenstadt, "The Protestant Ethic Thesis in an Analytical and Comparative Framework," in S. N. Eisenstadt (ed.), *The Protestant Ethic and Modernization* (New York: Basic Books, 1968).

25. William C. Fletcher, "Backwards from Reactionism: The De-Modernization of the Russian Orthodox Church," in Dunn (ed.), *Religion and Modernization,* p. 206.

26. Ibid., pp. 221–222.

27. Aidala, "Social Change," pp. 299, 301, 303, 306, 307, 311.

2. THE INTERPLAY OF RELIGIOUS POLICY AND NATIONALITIES POLICY

This chapter is a revised, updated, and slightly condensed version of a chapter entitled "The Interplay of Religious Policy and Nationalities Policy in the Soviet Union and Eastern Europe," which was first published in Pedro Ramet (ed.), *Religion and Nationalism in Soviet and East European Politics* (Durham, N.C.: Duke University Press, 1984) © 1984 by Duke University Press. It is used here by permission.

1. Summarized in Barbara Hargrove, *The Sociology of Religion* (Arlington Heights, Ill.: AHM, 1979), p. 4.

2. See Jean Jacques Rousseau, *A Discourse on Political Economy,* trans. G. D. H. Cole (Chicago: William Benton, 1952), pp. 371–375; and Georg Wilhelm Friedrich Hegel, *The Philosophy of Right,* trans. T. M. Knox (Oxford: Clarendon Press, 1952), p. 168.

3. Sigmund Freud, *Moses and Monotheism,* trans. Katherine Jones (New York: Knopf, 1939), pp. 21–43.

4. Ivan S. Lubachko, *Belorussia under Soviet Rule, 1917–1957* (Lexington: University Press of Kentucky, 1972), p. 159.

5. Vasyl Markus, "Religion in the Soviet Ukraine: A Political Problem of Modernizing Society," in Ihor Kamenetsky (ed.), *Nationalism and Human Rights in the USSR* (Littleton, Colo.: Libraries Unlimited, 1977), p. 156.

6. Ironically, however, as D. Kasić has pointed out, many Serbian Orthodox believers in Pavelić's Croatia were suspicious of the new church and felt that if they were going to change churches, they preferred to convert to Catholicism, which offered more reliable protection from *Ustaše* liquidations. See Fikreta Jelić-Butić, *Ustaše i NDH* (Zagreb: S. N. Liber and Školska knjiga, 1977), p. 178n; also Ante Pavelić, *Hrvatska Pravoslavna Crkva* (Madrid: Domovina, 1984).

7. V. Stanley Vardys, *The Catholic Church, Dissent and Nationality in Soviet Lithuania* (Boulder, Colo.: East European Monographs, 1978), pp. 11–13.

8. *Tercuman* (Istanbul, April 1, 1980), p. 3, trans. in Joint Publications Research Service (JPRS), *East Europe Report* No. 75548 (April 23, 1980), p. 15.

9. Hungarians constituted 96 percent of the Hungarian population in 1980, while Romanians accounted for 88 percent of the population of Romania in 1977. The Bulgarian regime denies the existence of any significant minorities in Bulgaria, but an impartial Western observer estimated in 1976 that ethnic minorities accounted for 13.8 percent of the Bulgarian population. See László Ribanszky, "Nationalities in Hungary: Few in Number but Pampered," *Radio Free Europe Research* (October 28, 1980), p. 2; Romanian Situation Report No. 20, *Radio Free Europe Research* (June 22, 1977); and John Georgeoff, "Ethnic Minorities in the People's Republic of Bulgaria," in George Klein and Milan J. Reban (eds.), *The Politics of Ethnicity in Eastern Europe* (Boulder, Colo.: East European Monographs, 1981), p. 79n.

10. See Dimitry Pospielovsky, "Some Remarks on the Contemporary Russian Nationalism and Religious Revival," in *Canadian Review of Studies in Nationalism*, vol. 11, No. 1 (Spring 1984), p. 73.

11. Quoted in Viktor Novak, *Velika optužba (Magnum Crimen)* (Sarajevo: Svjetlost, 1960), Vol. 2, p. 56.

12. *Katolički tjednik,* quoted in Fred Singleton, *Twentieth Century Yugoslavia* (New York: Columbia University Press, 1976), p. 197.

13. Lazar Milin, *Razgovori o veri,* quoted in *NIN* (February 20, 1972), p. 16.

14. See Hans Kohn, *Pan-Slavism: Its Meaning and Ideology,* 2d ed. (New York: Random House, 1960), p. 127 and passim.

15. Joseph F. Zacek, "Nationalism in Czechoslovakia," in Peter F. Sugar and Ivo J. Lederer (eds.), *Nationalism in Eastern Europe* (Seattle: University of Washington Press, 1970), p. 173.

16. The council has seven departments: for Orthodox churches (Russian, Geogian, Old Believers); for Islam and Buddhism; for the Catholic, Protestant, and Armenian-Apostolic churches, Judaism, and sects; for "International Contacts"; the legal department; bookkeeping; and a general department. See Albert Boiter, *Religion in the Soviet Union,* Washington Papers, Vol. 8, No. 78 (Beverly Hills: Sage Publications, 1980), p. 48.

17. On the structural aspects of Yugoslav religious policy, see Pedro Ramet, "The Dynamics of Yugoslav Religious Policy—Some Insights from Organization Theory," in Pedro Ramet (ed.), *Yugoslavia in the 1980s* (Boulder, Colo.: Westview Press, 1985).

18. There are some 500,000 Polish Uniates, mostly of Ukrainian descent. See

Markus, "Religion in the Soviet Ukraine," pp. 155–156; Gerhard Simon, "The Catholic Church and the Communist State in the Soviet Union and Eastern Europe," in Bohdan R. Bociurkiw and John W. Strong (eds.), *Religion and Atheism in the USSR and Eastern Europe* (London: Macmillan, 1975), p. 202; Rudolf Grulich, "Unierte Gläubige in kommunistisch regierten Ländern," in *Digest des Ostens* (1980), No. 11. pp. 1–51; *Družina* (Ljubljana, August 17, 1975), p. 1; and *Keston News Service* No. 155 (September 1, 1982), p. 10.

19. Michael Bourdeaux, "Roman Catholics and Uniates," in George Schöpflin (ed.), *The Soviet Union and Eastern Europe: A Handbook* (New York: Praeger, 1970), p. 476.

20. *Rabochaya gazeta* (Kiev, April 17, 1981), p. 3, trans. in JPRS, *Soviet Report* No. 78159 (May 26, 1981), p. 22.

21. Denis Dirscherl, "The Soviet Destruction of the Greek Catholic Church," in *Journal of Church and State,* vol. 12, No. 3 (Autumn 1970), pp. 423, 426.

22. See ibid., pp. 427–428; Yaroslav Bilinsky, *The Second Soviet Republic: The Ukraine after World War II* (New Brunswick, N.J.: Rutgers University Press, 1964), pp. 97–98; Bohdan R. Bociurkiw, "Religion and Nationalism in the Contemporary Ukraine," in George W. Simmonds (ed.), *Nationalism in the USSR and Eastern Europe* (Detroit: University of Detroit Press, 1977); Vasyl Markus, "Religion and Nationality: The Uniates of the Ukraine," in Bociurkiw and Strong (eds.), *Religion and Atheism;* and "Zur religiosen Unterdrückung in der Westukraine," in *Glaube in der 2. Welt,* Vol. 8, No. 9 (September 1980).

23. See Blahoslav Hruby, "Soviet Infiltration and Manipulation of the Russian Orthodox Church," in *Religion in Communist Dominated Areas,* Vol. 19, Nos. 4–11 (1980), pp. 146–147; and "Cadres of the Church and Legal Measures to Curtail Their Activities," a secret report by the Council on Religious Affairs, in two parts, in *Religion in Communist Dominated Areas,* Vol. 19, Nos. 9–11 (1980), pp. 149–161, and Vol. 20, Nos. 4–6 (1981), pp. 52–68.

24. *The Church and State Under Communism,* Vol. 2 (Rumania, Bulgaria, Albania), prepared by the Law Library of the Library of Congress (Washington, D.C.: Government Printing Office, 1965), pp. 1–2, 12.

25. *Univerzul* (October 15, 1948), as quoted in Emil Ciurea, "Religious Life," in Alexandre Cretzianu (ed.), *Captive Rumania* (London: Atlantic Press, 1956), p. 195.

26. "Zwischen Anpassung und Unterdrückung," in *Herder Korrespondenz,* Vol. 32, No. 8 (August 1978), p. 414.

27. Ion Ratiu, "The Uniates in Romania," in *The Tablet* (February 27, 1982), p. 199.

28. "Die Lage der griechisch-katholischen Ukrainer in Rumänien," *Glaube in der 2. Welt,* Vol. 5, Nos. 7–8 (July–August 1977), p. D54.

29. See Pedro Ramet, "Innenpolitische Determinanten der sowjetischen Interventionspolitik. Zu den Auswirkungen der tschechoslowakischen und polnischen Krise auf den Westen der UdSSR," in *Osteuropa,* Vol. 35, No. 3 (March 1985).

30. Michael Bourdeaux, "The Uniate Churches in Czechosolovakia," in *Religion in Communist Lands,* Vol. 2, No. 2 (March–April 1974), pp. 4–6; *Rude Pravo* (Prague, April 12, 1968), trans. in *Religion in Communist Dominated Areas,* Vol. 7, Nos. 7–8 (April 15–30, 1968), p. 78; Galia Golan, *The Czechoslovak Reform Movement* (Cambridge: Cambridge University Press, 1971), p. 292; and Markus, "Religion and Nationality: The Uniates of the Ukraine," p. 113.

31. Quoted in Eugen Steiner, *The Slovak Dilemma* (Cambridge: Cambridge University Press, 1973), p. 74.

32. Boiter, *Religion,* p. 72.

33. Zvi Gitelman, "Moscow and the Soviet Jews: A Parting of the Ways," in *Problems of Communism,* Vol. 29, No. 1 (January–February 1980), p. 21.

34. Boiter, *Religion,* p. 74.

35. *Los Angeles Times* (December 22, 1976), p. 19.

36. Michael Bourdeaux, "Jews," in Schöpflin (ed.), *The Soviet Union,* pp. 489–490. See also Bennett Kovrig, *The Hungarian People's Republic* (Baltimore: Johns Hopkins Press, 1970), p. 144.

37. *Neue Zürcher Zeitung* (August 15–16, 1982), p. 6.

38. Maxine Pollack, "Anti-Semitism in Poland," in *The Tablet* (January 30, 1982), pp. 99–100.

39. G. S., "Bulgarian Jews—a Doomed Minority," *Radio Free Europe Research* (May 3, 1985).

40. For a listing of Monophysite Churches and a discussion of the difference between Chalcedonian and Monophysite Churches, see Pedro Ramet, "Autocephaly and National Identity in Church-State Relations in Eastern Christianity," in Pedro Ramet (ed.), *Eastern Christianity and Politics in the Twentieth Century* (Durham, N.C.: Duke University Press, forthcoming).

41. Peter J. Babris, *Silent Churches* (Arlington Heights, Ill.: Research Publishers, 1978), p. 158.

42. All statistics from Ramet (ed.), *Eastern Christianity.*

43. *Europa Year Book 1972,* Vol. 1, pp. 1435–1436, cited in Burton Paulu, *Radio and Television Broadcasting in Eastern Europe* (Minneapolis: University of Minnesota Press, 1974), p. 463.

44. C. J. Peters, "The Georgian Orthodox Church," in Ramet (ed.), *Eastern Christianity.*

45. Official figures of the Council of the Russian Orthodox Church, as given in Salo Wittmayer Baron, *Modern Nationalism and Religion* (New York: Harper 1947), p. 200.

46. If the annexed territories are counted, then, as official Soviet figures show, there were some 4,225 licensed Orthodox churches in the USSR in 1941. See ibid., p. 206; and D. Konstantinow, "Die Russische Orthodoxe Kirche heute," in *Ost-Probleme,* Vol. 18, No. 13 (July 1, 1966), p. 388.

47. One of the best studies of the Russian Orthodox Church is Dimitry Pospielovsky, *The Russian Church under the Soviet Regime, 1917–1982,* 2 vols. (Crestwood, N.Y.: St. Vladimir's Seminary Press, 1984).

48. Boiter, *Religion,* p. 17; Konstantinow, "Die Russische," p. 388; Otto Luchterhandt, "Geknebelt, und dennoch lebensfähig: Die Russisch-Orthodoxe Kirche in der Ära Breschnew," in *Herder Korrespondenz,* Vol. 36, No. 5 (May 1982), p. 235; and Philip Walters, "The Russian Orthodox Church," in Ramet (ed.), *Eastern Christianity.*

49. "Cadres of the Church and Legal Measures," Part 1, p. 149.

50. See Novosti Press Agency (September 20, 1968), trans. in *Religion in Communist Dominated Areas,* Vol. 7, Nos. 17–18 (September 15–30, 1968), pp. 149–150.

51. "I Žukov i Nevski," trans. from the German original in *Stern* into Serbo-Croatian in *Duga* (December 8, 1979), p. 17.

52. Raoul Bossy, "Religious Persecutions in Captive Romania," in *Journal of Central European Affairs,* Vol. 15, No. 2 (July 1955), p. 162; and Ciurea, "Religious Life," p. 167.

53. Rumanian National Committee (Washington, D.C.), *Information Bulletin*

No. 46 (January 1953), p. 11; and Radio Vatican (January 6, 1953), as cited in Ciurea, "Religious Life," p. 173.

54. Bossy, "Religious Persecutions," p. 164.

55. Kenneth Jowitt, in *Revolutionary Breakthroughs and National Development: The Case of Romania, 1944–1965* (Berkeley: University of California Press, 1971, p. 198), insists that Romania's independent course should be dated from 1962, not from 1945 or even 1955.

56. Keith Hitchins, "The Romanian Orthodox Church and the State," in Bociurkiw and Strong (eds.), *Religion and Atheism,* pp. 314–325; and Miranda Villiers, "The Romanian Orthodox Church Today," in *Religion in Communist Lands,* Vol. 1, No. 3 (May–June 1973), pp. 4–5.

57. See, for instance, the review article by Mircea Muthu in *Steaua* (Cluj–Napoca, February 1982), p. 39, trans. in JPRS, *East Europe Report* No. 80679 (April 27, 1982), pp. 50–53.

58. Djoko Slijepčević, *Die bulgarische orthodoxe Kirche 1944–1965* (Munich: R. Oldenbourg, 1957), pp. 9, 18.

59. *Narodna mladež* (March 11, 1970), quoted in Wolf Oschlies, " 'Überwundene Religion?'—Zur Gegenwartssituation von Religion und Kirche in Bulgarien," in *Evangelische Theologie,* Vol. 35, No. 5 (September–October 1975), p. 442.

60. Thus, in early 1979, a statement signed by five Bulgarian Orthodox metropolitans attacked an article in the Yugoslav daily *Borba* for asserting that the Kresnen-Raslog uprising of 1878–79 had been Macedonian in character rather than Bulgarian. See *Tsurkoven vestnik* (February 1, 1979), pp. 4–6.

61. Vladimir M. Rodzianko, "The Golgotha of the Orthodox Church in Yugoslavia, 1941–1951," in *Eastern Churches Quarterly,* Vol. 10, No. 2 (Summer 1953), p. 71.

62. *The Church and State under Communism,* Vol. 3 (Yugoslavia), report of the US Senate Subcommittee to Investigate the Administration of the Internal Security Act and Other Internal Security Laws (Washington, D.C.: Government Printing Office, 1965), pp. 18, 21.

63. See ibid., pp. 21–22; and Radovan Popovitć, "Iza crkvenih dveri," in *NIN,* No. 1588 (June 7, 1981), p. 25.

64. Rudolf Trofenik, "Staat und Kirche in heutigen Jugoslawien," in *Osteuropa,* Vol. 8, Nos. 7–8 (July–August 1958), p. 496.

65. *The Church and State under Communism,* Vol. 3, p. 12.

66. See Patriarch German's interview with *8 Novosti* (June 6, 1981), excerpted in *Vesnik: Organ Saveza udruženog Pravoslavnog sveštenstva Jugoslavije* (July 1981), p. 3.

67. For an elaboration, see Pedro Ramet, "Religion and Nationalism in Yugoslavia," in Pedro Ramet (ed.), *Religion and Nationalism in Soviet and East European Politics* (Durham, N.C.: Duke University Press, 1984), pp. 159–163.

68. Interviews, Belgrade, July 1982.

69. Tanjug (October 20, 1981), trans. in Foreign Broadcast Information Service (FBIS), *Daily Report* (Eastern Europe), October 21, 1981, p. 15.

70. See *Pravoslavlje* (September 1, 1972, and September 15, 1972), as trans. in JPRS, *East Europe Report* No. 57287 (October 18, 1972), pp. 32–40.

71. Ciurea, "Religious Life," p. 174.

72. Peter A. Toma and Milan J. Reban, "Church-State Schism in Czechoslovakia," in Bociurkiw and Strong (eds.), *Religion and Atheism,* p. 280.

73. Trofenik, "Staat und Kirchen," p. 497. See also *Glas koncila* (September 13, 1981), p. 2.

74. Simon, "The Catholic Church," p. 205; and Stefan Rosada and Jozef Gwozdz, "Church and State in Poland," in Vladimir Gsovski (ed.), *Church and State behind the Iron Curtain* (New York: Praeger, 1955), p. 198.

75. Emmerich András, "The Cultural Lag in Society and Church in Hungary during the Post-War Period," in Norbert Greinacher and Virgil Elizondo (eds.), *Churches in Socialist Societies of Eastern Europe,* Concilium: Religion in the Eighties (New York: Seabury Press, 1982), p. 8.

76. George N. Shuster, *Religion behind the Iron Curtain* (New York: Macmillan, 1951), pp. 240–241; George Rosu, Mircea Vasiliu, and George Crisan, "Church and State in Romania," in Gsovski (ed.), *Church and State,* p. 284; and Jean G. H. Hoffmann, *Eglises du Silence* (Paris: La Table Ronde, 1967), p. 153.

77. Bernhard Tönnes, "Religious Persecution in Albania," in *Religion in Communist Lands,* Vol. 10, No. 3 (Winter 1982), p. 249; Bernhard Tönnes, "Der Glaube an Gott lebt auch in Albanien," in *Kirche in Not,* Vol. 29 (1981), p. 206; and Gjon Sinishta, "Grave Violations of Religious Rights in Albania," *Occasional Papers on Religion in Eastern Europe,* Vol. 3, No. 5 (July 1983), pp. 9–12.

78. See Caroline Ward, "Church and State in East Germany," in *Religion in Communist Lands,* Vol. 6, No. 2 (Summer 1978), p. 89.

79. *Uj Ember* (February 3, 1980), p. 1, trans. in JPRS, *East Europe Report* No. 75414 (April 1, 1980), pp. 22–25; and Vincent C. Chrypinski, "Church and State in Gierek's Poland," in Maurice D. Simon and Roger D. Kanet (eds.), *Background to Crisis: Policy and Politics in Gierek's Poland* (Boulder, Colo.: Westview Press, 1981), pp. 245–247.

80. *The Church and State under Communism,* Vol. 2, p. 22.

81. *Deutsche Tagespost* (December 18–19, 1953), as cited in Ciurea, "Religious Life," p. 190.

82. Paul Mailleux, "Catholics in the Soviet Union," in Richard H. Marshall, Jr. (ed.), *Aspects of Religion in the Soviet Union, 1917–1967* (Chicago: University of Chicago Press, 1971), pp. 363–364.

83. *The Church and State under Communism,* Vol. 2, p. 29.

84. Ibid., pp. 35, 37.

85. *The Church and State under Communism,* Vol. 3, p. 22. For a more detailed discussion of the early phase of church-state relations in Yugoslavia, see Pedro Ramet, "Catholicism and Politics in Socialist Yugoslavia," in *Religion in Communist Lands,* Vol. 10, No. 3 (Winter 1982); and Stella Alexander, *Church and State in Yugoslavia since 1945* (Cambridge: Cambridge University Press, 1979).

86. *Rheinischer Merkur* (February 17, 1978), p. 13; *Frankfurter Allgemeine* (June 18, 1975), p. 7; and Anton Hlinka, *Freedom Denied: Czechoslovakia after Helsinki,* trans. H. E. Oborg (Uhldingen-Muhlhofen: Stefanus, 1977?), p. 27.

87. András, "The Cultural Lag," pp. 8–9; and Emmerich András, "The Situation of the Catholic Clergy in Hungary," in Greinacher and Elizondo (eds.), *Churches in Socialist Societies,* pp. 58, 60.

88. Jan Nowak, "The Church in Poland," in *Problems of Communism,* Vol. 31, No. 1 (January-February 1982), p. 5.

89. Karl Hartmann, "Der Polnische Episkopat und die Oder-Neisse Gebiete," in *Osteuropa,* Vol. 21, No. 3 (March 1971), pp. 165–167; and Michael D. Kennedy and Maurice D. Simon, "Church and Nation in Socialist Poland," in Peter H.

Merkl and Ninian Smart (eds.), *Religion and Politics in the Modern World* (New York: New York University Press, 1983), pp. 133–134. See also Joachim Piegsa, "Die Rolle der Kirche in Polen," in *Politische Studien*, Vol. 33, No. 264 (July-August 1982).

90. See Janusz Bugajski, "Poland's Anti-Clergy Campaign," in *The Washington Quarterly*, Vol. 8, No. 4 (Fall 1985).

91. I have omitted Bulgaria from this listing because its Catholic Church is so small as to be insignificant—which makes its church unique among the Catholic churches of Eastern Europe.

92. Rudolf Grulich, "Katholische Kirche in Rumänien," in *Kirche in Not*, Vol. 26 (1978), p. 145.

93. *Pravda Ukrainy* (October 19, 1977), pp. 3–4; and *Život strany* (February 13, 1978), pp. 46–49, trans. in JPRS, *East Europe Report* No. 70937 (April 12, 1978), pp. 37–45.

94. *Pro fratribus* (1980), No. 34, p. 6.

95. *Chronicle of the Catholic Church in Lithuania* (June 29, 1977), reprinted in Vardys, *Catholic Church, Dissent and Nationality*, pp. 270–271.

96. Christel Lane, *Christian Religion in the Soviet Union* (London: George Allen & Unwin, 1978), p. 211; and Bohdan R. Bociurkiw, "Religious Dissent and the Soviet State," in Bociurkiw and Strong (eds.), *Religion and Atheism*, pp. 71, 73–74.

97. Malik Sabirovich Fazylov, *Religiya i natsional'nyye otnosheniya* (Alma Ata: Kazakhstan Publishing House, 1969), pp. 39, 71–74, 80.

98. I have developed this argument systematically, using statistical measures from all the Soviet republics, in "Linguistic Assimilation in Ukraine," in *Ukrainian Quarterly*, Vol. 35, No. 3 (Autumn 1979). See also Ivan Dzyuba, *Internationalism or Russification?* (New York: Monad Press, 1974); and Stephen M. Horak, "Belorussia: Modernization, Human Rights, Nationalism," in Kamenetsky (ed.), *Nationalism and Human rights*, pp. 144, 149.

99. E.g., I. A. Matsyavichius, "Katolitsizm i sovremennaya ideologicheskaya bor'ba," in *Voprosy filosofii*, No. 8 (August 1976), p. 162.

100. Quoted in Vardys, *Catholic Church, Dissent and Nationality*, pp. 158–159.

101. *Nauka i religiya*, No. 4 (April 1980), p. 60, as cited in Oxana Antić, "The Soviet Press on the Catholic Church in Lithuania," *Radio Liberty Research* (December 29, 1980), p. 2n; and Marite Sapiets, "Religion and Nationalism in Lithuania," in *Religion in Communist Lands*, Vol. 7, No. 2 (Summer 1979), p. 78.

102. Sapiets, "Religion and Nationalism in Lithuania," p. 82.

103. *Vestsi Akademii Navuk Belaruskai SSR*, Sryya Gramadskikh Navuk, No. 5 (1981), p. 137.

104. *Nauka i religiya*, No. 6 (June 1980), trans. in JPRS, *Soviet Report* No. 76263 (August 20, 1980), p. 65.

105. *Elta Information Bulletin* (May 1981), p. 15, and (February 1982), pp. 10–11.

106. See, for instance, *Tvorba* (March 24, 1982), p. 6, trans. in JPRS, *East Europe Report* No. 80972 (June 3, 1982), pp. 10–11; and *Pravda* (Bratislava, March 25, 1982), p. 3, trans. in FBIS, *Daily Report* (Eastern Europe), March 29, 1982, pp. D4–D6.

107. *Keston News Service* Nos. 151–154 (August 31, 1982), pp. 5–6.

108. All are 1971 figures, as reported in Smail Balic, "Eastern Europe: The

Islamic Dimensions," in *Journal of the Institute of Muslim Minority Affairs*, Vol. 1, No. 1 (Summer 1979), p. 31.

109. Zachary T. Irwin, "The Fate of Islam in the Balkans: A Comparison of Four State Policies," in Ramet (ed.), *Religion and Nationalism*, p. 218.

110. "News in Brief," *Religion in Communist Lands*, Vol. 5, No. 4 (Winter 1977), p. 272.

111. See Irwin, "The Fate of Islam," pp. 218–221.

112. *The Times* (London, February 8, 1985), p. 10, (February 16, 1985), p. 6, (February 20, 1985), p. 9, and (April 17, 1985), p. 9; *Frankfurter Allgemeine* (March 15, 1985), p. 7; and *Arabia* (March 1985), pp. 10–13.

113. Author's calculations from *Vestnik statistiki* (Moscow, 1980), No. 7, pp. 41–42. Tallying up the figures of all the traditionally Muslim groups listed by the Soviets, deducting 20 percent of the Kurds (who are non-Muslim), and adding in half of the Abkhaz yields a figure of 43,768,973, or 16.70 percent of the Soviet population of 262,084,654 in 1979. But this figure excludes the Muslim South Ossetians (who are listed with Orthodox North Ossetians in the census report), a small group of Muslim Georgians (once known as Ingiloy), Dungans, Iranians, and Adzhars, as well as Muslims among the Mari, Mordvins, Udmurts, and Chuvash, and less numerous Muslim peoples.

114. Ronald Wixman, "The Creation of National Territories and Languages among Soviet Muslims: How and Why?" oral presentation at the twentieth conference of the Western Slavic Association, Honolulu (March 18–21, 1982); and Alexandre Bennigsen, "Islamic or Local Consciousness among Soviet Nationalities?" in Edward Allworth (ed.), *Soviet Nationality Problems* (New York: Columbia University Press, 1971), pp. 178–179.

115. N. Ashirov, "Islam i natsional'nyye otnosheniya," in *Nauka i religiya* (1974), No. 2, trans. into German under the title "Islamische Probleme in Sowjetasien," in *Osteuropa*, Vol. 25, No. 4 (April 1975), p. A207.

116. R. Mavlyutov, "Musulmanskie prazniki i obryady," in *Nauka i religiya* (1978), No. 9, trans. into German under the title "Der Islam in der Sowjetunion," in *Osteuropa*, Vol. 30, No. 5 (May 1980), pp. A273–A277.

117. N. Ashirov, "Musulmanskaya propoved segodnya," in *Nauka i religiya* (1978), No. 12, trans. into German under the title "Der Islam in der Sowjetunion," p. A269.

118. *Turkmenskaya iskra* (May 30, 1976), trans. in *Current Digest of the Soviet Press*, Vol. 28, No. 23 (July 7, 1976), p. 1.

119. Peters, "The Georgian Orthodox Church."

120. David Koridze, "Über die Verbrechen im grusinischen Patriarchat," in *Glaube in der 2. Welt*, Vol. 5, No. 10 (October 1977), pp. 124–125; and Peter Reddaway, "The Georgian Orthodox Church: Corruption and Renewal," in *Religion in Communist Lands*, Vol. 3, Nos. 4–5 (July–October 1975), pp. 17, 19.

121. Reddaway, "The Georgian Orthodox Church," pp. 16, 21.

122. *Frankfurter Allgemeine* (August 25, 1981), p. 3.

123. Quoted in Peters, "The Georgian Orthodox Church."

124. Ibid. See also Peter Hauptmann, "Aus der Georgisch-Orthodoxen Kirche," in *Kirche im Osten*, Vol. 24 (1981), esp. pp. 183–185.

125. Peters, "The Georgian Orthodox Church."

126. *Keston News Service* No. 130 (September 11, 1981), pp. 5–6.

127. *Slovo Lektora* (May 1982), pp. 41–42; and Makhmadula Kholovich Kholov,

"The Vital Force of the Fraternal Union," in *Nauka i religiya* (1982), No. 8, trans. in JPRS, *Soviet Report* No. 82124 (October 29, 1982), pp. 45–46.

128. I am thinking of the struggle over the state's proposed concordat with the Vatican.

129. Interview, Belgrade, July 1982.

130. This proposition makes sense of the tendencies within the coopted Georgian Orthodox Church to sympathize with nationalist currents.

3. SOCIAL FUNCTIONS OF RELIGION IN THE USSR

1. Cited in Louis Schneider, *Sociological Approach to Religion* (New York: Wiley, 1970), p. 40.

2. See Marshall I. Goldman, *USSR in Crisis: The Failure of an Economic System* (New York: Norton, 1983), chapters 2, 4; and Konstantin M. Simis, *USSR: The Corrupt Society,* trans. Jacqueline Edwards and Mitchell Schneider (New York: Simon & Schuster, 1982).

3. See Robert K. Merton, *Social Theory and Social Structure* (Glencoe: Free Press, 1957).

4. This list is a rough composite drawn from Ronald L. Johnstone, *Religion in Society: A Sociology of Religion,* 2d ed. (Englewood Cliffs, N.J.: Prentice-Hall, 1983), pp. 64–68; and Thomas F. O'Dea and Janet O'Dea Aviad, *The Sociology of Religion,* 2d ed. (Englewood Cliffs, N.J.: Prentice-Hall, 1983), pp. 14–16.

5. This framework is loosely adapted from Kenneth Jowitt, "Inclusion and Mobilization in European Leninist Systems," in Jan F. Triska and Paul M. Cocks (eds.), *Political Development in Eastern Europe* (New York: Praeger, 1977); Alfred G. Meyer, *Communism,* 4th ed. (New York: Random House, 1984); and Robert C. Tucker, *The Soviet Political Mind: Studies in Stalinism and Post-Stalin Change* (New York: Praeger, 1963).

6. Gail Warshofsky Lapidus, *Women in Soviet Society: Equality, Development, and Social Change* (Berkeley: University of California Press, 1978); and Mikhail Stern with August Stern, *Sex in the USSR,* trans. Mark Howson and Cary Ryan (New York: Times Books, 1980), pp. 23–24.

7. E. H. Carr, *German-Soviet Relations between the Two World Wars, 1919–1939* (Baltimore: Johns Hopkins Press, 1951).

8. Thus Lenin, in 1923: "The absence of self-control in one's sexual life is a bourgeois phenomenon. The revolution requires the concentration of all one's forces, and wild sexual excesses are symptomatic of a reactionary outlook. We need minds that are healthy." Quoted in Stern, *Sex in the USSR,* pp. 32–33.

9. Basil Dmytryshyn, *USSR: A Concise History,* 3d ed. (New York: Scribner, 1978), pp. 134–135.

10. Felicity O'Dell, *Socialisation Through Children's Literature: The Soviet Example* (Cambridge: Cambridge University Press, 1978), pp. 147–149.

11. Georg von Rauch, *A History of Soviet Russia,* 6th ed., trans. Peter and Annette Jacobsohn (New York: Praeger, 1972), p. 238.

12. Marshall I. Goldman, "Gorbachev and Economic Reform," in *Foreign Affairs,* Vol. 64, No. 1 (Fall 1985), p. 61. See also Sidney I. Ploss, "A New Soviet Era?" in *Foreign Policy,* No. 62 (Spring 1986).

13. Keith Bush, "Gorbachev's Speech to the Twenty-Seventh Party Congress: The Economy," *Radio Liberty Research* (February 25, 1986), p. 3.

14. Francis Fukuyama, "Gorbachev and the Third World," in *Foreign Affairs,* Vol. 64, No. 4 (Spring 1986), pp. 715–721.

15. Roman Solchanyk, "Two Soviet Scholars Oppose Silence on Concept of Merger *(Sliyanie)* of Nations," *Radio Liberty Research* (March 10, 1986).

16. For discussion of these two churches, see Walter Kolarz, *Religion in the Soviet Union* (New York: St. Martin's, 1961), pp. 106–117, 124–127.

17. For discussion of *razmezhavanie,* see Teresa Rakowska-Harmstone, *Russia and Nationalism in Central Asia* (Baltimore: Johns Hopkins Press, 1970), pp. 26–27.

18. Jane Ellis, *The Russian Orthodox Church: A Contemporary History* (Bloomington: Indiana University Press, 1986), p. 4.

19. Quoted in David E. Powell, *Antireligious Propaganda in the Soviet Union: A Study of Mass Persuasion* (Cambridge, Mass.: MIT Press, 1975), p. 37.

20. Ibid., p. 36.

21. Ibid., p. 37.

22. Kolarz, *Religion in the Soviet Union,* p. 125.

23. Regarding the legal position of the church in the USSR, see Giovanni Codevilla, *Stato e Chiesa nell' Unione Sovietica* (Milan: Jaca Book, 1972).

24. Christel Lane, *The Rites of Rulers: Ritual in Industrial Society—the Soviet Case* (Cambridge: Cambridge University Press, 1981), pp. 231–233.

25. Ibid., pp. 21–22.

26. Borys Lewytzkyj, *"Sovetskij narod," "Das Sowjetvolk": Nationalitätenpolitik als Instrument des Sowjetsimperialismus* (Hamburg: Hoffmann und Campe Verlag, 1983), p. 90.

27. See V. Furov, "Cadres of the Church and Legal Measures to Curtail Their Activities: A Report by the Council on Religious Affairs," trans. Olga S. Hruby, in *Religion in Communist Dominated Areas,* Vol. 19 (1980), Nos. 9–11, and Vol. 20 (1981), Nos. 1–3.

28. V. D. Kobetskii, *Sotsiologichesko izuchenie religioznosti i ateizma* (Leningrad, 1978), trans. under the title "Study of the Processes of Overcoming Religiosity and of the Dissemination of Atheism," Part 3, in *Soviet Sociology,* Vol. 19, No. 2 (Fall 1980).

29. Malik Sabirovich Fazylov, *Religiya i natsional'nyye otnosheniya* (Alma Ata: Kazakhstan Publishing House, 1969).

30. See Christel Lane, *Christian Religion in the Soviet Union* (London: George Allen & Unwin, 1978).

31. Dimitry V. Pospielovsky, "Ethnocentrism, Ethnic Tensions, and Marxism Leninism," in Edward Allworth (ed.), *Ethnic Russia in the USSR: The Dilemma of Dominance* (New York: Pergamon, 1980), p. 131; and Meredith B. McGuire, *Religion: The Social Context* (Belmont, Calif.: Wadsworth, 1981), p. 217.

32. Powell, *Antireligious Propaganda,* pp. 104–118.

33. Lane, *Christian Religion,* pp. 36–39; and L. A. Serdobol'skaia, "Baptizm i sem'ia," in D. G. Danilov and V. N. Sherdakov (eds.), *Problemy ateisticheskogo vospitaniia* (Leningrad: Lenizdat, 1974), trans. under the title "The Baptist Movement and the Family," in *Soviet Review,* Vol. 17, No. 2 (Summer 1976), p. 105.

34. Serdobol'skaia, "Baptizm," p. 114.

35. N. S. Vasil'evskaia, "Opyt konkretno-sotsiologicheskogo issledovaniia otnosheniia k religii v sovremennoi gorodskoi sem'e," in *Voprosy nauchnogo ateizma* (1972, No. 3), trans. in *Soviet Review,* Vol. 16, No. 1 (Spring 1975), p. 79; and A. A. Lebedev, "Sekuliarizatsiia naseleniia sotsialisticheskogo goroda," in *K*

obshchestvu svobodnomu ot religii (Moscow: Mysl, 1970), trans. under the title "The Secularization of the Population of a Socialist City," in *Soviet Review,* Vol. 14, No. 3 (Fall 1973), p. 66.

36. *Voprosy nauchnogo ateizma* (1973, No. 14), p. 25.

37. For brief discussions, see Tönu Parming, "Roots of Nationality Differences," and Christopher Doersam, "Sovietization, Culture, and Religion," both in Edward Allworth (ed.), *Nationality Group Survival in Multi-Ethnic States: Shifting Support Patterns in the Soviet Baltic Region* (New York: Praeger, 1977).

38. Documented in Ellis, *Russian Orthodox Church.*

39. Julia Wishnevsky, "Neo-Nazis in the Soviet Union," *Radio Liberty Research* (July 11, 1985), esp. pp. 8–9. According to Pospielovsky ("Ethnocentrism," p. 130), there is "a chauvinistic, racist, neo-Nazi wing within the Komsomol."

40. See Maria Broxup, "Recenti sviluppi nell'Islam sovietico," in *Russia Cristiana,* Vol. 9, No. 5 (September–October 1984).

41. See Boris Chichlo, "The Cult of the Bear and Soviet Ideology in Siberia," in *Religion in Communist Lands,* Vol. 13, No. 2 (Summer 1985).

42. Yu. V. Arutiunian, "Konkretno-sotsiologicheskoe issledovanie natsional'nykh otnoshenii," in *Voprosy filosofii* (1969, no. 12), quoted in Gail W. Lapidus, "The Nationality Question and the Soviet System," in Erik P. Hoffmann (ed.), *The Soviet Union in the 1980s* (New York: Academy of Political Science, 1984), p. 106.

4. CATHOLICISM AND NATIONAL CULTURE
IN POLAND, CZECHOSLOVAKIA,
AND HUNGARY

1. Andrzej Micewski, *Katholische Gruppierungen in Polen: Pax und Znak, 1945–1976,* trans. from Polish by Wolfgang Grycz (Munich and Mainz: Kaiser and Grunewald, 1978), p. 69.

2. William J. Brazill, *The Young Hegelians* (New Haven: Yale University Press, 1970), pp. 277–278.

3. For a detailed analysis of this subject in the Yugoslav context, see Pedro Ramet, "Apocalypse Culture and Social Change in Yugoslavia," in Pedro Ramet (ed.), *Yugoslavia in the 1980s* (Boulder, Colo.: Westview Press, 1985). See also Arnold Hauser, *The Social History of Art* (London: Routledge & Kegan Paul, 1952).

4. Najdan Pašić, "Faktori formiranja nacija na Balkanu i kod Južnih Slovena," in *Pregled* (1971), No. 5, as cited in Tomislav J. Šagi-Bunić, *Katolička crkva i hrvatski narod* (Zagreb: Kršćanska sadašnjost, 1983), pp. 23–25.

5. Šagi-Bunić, *Katolička crkva,* p. 11.

6. See "Brief des Episcopats über die Pflichten der Katholiken in Polen gegenüber der Nationalen und Religiosen Kultur," in *Dokumentation Ostmitteleuropa,* Vol. 4 (28), No. 6 (December 1978), pp. 335–338.

7. Wieslaw Muller et al., *Kosciol w Polsce,* Vol. 2: *Wieki XVI-XVIII* (Krakow: Znak, 1969), p. 16.

8. Ibid., p. 21.

9. Ibid., pp. 26–27.

10. Ibid., pp. 28–29.

11. Ibid., p. 28.

12. Lawrence Wolff, *Poland and the Vatican in the Age of Partitions: European Enlightenment, Roman Catholicism, and the Development of Polish Nationalism* (Ph.D. diss., Stanford University, 1984), pp. 45–47, 89. But see also p. 4.

13. V. Stanley Vardys, *The Catholic Church, Dissent and Nationality in Soviet Lithuania* (Boulder, Colo.: East European Monographs, 1978), pp. 4–5.

14. Norman Davies, *God's Playground: A History of Poland*, Vol. 2 [1795 to the Present] (New York: Columbia University Press, 1982), p. 62.

15. There was also a period of relative toleration of both Latin and Uniate rites of the Catholic Church, beginning with the reign of Tsar Paul I (1796–1801) and continuing, to some extent, during the reign of Alexander I (1801–25). See ibid., p. 86; and Dennis J. Dunn, *The Catholic Church and the Soviet Government, 1939–1949* (Boulder, Colo.: East European Monographs, 1977), pp. 8–10.

16. Davies, *God's Playground*, Vol. 2, pp. 86–87.

17. Ibid., p. 210.

18. Vardys, *Catholic Church*, pp. 12–13.

19. Davies, *God's Playground*, Vol. 2, p. 99.

20. See Sebastian Haffner, *The Rise and Fall of Prussia*, trans. Ewald Osers (London: Weidenfeld & Nicolson, 1980).

21. Davies, *God's Playground*, Vol. 2, pp. 126–127.

22. Quoted in ibid., p. 134.

23. Among a large number of excellent works dealing with Habsburg Austria, the following deserve mention: Edward Crankshaw, *The Fall of the House of Habsburg* (New York: Viking, 1963); Oscar Jaszi, *The Dissolution of the Habsburg Monarchy* (Chicago: University of Chicago Press, 1928); C. A. Macartney, *The Habsburg Empire, 1790–1918* (London: Weidenfeld & Nicolson, 1968); Arthur J. May, *The Hapsburg Monarchy, 1867–1914* (Cambridge, Mass.: Harvard University Press, 1960); and Adam Wandruszka, *The House of Habsburg*, trans. Cathleen and Hans Epstein (New York: Doubleday, 1964).

24. Davies, *God's Playground*, Vol. 2, p. 142.

25. Ibid., pp. 212–213.

26. Ibid., pp. 216–217.

27. See Suzanne Gwen Hruby, Leslie Laszlo, and Stevan K. Pavlowitch, "Minor Orthodox Churches in Eastern Europe," in Pedro Ramet (ed.), *Eastern Christianity and Politics in the Twentieth Century* (Durham, N.C.: Duke University Press, forthcoming).

28. Davies, *God's Playground*, Vol. 2, p. 404.

29. Ibid., pp. 419–420.

30. Quoted in Micewski, *Katholische Gruppierungen*, p. 219.

31. Oscar Halecki (ed.), *Poland* (New York: Praeger, 1957), p. 208.

32. Cited in Bogdan Szajkowski, *Next to God . . . Poland: Politics and Religion in Contemporary Poland* (New York: St. Martin's, 1983), p. 17.

33. Vincent C. Chrypinski, "Church and Nationality in Postwar Poland," in Pedro Ramet (ed.), *Religion and Nationalism in Soviet and East European Politics* (Durham, N.C.: Duke University Press, 1984), p. 128.

34. Szajkowski, *Next to God*, pp. 31–32.

35. Quoted in Adam Bromke, "A New Juncture in Poland," in *Problems of Communism*, Vol. 25, No. 5 (September-October 1976), pp. 11–12.

36. Chrypinski, "Church and Nationality," p. 130.

37. Szajkowski, *Next to God*, p. 87.

38. Alain Touraine, Francois Dubet, Michel Wievorka, and Jan Strzelecki, *Solidarity: Poland, 1980–81,* trans. David Denby (Cambridge: Cambridge University Press, 1983), p. 45.

39. Quoted in Szajkowski, *Next to God,* p. 168.

40. Jozef Archbishop Glemp, "Homily Delivered on 26 August 1982 at Jasna Gora, Czestochowa," trans. in *Communist Affairs,* Vol. 2, No. 2 (April 1983), pp. 252–253.

41. See chapter 8.

42. Touraine et al., *Solidarity,* p. 46.

43. Robert A. Kann and Zdenek V. David, *The Peoples of the Eastern Habsburg Lands, 1526–1918* (Seattle: University of Washington Press, 1984), p. 138.

44. F. M. Mayer-Kaindl and Hans Pirchegger, *Geschichte und Kulturleben Österreichs, von 1493 bis 1792,* 5th ed. (Vienna: Wilhelm Braumüller, 1960), p. 150; and Robert A. Kann, *A History of the Habsburg Empire, 1526–1918* (Berkeley: University of California Press, 1974), pp. 133–134.

45. Mayer-Kaindl and Pirchegger, *Geschichte,* pp. 315–324; Kann, *A History,* p. 188; and Macartney, *The Habsburg Empire,* p. 120.

46. For details, see Macartney, *The Habsburg Empire,* p. 458.

47. Leslie Laszlo, *Church and State in Hungary, 1919–1945* (Ph.D. diss., Columbia University, 1973), pp. 20–21.

48. Ibid., pp. 27–28, 30, 33–34.

49. Ibid., p. 39.

50. Ibid., p. 458.

51. Ibid., pp. 214–215.

52. Leslie Laszlo, "Religion and Nationality in Hungary," in Ramet (ed.), *Religion and Nationalism,* p. 142.

53. Quoted in Mihály Bucsay, "Kirche und Gesellschaft in Ungarn 1848–1945 unter besonderer Berücksichtigung des Problems des Nationalismus," in *Kirche im Osten,* Vol. 18 (1975), p. 106.

54. Joseph Rothschild, *East Central Europe between the Two World Wars* (Seattle: University of Washington Press, 1974), p. 193; and Leslie Laszlo, "Nationality and Religion in Hungary, 1867–1918," in *East European Quarterly,* Vol. 17, No. 1 (March 1983), p. 47.

55. Friedrich Hainbuch, *Kirche und Staat in Ungarn nach dem Zweiten Weltkrieg* (Munich: Dr. Rudolf Trofenik Verlag, 1982), pp. 9, 26–29.

56. Ibid., p. 37; and Steven Polgar, "A Summary of the Situation of the Hungarian Catholic Church," in *Religion in Communist Lands,* Vol. 12, No. 1 (Spring 1984), p. 15.

57. Hainbuch, *Kirche und Staat,* pp. 46, 71.

58. The Catholic Church had 6,900 priests in 1945, 4,500 in 1963; thirty seminaries in 1945, six in 1963; 3,163 elementary schools in 1945, none in 1963; forty-nine high schools in 1945, eight in 1963; nine hospitals in 1945, four in 1963; sixty-eight newspapers and journals in 1945, four in 1963; fifty publishing houses in 1945, two in 1963; about 4,000 lay organizations and associations in 1945, one in 1963.

59. Polgar, "A Summary," p. 20.

60. Quoted in Trevor Beeson, *Discretion and Valour: Religious Conditions in Russia and Eastern Europe,* rev. ed. (Philadelphia: Fortress Press, 1982), p. 284.

61. For example, Ferenc Magyar, editor of the Hungarian Catholic weekly, *Uj*

Ember, was awarded the Golden Medallion of the Order of Merit for Labor in 1986 by the chairman of the State Office for Church Affairs, Imre Miklos. See *Keston News Service* No. 242 (January 23, 1986), p. 11.

62. Ibid. No. 228 (June 27, 1985), p.9. Four Protestant church leaders were also elected.

63. Hainbuch, *Kirche und Staat,* pp. 4–6, 102–103.

64. Emmerich András, "Die Kirche in Ungarn," in Paul Lendvai (ed.), *Religionsfreiheit und Menschenrechte* (Graz: Verlag Styria, 1983), p. 158.

65. Alfred Reisch, "State Secretary for Church Affairs Goes on Television," *Radio Free Europe Research* (June 1, 1984), p. 25.

66. Laszlo, "Religion and Nationality," p. 146; and *Uj Ember* (Budapest, September 4, 1983), trans. in Joint Publications Research Service (JPRS), *East Europe Report* No. 84606 (October 25, 1983), p. 16.

67. *Kritika* (Budapest, September 1983), trans. in JPRS, *East Europe Report* No. 84830 (November 28, 1983), p. 120.

68. Ibid., p. 119.

69. Laszlo, "Religion and Nationality," p. 147.

70. The term is borrowed from Alexander Tomsky, "*Modus Moriendi* of the Catholic Church in Czechoslovakia," in *Religion in Communist Lands,* Vol. 10, No. 1 (Spring 1982).

71. According to official statistics of the Institute for Scientific Atheism, Brno, as cited in *Profil* (Vienna, July 15, 1985), p. 40.

72. Matthew Spinka, "The Religious Situation in Czechoslovakia," in Robert J. Kerner (ed.), *Czechoslovakia* (Berkeley: University of California Press, 1945), pp. 284–285.

73. Ibid., p. 285.

74. R. J. W. Evans, *The Making of the Habsburg Monarchy, 1550–1700* (Oxford: Clarendon Press, 1979), pp. 67–68.

75. Joseph F. Zacek, "Nationalism in Czechoslovakia," in Peter F. Sugar and Ivo J. Lederer (eds.), *Nationalism in Eastern Europe* (Seattle: University of Washington Press, 1970), p. 174; and Kann, *A History,* p. 112.

76. Quoted in Jaszi, *Dissolution,* p. 49.

77. Zacek, "Nationalism in Czechoslovakia," p. 174.

78. Quoted in Anthony Rhodes, *The Vatican in the Age of the Dictators, 1922–1945* (London: Hodder & Stoughton, 1973), pp. 141–142.

79. Tomsky, "*Modus Moriendi,*" p. 25. On the "Los von Rom" current, see Ludvik Nemec, *Church and State in Czechoslovakia* (New York: Vantage, 1955), pp. 117–131.

80. Rothschild, *East Central Europe,* p. 108.

81. Rhodes, *The Vatican,* p. 89.

82. Laszlo, *Church and State,* p. 234.

83. Anna Josko, "The Slovak Resistance Movement," in Victor S. Mamatey and Radomir Luža (eds.), *A History of the Czechoslovak Republic, 1918–1948* (Princeton, N.J.: Princeton University Press, 1973), p. 369.

84. Anton Hlinka, "Zur Lage der Katholischen Kirche in der Slowakei—Pt. I: Geschichtliche Sicht," in *Glaube in der 2. Welt,* Vol. 6, No. 3 (March 1978), p. 2.

85. Hlinka, "Zur Lage der Katholischen Kirche in der Slowakei—Pt. II: Hauptmomente der Auseinandersetzung zwischen Kirche und Staat," in *Glaube in der 2. Welt,* Vol. 6, No. 4 (April 1978), p. 16.

86. Ibid., p. 18; and *Rheinischer Merkur* (Bonn, February 17, 1978), p. 13.

87. Regarding the latter, see Michael Bourdeaux, "The Uniate Churches in Czechoslovakia," in *Religion in Communist Lands,* Vol. 2, No. 2 (March–April 1974).

88. Hlinka, "Zur Lage der Katholischen Kirche in der Slowakei—Pt. III: Die Dekade 1968–1978," in *Glaube in der 2. Welt,* Vol. 6, No. 5 (May 1978), p. 35.

89. Ibid., pp. 44–45.

90. *Rheinischer Merkur* (June 10, 1983), trans. in JPRS, *East Europe Report* No. 83906 (July 15, 1983), p. 25.

91. See also Pedro Ramet, "The Czechoslovak Church under Pressure," in *The World Today,* Vol. 38, No. 9 (September 1982).

92. *Učitelske Noviný* (Bratislava, October 21, 1982), quoted in Czechoslovakia/Situation Report, *Radio Free Europe Research* (December 3, 1982), p. 6.

93. Radio Prague (April 10, 1985), quoted in Czechoslovakia/Situation Report, *Radio Free Europe Research* (May 13, 1985), p. 3.

94. *Večerni Praha* (February 19, 1985), quoted in Czechoslovakia/Situation Report, *Radio Free Europe Research* (April 19, 1985), p. 3.

95. J. P. Hensley, "Slovakia's Catholic Resurgence," in *New Leader* (July 1–15, 1985), p. 10; and *Profil* (July 15, 1985), p. 40.

96. Czechoslovakia/Situation Report, *Radio Free Europe* (March 10, 1986), p. 10.

5. CHURCH AND PEACE IN THE GERMAN DEMOCRATIC REPUBLIC

This chapter is a revised and updated version of an article that appeared under the title "Church and Peace in the GDR," in *Problems of Communism,* Vol. 33, No. 4 (July–August 1984).

1. On East German foreign policy, see Melvin Croan, *East Germany: The Soviet Connection,* Washington Papers, Vol. 4, No. 36 (Beverly Hills: Sage Publications, 1976), especially pp. 1–13.

2. Kurt Sontheimer and Wilhelm Bleek, *The Government and Politics of East Germany,* trans. Ursula Price (London: Hutchinson University Library, 1975); Harmut Zimmerman, "The GDR in the 1970s," in *Problems of Communism,* Vol. 27, No. 2 (March–April 1978), pp. 7–8; Max L. Stackhouse, "The Religious Situation in the German Democratic Republic," *Occasional Papers on Religion in Eastern Europe* (OPREE), Vol. 1, No. 1 (February 1981), p. 1; and David Childs, *The GDR: Moscow's German Ally* (London: George Allen & Unwin, 1983), pp. 156–163.

3. In 1946, of a total population of seventeen million in the Soviet zone of occupation, fifteen million were members of the Evangelical Church and 1.75 million were Catholics. In March 1983, the Evangelical Church still claimed 7.7 million believers, while the Catholic Church numbered 1.2 million adherents; Otto Luchterhandt, *Die Gegenwartslage der Evangelischen Kirche in der DDR* (Tübingen: J.C.B. Mohr, 1982), p. 3; and *Archiv der Gegenwart* (June 29, 1983), p. 26770.

4. Sontheimer and Bleek, *Government and Politics,* p. 21; and Adam B. Ulam, *The Rivals* (New York: Viking, 1975).

5. Trevor Beeson, *Discretion and Valour: Religious Conditions in Russian and Eastern Europe,* rev. ed. (Philadelphia: Fortress Press, 1982), pp. 212–213.

6. Sontheimer and Bleek, *Government and Politics,* pp. 123–124.

7. Luchterhandt, *Die Gegenwartslage,* p. 16.

8. Albrecht Schönherr, at a church synod in Eisenach (1971), quoted by himself in Albrecht Schönherr, "Opportunities and Problems of Being a Christian in a Socialist Society," in Norbert Greinacher and Virgil Elizondo (eds.), *Churches in Socialist Societies of Eastern Europe,* Concilium: Religion in the Eighties (New York: Seabury, 1982), pp. 47–48.

9. Luchterhandt, *Die Gegenwartslage,* pp. 15, 83–84.

10. Ibid., pp. 17–18.

11. Quoted in Ibid., p. 32.

12. Reinhard Henkys, "Kirche in der Deutschen Demokratischen Republik," in Paul Lendvai (ed.), *Religionsfreiheit und Menschenrechte* (Graz: Verlag Styria, 1983), p. 172.

13. *Christian Science Monitor* (March 21, 1980), p. 7; and *Frankfurter Allgemeine* (May 30, 1981), p. 9.

14. Beeson, *Discretion and Valour,* p. 198.

15. Quoted in Gisela Helwig, "Zwischen Opposition und Opportunismus: Zur Lage der Kirche in der DDR," in *Deutschland Archiv,* Vol. 9, No. 6 (June 1976), p. 578.

16. Quoted in *Frankfurter Rundschau* (March 3, 1983), p. 2, trans. in Foreign Broadcast Information Service (FBIS), *Daily Report* (Eastern Europe), March 7, 1983, p. E2.

17. Quoted in Luchterhandt, *Die Gegenwartslage,* p. 79.

18. Childs, *The GDR,* p. 190.

19. *Die Welt* (Hamburg, November 6, 1981), p. 1.

20. *Frankfurter Allgemeine* (September 27, 1978), p. 1.

21. *Ibid.* (August 26, 1981), p. 2; *Christian Science Monitor* (September 4, 1981), p. 2, and (September 12, 1981), p. 1; and *Der Spiegel* (November 16, 1981), p. 63.

22. Klaus Ehring and Martin Dallwitz, *Schwerter zu Pflugscharen* (Hamburg: Rowohlt Taschenbuch Verlag, 1982), p. 96. Already in 1968, the Soviet invasion of Czechoslovakia had produced widespread revulsion among East German youth, and the burgeoning rock music scene provided a forum in which a counterculture could develop. The banning of the outspoken rock group Renft Combo in 1974 dampened but did not eliminate the political overtones in the rock counterculture. In fact, the roots of the unofficial peace movement in the GDR must be traced, in part, to the rock scene; see pp. 90–91. See also Pedro Ramet, "Disaffection and Dissent in East Germany," in *World Politics,* Vol. 37, No. 1 (October 1984), especially pp. 91–93.

23. *Die Zeit* (September 23, 1983), pp. 17–19, trans. in Joint Publications Research Service (JPRS), *East Europe Report* No. 84894 (December 7, 1983), pp. 9–26.

24. *Rheinische Merkur* (November 27, 1981); and Peter Wensierski, "Friedensbewegung in der DDR," in *Das Parlament* (Bonn, April 30, 1983), pp. 3–15.

25. Interview with Stefan Heym ("Plotzlich hebt sich der Boden"), in *Der Spiegel* (May 31, 1982), p. 100.

26. Peter Hebblethwaite, "The GDR: Servant or Subservient Church?" in *Religion in Communist Lands,* Vol. 6, No. 2 (Summer 1978), p. 98; and Stephen R. Bowers, "Private Institutions in Service to the State: The German Democratic Republic's Church in Socialism," in *East European Quarterly,* Vol. 16, No. 1 (March 1982), p. 79.

27. *Frankfurter Rundschau* (October 7, 1981).

28. *Die Tageszeitung* (West Berlin, April 12,1983), trans. in JPRS, *East Europe Report* No. 83558 (May 26, 1983), p. 38.

29. *Frankfurter Allgemeine* February 24, 1981), p. 3; *Die Welt* (August 21, 1981), p. 4; and *Neue Zürcher Zeitung* (September 29, 1981), p. 4.

30. *Neuer Weg* (East Berlin), Vol. 38, No. 7 (March 24, 1983), trans. in JPRS, *East Europe Report* No. 83700 (June 16, 1983), p. 42.

31. *Standpunkt*, Vol. 11, No. 6 (June 1983), in *DDR Report* (Bonn), Vol. 16, No. 8 (August 1983), p. 461. For a report on a two-day symposium of peace, organized by the Christian Peace Council, see *Neues Deutschland* (East Berlin, January 31, 1984), p. 3.

32. Wensierski, "Friedensbewegung," pp. 3–6.

33. "Plötzlich hebt sich der Boden," pp. 94, 100; and Ronald D. Asmus, "Is There a Peace Movement in the GDR?" in *Orbis*, Vol. 27, No. 2 (Summer 1983), p. 303.

34. Theo Mechtenberg, "Die Friedensverantwortung der Evangelischen Kirchen in der DDR," in *Deutsche Studien*, Vol. 19, No. 74 (June 1981), p. 179.

35. Gisela Helwig, "Zur Friedensverantwortung der Kirchen," in *Deutschland Archiv*, Vol. 13, No. 4 (April 1980), p. 350; and Luchterhandt, *Die Gegenwartslage*, p. 87.

36. *Frankfurter Allgemeine* (December 13, 1980), p. 9, trans. in JPRS, *East Europe Report* No. 77355 (February 9, 1981), p. 10.

37. Quoted in Henkys, "Kirche," p. 177.

38. *Frankfurter Allgemeine* (May 30, 1981), p. 10; and "Notes on Church-State Relations," in *Journal of Church and State*, Vol. 23, No. 1 (Winter 1981), p. 166.

39. DPA (Hamburg, April 28, 1981), trans. in FBIS, *Daily Report* (Eastern Europe), April 29, 1981, p. E1; and *Keston News Service* No. 127 (August 3, 1981), p. 12.

40. *Süddeutsche Zeitung* (Munich, September 8, 1982), p. 3, trans. in JPRS, *East Europe Report* No. 81941 (October 7, 1982), p. 42; and *Keston News Service* Nos. 151–154 (August 31, 1982), p. 20. The reference by Radio Moscow might have been prompted by the fact that a Soviet memorial with the same words stands before the UN building in New York.

41. *Der Spiegel* (February 22, 1982), p. 28; *Facts on File* (February 26, 1982), p. 122; *Der Spiegel* (March 29, 1982), p. 35; and *Die Welt* (June 21, 1982), p. 5.

42. Horst Dähn, *Konfrontation oder Kooperation? Das Verhältnis von Staat und Kirche in der SBZ/DDR 1945–1980* (Opladen: Westdeutscher Verlag, 1982), pp. 167–171.

43. Excerpted in *Der Spiegel* (February 22, 1982), p. 30.

44. *Frankfurter Rundschau* (November 10, 1981).

45. Quoted in *Süddeutsche Zeitung* (September 8, 1982), p. 3, trans. in JPRS, *East Europe Report* No. 81941 (October 7, 1982), 42. See also *Die Presse* (Vienna, Janaury 12, 1982), p. 2, trans. in FBIS, *Daily Report* (Eastern Europe), January 14, 1982, p. E7.

46. *Keston News Service* Nos. 144–145 (April 25, 1982), p. 6.

47. *Der Spiegel* (September 20, 1982), p. 54.

48. Quoted in *Rheinischer Merkur* (July 2, 1982), p. 18, trans. in JPRS, *East Europe Report* No. 81546 (August 16, 1982), p. 10.

49. Quoted in *Der Spiegel* (September 20, 1982), p. 54

50. For more details, see ibid. (March 29, 1982), p. 35; *Süddeutsche Zeitung* (August 28/29, 1982); and *Neue Zürcher Zeitung* (February 24, 1983), p. 3.

51. *Standpunkt,* Vol. 10, No. 11 (November 1982), pp., 2, 3.

52. *Rheinischer Merkur* (July 2, 1982), p. 18, trans. in JPRS, *East Europe Report* No. 81546 (August 16, 1982), p. 10; DPA (September 29, 1982), trans. in FBIS, *Daily Report* (Eastern Europe), September 30, 1982, p. E4; and *Neue Zürcher Zeitung* (September 30, 1982), p. 4.

53. *Mecklenburgische Kirchenzeitung* (July 8, 1984), p. 1, trans. in JPRS, *East Europe Report* No. EPS-84-106 (August 29, 1984), p. 5; and *Keston News Service* No. 200 (May 24, 1984), pp. 10–11.

54. *Der Spiegel* (November 8, 1982), p. 16; and *Keston News Service* No. 163 (December 2, 1982), p. 5–6.

55. *Wall Street Journal* (June 22, 1983), p. 31; and *Neue Zürcher Zeitung* (September 2, 1983), p. 2.

56. Gerhard Götting, general secretary of the CDU-East, quoted in *Frankfurter Allgemeine* (February 18, 1983), p. 5.

57. *Die Tageszeitung* (November 1, 1983), p. 9, trans. in JPRS, *East Europe Report* No. 84862 (December 2, 1983), p. 14.

58. *Der Spiegel* (February 6, 1984), pp. 29–30; and *Keston News Service* No. 198 (May 3, 1984), p. 7.

59. *Neue Zürcher Zeitung* (April 12, 1984), p. 3; *Der Spiegel* (April 23, 1984), p. 44; and *Frankfurter Allgemeine* (May 5, 1984), p. 4.

60. *Frankfurter Allgemeine* (September 21, 1983), p. 2.

61. *Keston News Service* No. 185 (October 20, 1983), p. 8.

62. *Standpunkt,* Vol. 11, No. 6 (June 1983), in *DDR Report,* Vol. 16, No. 8 (August 1983), p. 46.

63. *Neues Deutschland* (October 22–23, 1983), p. 2.

64. ARD Television (Hamburg, July 8, 1984), trans. in FBIS, *Daily Report* (Eastern Europe), July 10, 1984, p. E15; B. V. Flow, "The East German Protestant Church: Variations on the Theme of Peace," *Radio Free Europe Research* (November 21, 1985), pp. 1–5.

65. Matthew Boyse, "East German Lutheran Synod Calls for Human Rights Improvements," *Radio Free Europe Research* (October 4, 1985), pp. 2–3; DPA (September 22, 1984), trans. in FBIS, *Daily Report* (Eastern Europe), September 25, 1984, p. E14.

66. A point denied by the SED until the late 1970s. See Werner Volkmer, "East Germany: Dissenting Views during the Last Decade," in Rudolf L. Tökes (ed.), *Opposition in Eastern Europe* (London: Macmillan, 1979), pp. 116–117.

67. Bishop Johannes Hempel, quoted in *Die Welt* (October 18, 1982), p. 3.

68. DPA (January 12, 1982).

69. *Christian Science Monitor* (May 21, 1980), p. 7.

70. Nancy Lukens, "The Churches in the German Democratic Republic: Notes of an Interested Observer," OPREE, Vol. 2, No. 1 (February 1982), pp. 5–6.

71. Quoted in Ronald D. Asmus, Evangelical Churches in the FRG and GDR Issue a Peace Declaration," *Radio Free Europe Research* (August 20, 1982), p. 1.

72. For membership figures, see note 3, this chapter. Today only 20 percent of the East German population as a whole and only 10 percent of East German youth are believers. See Peter Wensierski, "Theses on the Role of the Church in the GDR," *Kirche im Sozialismus,* Vol. 7, No. 10 (1981), trans. Norman C. Robinson for OPREE, Vol. 3, No. 4 (May 1983), p. 23.

73. *Süddeutsche Zeitung* (May 20, 1980), p. 4; *Rheinischer Merkur* (May 29, 1981), p. 18, (January 15, 1982), p. 18, and (September 10, 1982), p. 20.

74. *Frankfurter Allgemeine* (April 9, 1984), p. 4.

75. Luchterhandt, *Die Gegenwartslage,* p. 50.

76. *Neue Zürcher Zeitung* (September 8, 1982), p. 4.

77. See Horst Dähn, "Die Kirchen im Spannungsfeld von Loyalität und Opposition in der DDR," in *Deutsche Studien,* Vol. 22, No. 88 (December 1984), esp. pp. 332–336; and Pedro Ramet, "East Germany: Strategies of Church-State Coexistence," in *Religion in Communist Dominated Areas,* Vol. 24, No. 2 (Spring 1985), pp. 38–39.

78. Quoted in Norman Davies, *God's Playground: A History of Poland,* Vol. 2 (New York: Columbia University Press, 1982), p. 213.

79. Klemens Richter, "Veränderte Haltung der DDR-Katholiken," in *Deutschland Archiv,* Vol. 16, No. 5 (May 1983), pp. 454–455.

80. The text of the letter is published in *Frankfurter Allgemeine* (January 4, 1983), p. 5, trans. in FBIS, *Daily Report* (Eastern Europe), January 10, 1983, pp. E1–E4.

81. Quoted in *Frankfurter Allgemeine* (November 3, 1983), p. 5, trans. in JPRS, *East Europe Report* No. EPS–84–031 (March 1, 1984), p. 32.

82. See Ramet, "East Germany: Strategies," p. 40.

6. FACTIONALISM IN THE CROATIAN CHURCH-STATE RELATIONSHIP

This chapter was originally published as an article entitled "Factionalism in Church-State Interaction: The Croatian Catholic Church in the 1980s" in *Slavic Review,* Vol. 44, No. 2 (Summer 1985). The research for this chapter was made possible through the assistance of a research grant from the American Council of Learned Societies, financed in part by the National Endowment for the Humanities.

1. A recent work sensitive to this complexity is Otto Luchterhandt, *Die Gegenwartslage der Evangelischen Kirche in der DDR* (Tübingen: J.C.B. Mohr, 1982).

2. John Anderson, "Soviet Religious Policy under Brezhnev and After," in *Religion in Communist Lands,* Vol. 11, No. 1 (Spring 1983); Bohdan R. Bociurkiw, "Soviet Religious Policy in the Ukraine in Historical Perspective," *Occasional Papers on Religion in Eastern Europe* (OPREE), Vol. 2, No. 3 (June 1982), pp. 1–2; Christopher Cviic, "Recent Developments in Church-State Relations in Yugoslavia," in *Religion in Communist Lands,* Vol. 1, No. 2 (March–April 1973), p. 7; Dionisie Ghermani, "Die Katholische Kirche in Kroatien/Slowenien," in *Kirche in Not,* Vol. 27 (1979), p. 91; Rudolf Grulich, "Probleme der Religionsfreiheit in Jugoslawien," in *Kirche in Not,* Vol. 25 (1977), p. 81; Josip Horak, "Church, State, and Religious Freedom in Yugoslavia: An Ideological and Constitutional Study," in *Journal of Church and State,* Vol. 19, No. 2 (Spring 1977), p. 286; Leslie Laszlo, "Religion in a Communist Consumer Society: The Case of Kadar's Hungary," OPREE, Vol. 1, No. 5 (September 1981), esp. p. 2; Trevor Beeson, *Discretion and Valour: Religious Conditions in Russia and Eastern Europe,* rev. ed. (Philadelphia: Fortress Press, 1982), p. 8; Emmerich Andras, "The Hungarian Practice of Christian-Marxist Dialogue," OPREE, Vol. 2, No. 5 (August 1982); Zyrill Boldirev, "Staat und Kirche in Polen," in *Osteuropa,* Vol. 11, No. 1 (January 1961), p. 15 and passim; Raoul Bossy, "Religious Persecutions in Captive Romania," in *Journal of Central European Affairs,* Vol. 15, No. 2 (July 1955); Michael Bourdeaux, "The Black Quinquennium: The Russian Orthodox Church 1959–1964," in *Religion in Communist Lands,* Vol. 9, Nos. 1–2 (Spring

1981); Marie Broxup, "Recent Developments in Soviet Islam," in *Religion in Communist Lands*, Vol. 11, No. 1 (Spring 1983); Emil Ciurea, "Religious Life," in Alexandre Cretzianu (ed.), *Captive Rumania* (London: Atlantic Press, 1956); George A. Glass, "Church-State Relations in East Germany: Expanding Dimensions of an Unresolved Problem," in *East Central Europe*, Vol. 6, Pt. 2 (1979); Rudolf Grulich, "Die Katholische Kirche in Kroatien und Slowenien," in *Kirche in Not*, Vol. 23 (1975); Rudolf Grulich, *Kreuz, Halbmond und Roter Stern: Zur Situation der Katholischen Kirche in Jugoslawien* (Munich: Fund-Druck, 1979); Wolfgang Grycz, "Katholische Kirche in der Volksrepublik Polen," in *Kirche in Not*, Vol. 23 (1975); Wolfgang Grycz, "Katholische Kirche in Jugoslawien," in *Kirche in Not*, Vol. 20 (1971); Andrew Harsanyi, "The Reformed Church in Hungary Today," OPREE, Vol. 2, No. 5 (August 1982); Karl Hartmann, "Dialog zwischen Staat und Kirche nach dem Machtwechsel in Polen," in *Osteuropa*, Vol. 22, No. 2 (February 1972); Karl Hartmann, "Stagnation in den Beziehungen zwischen Kirche und Staat in Polen," in *Osteuropa*, Vol. 27, No. 1 (January 1977); Alf Johansen, "The Russian Orthodox Church as Reflected in Orthodox and Atheist Publications in the Soviet Union," OPREE, Vol. 3, No. 2 (February 1983); Dimitry Konstantinov, "The Russian Orthodox Church in the USSR: 1977–1979," in *The Orthodox Monitor* (January–June 1981); David Kowalewski, "The Catholic Church and the Cuban Regime," in *Religion in Communist Lands*, Vol. 11, No. 1 (Spring 1983); Peter Maser, "Suffering from the Church? Aspects of Uneasiness at the Church Basis," OPREE, Vol. 3, No. 1 (January 1983); Michael B. Petrovich, "Yugoslavia: Religion and the Tensions of a Multinational State," in *East European Quarterly*, Vol. 6, No. 1 (March 1972); Joachim Piegsa, "Die Rolle der Kirche in Polen," in *Politische Studien*, Vol. 33, No. 264 (July–August 1982); Earl A. Pope, "The Romanian Orthodox Church," OPREE, Vol. 1, No. 3 (June 1981); Josef Rabas, "The Roman Catholic Church in Czechoslovakia," OPREE, Vol. 2, No. 6 (September 1982); Pedro Ramet, "Catholicism and Politics in Socialist Yugoslavia," in *Religion in Communist Lands*, Vol. 10, No. 3 (Winter 1982); Pedro Ramet, "The Czechoslovak Church under Pressure," in *The World Today*, Vol. 38, No. 9 (September 1982); Irwin T. Sanders, "Church-State Relationships in Southeastern Europe (with Special Reference to the Orthodox Church)," in *East European Quarterly*, Vol. 16, No. 1 (March 1982); George Schöpflin, "Poland: Troubled Relations between Church and State," in *Religion in Communist Lands*, Vol. 2, Nos. 4–5 (July–October 1974), esp. p. 6; Gjon Sinishta, "Grave Violations of Religious Rights in Albania," OPREE, Vol. 3, No. 5 (July 1983); Hansjakob Stehle, "Church and Pope in the Polish Crisis," in *The World Today*, Vol. 38, No. 4 (April 1982); Peter A. Toma and Milan J. Reban, "Church-State Schism in Czechoslovakia," in Bohdan R. Bociurkiw and John W. Strong (eds.), *Religion and Atheism in the USSR and Eastern Europe* (London: Macmillan, 1975); Alex Tomsky, "Poland's Church on the Road to Gdansk," in *Religion in Communist Lands*, Vol. 9, Nos. 1–2 (Spring 1981); Bernhard Tönnes, "Der Glaube an Gott lebt auch in Albanien," in *Kirche in Not*, Vol. 29 (1981); Rudolf Urban, "Staat und Kirche in der Tschechoslowakei," in *Osteuropa*, Vol. 28, No. 7 (July 1978); and James Will, "Reflections on the Role of the Catholic Church in Mediating the Present Crisis in Poland," OPREE, Vol. 2, No. 6 (September 1982).

3. Stella Alexander, *Church and State in Yugoslavia since 1945* (Cambridge: Cambridge University Press, 1979); Emmerich András, "Offene Konflikte in Ungarns Kirche," in *Herder Korrespondenz*, Vol. 36, No. 4 (April 1982); Stephen R. Bowers, "Private Institutions in Service to the State: The German Democratic

Republic's Church in Socialism," in *East European Quarterly*, Vol. 16, No. 1 (March 1982), p. 83; George Cushing, "Protestantism in Hungary," in *Religion in Communist Lands*, Vol. 10, No. 2 (Autumn 1982), John C. Cort, "The Catholic Church and Socialism," in *Dissent* (Spring 1982); Peter Grose, "God and Communism," in Harrison E. Salisbury (ed.), *The Soviet Union: The Fifty Years* (New York: New York Times, 1967); Michael Aksenov Meerson, "The Russian Orthodox Church 1965–1980," in *Religion in Communist Lands*, Vol. 10, No. 1 (Spring 1982); Jozef Nechlubyl, "Wird die Kirche in den Untergrund gezwungen?" in *Herder Korrespondenz*, Vol. 35, No. 7 (July 1981); Alexander Tomsky "*Modus Moriendi* of the Catholic Church in Czechoslovakia," in *Religion in Communist Lands*, Vol. 10, No. 1 (Spring 1982); and Diethild Treffert, "Ungarn: Einigkeit— das Schlüsselproblem der Kirche," in *Herder Korrespondenz*, Vol. 35, No. 3 (March 1981).

4. For example, Peter Wensierski, "Theses on the Role of the Church in the GDR," OPREE, Vol. 3, No. 4 (May 1983), p. 26.

5. Bohdan R. Bociurkiw, "The Shaping of Soviet Religious Policy," in *Problems of Communism*, Vol. 22, No. 3 (May–June 1973), pp. 41, 50; C. D. Kernig, "Religionsfreiheit in kommunistischer Theorie und Praxis," in *Kirche in Not*, Vol. 20 (1971), pp. 23–24; and Jure Kristo, "Relations between the State and the Roman Catholic Church in Croatia, Yugoslavia in the 1970s and 1980s," OPREE, Vol. 2, No. 3 (June 1982).

6. See Pedro Ramet, "Religion and Nationalism in Yugoslavia," in Pedro Ramet (ed.), *Religion and Nationalism in Soviet and East European Politics* (Durham, N.C.: Duke University Press, 1984); and Pedro Ramet, "From Strossmayer to Stepinac: Croatian National Ideology and Catholicism," in *Canadian Review of Studies in Nationalism*, Vol. 12, No. 1 (Spring 1985).

7. *Glaube in der 2. Welt* (March 1982), p. 84; AKSA (March 31, 1978); *The Tablet* (July 26, 1980), p. 735. The figure of 6.8 million Catholics is also given in Gabrijel Štokalo, *Adresar Katoličke crkve u SFRJ* (Zagreb: Kršćanska sadašnjost, 1981), as cited in Chris Cviic, "Die Katholische Kirche in Jugoslawien," in Paul Lendvai (ed.), *Religionsfreiheit und Menschenrechte* (Graz: Verlag Styria, 1983), p. 215.

8. Grulich, "Probleme der Religionsfreiheit," p. 82; *Kirche im Osten*, Vol. 24 (1981), pp. 143–144; and Rudolf Grulich, "Unierte Gläubige in kommunistisch regierten Ländern," in *Digest des Ostens* (1980), No. 11, p. 5. See also *Opći šematizam katoličke crkve u Jugoslaviji 1974* (Zagreb: Biskupska konferencija Jugoslavije, 1975), pp. 33–638.

9. Srdjan Vrcan, "Vezanost ljudi za religiju i crkvu u nas," in *Naše teme*, Vol. 19, Nos. 7–8 (July–August 1975), pp. 1218–1239.

10. AKSA (March 5, June 25, and July 9, 1982).

11. Cviic, "Die Katholische Kirche in Jugoslawien," p. 224.

12. AKSA (April 23, 1982); and N. Gerald Shenk, "Some Social Expectations of Christians in Yugoslavia with Primary Emphasis on the Protestant Churches," OPREE, Vol. 1, No. 4 (August 1981), pp. 5–6.

13. Quoted in Tomislav Ivančić, "Vjera kršćanina u ateističkom ambijentu," in *Crkva u svijetu*, Vol. 16, No. 4 (1981), p. 317.

14. Ibrahim Bakić, "Odnos Saveza komunista Jugoslavije prema religiji," in *Opredjeljenja*, Vol. 6, Nos. 10–11 (October–November 1978), pp. 74–75, 77.

15. Radio Belgrade (June 24, 1975), trans. in Foreign Broadcast Information Service (FBIS), *Daily Report* (Eastern Europe), June 25, 1975; and Tanjug (March

5, 1981), trans. in FBIS, *Daily Report* (Eastern Europe), March 10, 1981, pp. I11–I12.

16. Quoted in AKSA (July 3, 1981).

17. *Digest des Ostens* (1977), Nos. 11–12, pp. 25–26; Grulich, "Probleme der Religionsfreiheit," pp. 91–92; and "Informationsdienst," in *Glaube in der 2. Welt* (August 1979), p. 8.

18. *Politika* (February 11, 1981), p. 7; *Slobodna Dalmacija* (February 19, 1981), summarized and excerpted in Tanjug (February 19, 1981), trans. in FBIS, *Daily Report* (Eastern Europe), February 20, 1981, p. I4; and *Politika* (April 13, 1981), p. 6.

19. Grycz, "Katholische Kirche in Jugoslawien," pp. 88–89; and Grulich, "Die Katholische Kirche in Kroatien und Slowenien," p. 95.

20. *Danas* (January 11, 1983), summarized in *Nova Hrvatska* (London, January 30, 1983), p. 7; and *Frankfurter Allgemeine* (February 23, 1983), trans. into Croatian in *Nova Hrvatska* (March 13, 1983), p. 16.

21. *Süddeutsche Zeitung* (October 29, 1981); and *Nova Hrvatska* (March 13, 1983), p. 5.

22. *Vjesnik* (November 28, 1981), quoted in Zdenko Antic, "Calls for Moderation in Relations with Churches in Yugoslavia," *Radio Free Europe Research* (December 3, 1981).

23. Interview, Belgrade, July 1982.

24. AKSA (July 16, 1982).

25. *Danas* (July 13, 1982), pp. 9–10.

26. Ibid. (July 20, 1982), pp. 13–14, 42.

27. ASKA (March 26, 1982).

28. Responding to these currents, *Glas koncila* welcomed what it chose to view as evidence of a desire among some Yugoslav party officials to understand and accept the church and lent its support to the idea of depoliticization of the religious sphere, adding that the Christian religion has no political program to advance and hence need not be in conflict with a socialist system. See *Glas koncila* (July 18, 1982), p. 2.

29. Paul Mojzes, *Christian-Marxist Dialogue in Eastern Europe* (Minneapolis: Augsburg, 1981), p. 144.

30. Ivica Račan, "Politika saveza komunista prema crkvi i religiji," in *Naše teme,* Vol. 20, No. 6 (June 1976), p. 967.

31. 31. Ivan Cvitković, *Marksistička misao i religija* (Sarajevo: Svjetlost, 1980), p. 136.

32. Mojzes, *Christian-Marxist Dialogue,* p. 129; and interviews, Belgrade, July 1982.

33. AKSA (December 4, 1981).

34. Cviic, "Die Katholische Kirche in Jugoslawien," p. 231.

35. AKSA (December 11, 1982).

36. *Vjesnik* (May 28, 1970), p. 9.

37. In response, some forty-three "loyalist" priests wrote an open letter condemning the sixteen "rebels." See *Ekonomska politika* (October 18, 1971), p. 20, trans. in JPRS, *Translations on Eastern Europe* No. 54538 (November 22, 1971), pp. 78–79.

38. See John V. A. Fine, Jr., *The Bosnian Church: A New Interpretation,* East European Monographs (New York: Columbia University Press, 1975), p. 185; Fra Dr Berislav Gavranović, *Uspostava redovite katoličke hijerarhije u Bosni i Her-*

cegovini 1881 godine (Belgrade: Filosofski fakultet, 1935), pp. 7–8; and *Glas koncila* (July 18, 1982), p. 2.

39. *Vjesnik u srijedu* (May 6, 1970), pp. 10–11; and *The Tablet* (August 18, 1976), p. 795.

40. Kristo, "Relations between the State," p. 29; and *Frankfurter Allgemeine* (October 17, 1979), p. 10.

41. *Komunist* (September 23, 1983), trans. in JPRS, *East Europe Report* No. 84627 (October 27, 1983), pp. 80–81.

42. *Keston News Service*, No. 198 (May 3, 1984), pp. 8–9; see also *Danas* (September 20, 1983), as cited in AKSA (September 23, 1983).

43. Stella Alexander, "The Catholic Church in Yugoslavia since John Paul II," paper presented at Notre Dame University, April 1980, p. 8.

44. Interview, Zagreb, July 1982.

45. Interview, Ljubljana, July 1982.

46. For more details on the dispute regarding these committees, see Ramet, "Catholicism and Politics in Socialist Yugoslavia," p. 266.

47. *Nova Hrvatska* (February 13, 1983), p. 5.

48. *Vjesnik* (March 25, 1980), p. 5.

49. *Nova Hrvatska* (March 13, 1983), p. 4.

50. *Glas koncila* (January 9, 1983), p. 4.

51. Frane Franić, *Putovi dijaloga* (Split: Crkva u svijetu, 1973), p. 179.

52. *Borba* (May 28, 1981), p. 6; and *Slobodna Dalmacija* (August 1, 1981), summarized in AKSA (August 7, 1981).

53. Interview, Zagreb, July 1982.

54. *Glas koncila* (January 9, 1983), p. 1 (my emphasis).

55. AKSA (February 8, 1980).

56. Interview, Zagreb, July 1982.

57. Zdenko Antic, "New Conflict within the Catholic Church in Yugoslavia," *Radio Free Europe Research* (June 8, 1978), p. 1; *Frankfurter Allgemeine* (July 23, 1980), p. 5.

58. *Crkva u svijetu* (1982), no. 3, pp. 278–279; and *Frankfurter Allgemeine* (February 8, 1983), p. 10.

59. *Vjesnik: Sedam dana* (July 31, 1982), pp. 14–15.

60. Ibid. (August 7, 1982), pp. 2, 20.

61. *Nova Hrvatska* (October 24, 1982), p. 12.

62. *Frankfurter Allgemeine* (July 5, 1983), p. 8.

63. Reinhard Lauer, "Genese und Funktion des illyrischen Ideologems in den südslawischen Literaturen (16. bis Anfang des 19. Jahrhunderts)," in Klaus-Detlev Grothusen (ed.), *Ethnogenese und Staatsbildung in Südosteuropa* (Göttingen: Vandenhoeck und Ruprecht, 1974), pp. 135–136; and Charles Joseph Slovak III, *Josip Juraj Strossmayer, A Balkan Bishop: The Early Years, 1815–1854* (Ph.D. diss., University of Illinois at Urbana-Champaign, 1974), p. 72.

64. Quoted in *Nova Hrvatska* (January 30, 1983), p. 12.

65. *Keston News Service*, No. 191 (January 26, 1984), p. 5.

66. The declaration is translated into German in *Kroatische Berichte*, Vol. 6, No. 6 (November–December 1981), p. 13.

67. *Nova Hrvatska* (December 19, 1982), p. 5, and (July 17, 1983), p. 10.

68. *Glas koncila* (January 9, 1983), p. 6.

69. *That's Yugoslavia* (1982), no. 4, p. 11.

70. *Danas* (July 5, 1983), as reported in Sandra Oestreich, "Yugoslav Papers

Report on the Case of Marija Car," in *Keston News Service,* No. 184 (October 6, 1983), p. 14.

71. See Cviic, "Die Katholische Kirche in Jugoslawien," pp. 230–231; *Komunist* (September 23, 1983), p. 4, trans. in JPRS, *East Europe Report* No. 84627 (October 27, 1983), pp. 80–81; and *Glas koncila* (May 29, 1983), p. 2.

7. ORGANIZATION THEORY AND THE BULGARIAN AND SERBIAN ORTHODOX CHURCHES

1. D. S. Pugh (ed.), *Organization Theory* (Harmondsworth: Penguin, 1971), p. 9.

2. I have previously applied organization theory to the study of church-state relations in "The Dynamics of Yugoslav Religious Policy: Some Insights from Organization Theory," in Pedro Ramet (ed.), *Yugoslavia in the 1980s* (Boulder, Colo.: Westview Press, 1985).

3. Otto Luchterhandt, "State Authorities for Religious Affairs in Soviet Bloc Countries," in *Religion in Communist Lands,* Vol. 13, No. 1 (Spring 1985), esp. pp. 54–57.

4. See Charles Perrow, "The Analysis of Goals in Complex Organizations," and D. Katz and R. L. Kahn, "The Definition and Identification of Organizations," both in Joseph A. Litterer (ed.), *Organizations: Structure and Behavior,* 3d ed. (New York: Wiley, 1980).

5. This combines three hypotheses listed separately in Philip Selznick, "The Informal Organization," in Litterer (ed.), *Organizations,* p. 209.

6. Ibid., p. 210.

7. Peter M. Blau, "A Formal Theory of Differentiation in Organizations," in Litterer (ed.), *Organizations,* pp. 380, 383.

8. Ibid., p. 379.

9. See Herbert A. Simon, *Administrative Behavior,* 3d ed. (New York: Free Press, 1976), pp. 214–215.

10. Djoko Slijepčević, *Die bulgarische orthodoxe Kirche 1944–1956* (Munich: R. Oldenbourg, 1957), p. 6.

11. Quoted in ibid., pp. 7–8.

12. See Bulgaria/Situation Report, *Radio Free Europe* (November 3, 1982), pp. 11–12; William C. Fletcher, *Religion and Soviet Foreign Policy, 1945–1970* (London: Oxford University Press, 1973); and Spas T. Raikin, "Nationalism and the Bulgarian Orthodox Church," in Pedro Ramet (ed.), *Religion and Nationalism in Soviet and East European Politics* (Durham, N.C.: Duke University Press, 1984), p. 191.

13. *The Church and State under Communism,* Vol. 2 (Rumania, Bulgaria, Albania), prepared by the Law Library of the Library of Congress (Washington, D.C.: Government Printing Office, 1965), pp. 28–30.

14. Quoted in Slijepčević, *Die bulgarische orthodoxe Kirche,* p. 10.

15. Quoted in ibid.

16. Ibid., p. 12.

17. Wolf Oschlies, "'Überwundene Religion?' Zur Gegenwartssituation von Religion und Kirche in Bulgarien," in *Evangelische Theologie,* Vol. 35, No. 5 (September–October 1975), p. 452. It seems likely that the 1971 Central Commit-

tee resolution calling for wider introduction of new socialist rituals to displace existing religious ones was undertaken at Soviet instigation.

18. Wolf Oschlies, "Kirche und Religion in Bulgarien," in Paul Lendvai (ed.), *Religionsfreiheit und Menschenrechte* (Graz: Verlag Styria, 1983), pp. 189–190.

19. Reprinted in full in Erich Weingartner (ed.), *Church within Socialism: Church and State in East European Socialist Republics* (Rome: IDOC, 1976), pp. 120–123.

20. Quoted in Slijepčević, *Die bulgarische orthodoxe Kirche,* p. 17.

21. *Corriere della Sera* (Milan, May 12, 1984), p. 4.

22. Totju P. Kosev, "Patriarch Kiril Zum Gedächtnis," in *Kirche im Osten,* Vol. 15 (1972), p. 14.

23. *Sofia News* (October 31, 1984), excerpted and summarized in *Keston News Service* No. 214 (December 6, 1984), p. 15.

24. "News in Brief," in *Religion in Communist Lands,* Vol. 9, Nos. 1–2 (Spring 1981), p. 67: Werner Völker, "Aus der Bulgarisch-Orthodoxen Kirche," in *Kirche im Osten, Vol. 25 (1980), p. 154;* and "Zhivot v mir i dobra volya," in *Rodolyubie* (1983), Nos. 7–8, inside cover.

25. This controversial matter is more fully explored in Suzanne Hruby, Leslie Laszlo, and Stevan K. Pavlowitch, "Minor Orthodox Churches in Eastern Europe," in Pedro Ramet (ed.), *Eastern Christianity and Politics in the Twentieth Century* (Durham, N.C.: Duke University Press, forthcoming).

26. Quoted in Werner Völker, "Zum gegenwärtigen Verhältnis von Kirche und Staat in Bulgarien," in *Ostkirchliche Studien,* Vol. 31, No. 1 (March 1982), p. 53.

27. As discussed in Alf Johansen, "The Bulgarian Orthodox Church," in *Occasional Papers on Religion in Eastern Europe,* Vol. 1, No. 7 (December 1981), pp. 8–9.

28. Peter J. Babris, *Silent Churches* (Arlington Heights, Ill.: Research Publishers, 1978), p. 330.

29. *Duhovna kultura* (1984), No. 9, trans. in *Keston News Service* No. 219 (February 21, 1985), p. 16.

30. Rosemary Stewart, *The Reality of Organizations* (Garden City, N.Y.: Doubleday, 1972), pp. 142–143.

31. Dennison I. Rusinow, *The Yugoslav Experiment, 1948–1974* (Berkeley: University of California Press, 1977), p. 227.

32. See Simon, *Administrative Behavior,* pp. 154–171.

33. William G. Scott, *Organization Theory: A Behavioral Analysis for Management* (Homewood, Ill.: Richard D. Irwin, 1967), pp. 301-322.

34. On these several points, see Pedro Ramet, *Nationalism and Federalism in Yugoslavia, 1963–1983* (Bloomington: Indiana University Press, 1984), pp. 144–175; Wolfgang Höpken, "Party Monopoly and Political Change: The League of Communists since Tito's Death," Dennison Rusinow, "Nationalities Policy and the 'National Question,' " and Pedro Ramet, "The Yugoslav Press in Flux"—all in Ramet (ed.), *Yugoslavia in the 1980s.*

35. Rastko Vidić, *The Position of the Church in Yugoslavia* (Belgrade: Jugoslavija, 1962), p. 134.

36. Comments by Paul Mojzes, at the Third World Congress of Slavicists, Washington, D.C., November 1, 1985.

37. Ivan Lazić, "Donošenje novih republičkih i pokrajinskih zakona o pravnom položaju vjerskih zajednica u SFRJ," in *Naša zakonitost* (Zagreb), Vol. 30 (1976), Nos. 11–12, p. 71.

38. In Serbia, every religious publication, including the biweekly newspaper, *Pravoslavlje,* must be submitted to the authorities for clearance fifteen days prior to publication. In Croatia, on the other hand, the authorities are content to receive copies of *Glas koncila* (the leading Catholic weekly) and other church publications upon appearance in print.

39. For details regarding these laws, see Stella Alexander, "Yugoslavia: New Legislation on the Legal Status of Religious Communities," in *Religion in Communist Lands,* Vol. 8, No. 2 (Summer 1980).

40. Tanjug (May 5, 1982), trans. in Foreign Broadcast Information Service (FBIS), *Daily Report* (Eastern Europe), May 7, 1982, p. 115.

41. For details, see Ramet, "The Dynamics of Yugoslav Religious Policy," esp. pp. 168–174, 175–177.

42. See, for example, *Oslobodjenje* (Sarajevo, October 21, 1981), p. 4; and *Politika* (Belgrade, October 21, 1981), p. 6.

43. *Borba* (October 25, 1984), trans. into German under the title "Die Partei und die Glaubigen," in *Osteuropa,* Vol. 35, Nos. 7–8 (July–August 1985), p. A418.

44. *Oslobodjenje* (September 18–24, 1981).

45. *Vjesnik—Sedam dana* (November 7, 1981), p. 12, trans. in Joint Publications Research Service (JPRS), *East Europe Report* No. 79591 (December 4, 1981), p. 130.

46. *Danas* (Zagreb, February 21, 1984), trans. in JPRS, *East Europe Report* No. EPS–84–053 (April 25, 1984), pp. 78–79.

47. Zdenko Antić, "Growing Tension in Church-State Relations," *Radio Free Europe Research* (May 28, 1985), p. 36.

48. Stella Alexander, *Church and State in Yugoslavia since 1945* (Cambridge: Cambridge University Press, 1979), p. 282.

49. *Nova Makedonija, Sabota* supplement (Skopje, October 10, 1981), p. 5, trans. in JPRS, *East Europe Report* No. 79748 (December 29, 1981), pp. 37–41.

50. *Rheinischer Merkur* (November 13, 1981).

51. See *Vjesnik* (April 30–May 3, 1983), p. 11, trans. in JPRS, *East Europe Report* No. 83700 (June 16, 1983), p. 108.

52. *The Economist* (September 15, 1984), p. 51.

53. See, for example, the report in *Kirche und Leben* (January 6, 1980), p. 1.

8. RELIGIOUS FERMENT, 1978—84

This chapter is a revised version of an article that originally appeared under the title "Religious Ferment in Eastern Europe," in *Survey,* Vol. 28, No. 4 (Winter 1984).

1. Bohdan R. Bociurkiw, "Religion and Nationalism in the Contemporary Ukraine," in George W. Simmonds (ed.), *Nationalism in the USSR and Eastern Europe* (Detroit: University of Detroit Press, 1977), p. 86.

2. Karl Hartmann, "Stagnation in den Beziehungen zwischen Kirche und Staat in Polen," in *Osteuropa,* Vol. 28, No. 10 (October 1978), pp. 883–885.

3. Witold Zdaniewicz, *Kosciol Katolicki w Polsce 1945–1978* (Poznan: Pallotinium, 1979), p. 21, cited in Jan Nowak, "The Church in Poland," in *Problems of Communism,* Vol. 31, No. 1 (January-February 1982), p. 3.

4. *Los Angeles Times* (May 12, 1983), Part I-C, p. 1; *Christian Science Monitor* (May 6, 1983), p. 3; *Aktuelnosti Kršćanske Sadašnjosti* (AKSA), Zagreb, May 20, 1983; and *Keston News Service* No. 142 (March 12, 1982), p. 1.

5. Keston News Service No. 185 (October 20, 1983), No. 187 (November 17, 1983), No. 188 (December 1, 1983), No. 190 (January 12, 1984), p. 7, and No. 194 (March 8, 1984), p. 4.

6. *New York Times* (October 16, 1983), p. 6; *Christian Science Monitor* (October 17, 1983), p. 2; and *Corriere della Sera* (Milan, March 17, 1984), p. 8.

7. *Foreign Report* (February 17, 1983), p. 3. See also *Frankfurter Allgemeine* (April 6, 1984), p. 1.

8. *Corriere della Sera* (March 4, 1984), p. 9; and *Der Spiegel* (February 6, 1984), p. 121.

9. *Neue Zürcher Zeitung* (January 24, 1984), p. 4; *The Times* (London, February 22, 1984), p. 6; and *Washington Post* (February 22, 1984), p. A15, and (February 23, 1984), pp. A21, A30.

10. *Vjesnik* (Zagreb, December 27, 1983), p. 2; *The Times* (January 5, 1984), p. 6; *Die Zeit* (January 27, 1984), p. 5; and *Frankfurter Allgemeine* (April 14, 1984), p. 5.

11. See Pedro Ramet, "Catholicism and Politics in Socialist Yugoslavia," in *Religion in Communist Lands,* Vol. 10, No. 3 (Winter 1982).

12. See, in particular, H. H. Hiking and M. T. Svije čki, "Katolička crkva i demokratska opozicija," in *Gledišta* (Belgrade), Vol. 22, Nos. 5–6 (May–June 1981).

13. See "317 polnische katholiken ermutigen Kardinal Tomášek zum Einsatz für 'Charta 77,'" in *Glaube in der 2. Welt,* Vol. 7, No. 10 (October 1979), p. II.

14. See "Nadbiskup Kuharić—kardinal," in *Nova Hrvatska* (January 16, 1983), p. 5; and "Kardinal Kuharić—'Primas Croatiae'?" in *Nova Hrvatska* (February 13, 1983), p. 4.

15. Quoted in *Los Angeles Times* (October 21, 1978), p. 6.

16. *Glas koncila* (Zagreb, October 23, 1983), pp. 3, 10, and (November 20, 1983), p. 6.

17. Quoted in *New York Times* (December 25, 1978).

18. Paul Lendvai, *The Bureaucracy of Truth: How Communist Governments Manage the News* (Boulder, Colo.: Westview Press, 1981), p. 99.

19. Margaret Budy, "Nine Days that Shook E. Europe," in *Soviet Analyst,* Vol. 8, No. 13 (June 28, 1979), p. 7.

20. *Frankfurter Rundschau* (June 1, 1979).

21. Quoted in Budy, "Nine Days," p. 7.

22. Special report of the Lutheran Council USA (March 23, 1981); and *Frankfurter Allgemeine* (August 3, 1981), p. 2.

23. Poland/Situation Report, *Radio Free Europe Research* (May 29, 1981), p. 9.

24. *Vjesnik* (January 10, 1980), p. 2.

25. Peter A. Toma and Milan J. Reban, "Church-State Schism in Czechoslovakia," in Bohdan R. Bociurkiw and John W. Strong (eds.), *Religion and Atheism in the USSR and Eastern Europe* (London: Macmillan, 1975), pp. 286–287.

26. *Christian Science Monitor* (August 24, 1981), p. 4.

27. KNA (November 3, 1981); and *Daily Telegraph* (London, March 6, 1981).

28. *Rheinischer Merkur* (November 2, 1979), p. 24, trans. in Joint Publications Research Service (JPRS), *East Europe Report* No. 74973 (January 21, 1980), pp. 5–10; and Czechoslovakia/Situation Report, *Radio Free Europe Research* (April 6, 1984), p. 10.

29. See, for instance, the article by Bohus Kuchar in *Pravda* (Bratislava, February 3, 1972), trans. in *Religion in Communist Dominated Areas,* Vol. 11, Nos. 7–9 (July-September 1972), pp. 100–102.

30. *Muenchner Merkur* (August 13, 1981); *Stuttgarter Zeitung* (August 28, 1982); *Frankfurter Rundschau* (April 13, 1983); and Czechoslovakia/Situation Report, *Radio Free Europe Research* (May 11, 1984). See also *Czechoslovak Newsletter* (May 1984), which claims that "the neo-Stalinist regime of Gustav Husak [through] its antireligious stance is producing a backlash, a revival of religious feeling among the population."

31. For more on these points, see *Rheinischer Merkur* (November 2, 1979), p. 24.

32. *Pravda* (Bratislava, December 29, 1980), trans. in Foreign Broadcast Information Service (FBIS), *Daily Report* (Eastern Europe), January 5, 1981, p. D4.

33. *Keston News Service* No. 113 (January 16, 1981), p. 2.

34. For more on the Czechoslovak situation, see Pedro Ramet, "The Czechoslovak Church under pressure," in *The World Today,* Vol. 38, No. 9 (September 1982).

35. *Keston News Service* No. 193 (February 23, 1984), p. 11, and No. 201 (June 7, 1984), p. 6; and Czechoslovakia/Situation Report, *Radio Free Europe Research* (May 11, 1984), p. 10.

36. *Die Presse* (Vienna, April 27, 1983), p. 3, trans. in JPRS, *East Europe Report* No. 83734 (June 22, 1983), p. 20; and *Keston News Service* No. 179 (July 28, 1983), p. 6.

37. *Keston News Service* No. 186 (November 3, 1983), p. 10, No. 192 (February 9, 1984), p. 3, and No. 196 (April 5, 1984), p. 2.

38. Reported in DPA (Hamburg, July 10, 1982).

39. See Alexander Tomsky, "*Modus Moriendi* of the Catholic Church in Czechoslovakia," in *Religion in Communist Lands,* Vol. 10, No. 1 (Spring 1982).

40. *Stuttgarter Zeitung* (August 28, 1982); and Radio Vatican (December 3, 1982), trans. in FBIS, *Daily Report* (Eastern Europe), December 6, 1982, pp. D2–D3.

41. *Rude pravo* (December 17, 1982), trans. in FBIS, *Daily Report* (Eastern Europe), December 20, 1982, p. D1.

42. *Pravda* (Bratislava, January 21, 1983), trans. in FBIS, *Daily Report* (Eastern Europe), January 25, 1983, p. D2.

43. *Kurier* (Vienna, November 12, 1982), trans. in FBIS, *Daily Report* (Eastern Europe), November 15, 1982, p. D1.

44. AKSA (April 4, 1984). See also *The Times* (April 26, 1984), p. 6.

45. See Pedro Ramet, "Opening Old Wounds in Yugoslavia," in *Commonweal* (June 19, 1981), pp. 368–369; and "Alojzije Stepinac: 'Iz vječnosti svijetli i grije svjetlo jednog ljudskog srca,' " in *Hrvatska revija,* Vol. 34, No. 2 (June 1984), pp. 281–290.

46. See *Frankfurter Allgemeine* (June 21, 1979), p. 6.

47. Radio Vatican (December 30, 1980), trans. in FBIS, *Daily Report* (Eastern Europe), December 31, 1980, p. 15; *Frankfurter Allgemeine* (January 27, 1981), p. 4; *Kroatische Berichte* (January–April 1981), pp. 9–13; and interviews conducted by the author in Zagreb, July 1982.

48. Tanjug (March 5, 1981), trans. in FBIS, *Daily Report* (Eastern Europe), March 10, 1981, p. I11.

49. Ibid. See also *Politika* (Belgrade, March 12, 1981), p. 6.

50. A high-ranking party official in Belgrade admitted to me in July 1982 that Baltić's charge was unfounded and absurd. See also *Oslobodjenje* (Sarajevo, July 28, 1981); *Frankfurter Allgemeine* (July 29, 1981), p. 3; and *Süddeutsche Zeitung* (July 29, 1981), p. 6.

51. Tanjug (August 6, 1981), trans. in FBIS, *Daily Report* (Eastern Europe), August 7, 1981, p. 115; and *Frankfurter Allgemeine* (July 9, 1981), p. 3.

52. Interviews, Zagreb, July 1982. After numerous people who had approached the Crnica hill where the apparition was supposed to have taken place claimed to have been miraculously cured of ailments, the authorities placed a cordon around the hill, with armed guards, to prevent people from approaching it. See Christopher Cviic, "A Fatima in a Communist Land?" in *Religion in Communist Lands,* Vol. 10, No. 1 (Spring 1982), pp. 5–6. See also *Frankfurter Allgemeine* (September 2, 1981), p. 10; *Die Presse* (September 15, 1981); and *Večernje novosti* (October 12, 1981).

53. Cited in *Glas koncila* (August 30, 1981), p. 2, trans. in JPRS, *East Europe Report,* No. 79195 (October 13, 1981), p. 51. See also *Vjesnik—Sedam dana* (October 24, 1981), p. 2; and AKSA (September 17, 1982).

54. *Glas koncila,* reflecting the official stance of the Vatican and of the Zagreb archbishopric, cautiously declined to endorse either the alleged appearances of the Madonna or the attendant miracle cures being reported. See *Glas koncila* (May 1, 1983), pp. 2, 17.

55. *Politika* (September 4, 1981), p. 11; and *Oslobodjenje* (September 19, 1981).

56. *Oslobodjenje* (September 18–24, 1981); and Tanjug (October 20, 1981), trans. in FBIS, *Daily Report* (Eastern Europe), October 21, 1981, p. 15.

57. *Slobodna Dalmacija* (Split, July 16, 1983), summarized in AKSA (July 22, 1983).

58. *Frankfurter Allgemeine* (December 13, 1980), p. 9, and (January 3, 1981), p. 4. See also George A. Glass, "Church-State Relations in East Germany: Expanding Dimensions of an Unresolved Problem," in *East Central Europe,* Vol. 6, Pt. 2 (1979), pp. 243–246.

59. Glass, "Church-State Relations in East Germany," p. 248.

60. *Die Welt* (January 29, 1981), p. 5, trans. in FBIS, *Daily Report* (Eastern Europe), January 30, 1981, p. E4. See also Robert F. Goeckel, "Zehn Jahre Kirchenpolitik unter Honecker," in *Deutschland Archiv,* Vol. 14, No. 9 (September 1981), p. 942.

61. Quoted in Gisela Helwig, "Zwischen Opposition und Opportunismus: Zur Lage der Kirche in der DDR," in *Deutschland Archiv,* Vol. 9, No. 6 (June 1976), p. 577.

62. *Frankfurter Allgemeine* (December 13, 1980), p. 9.

63. Eberhard Poppe, "Basic Rights of Citizens in Socialist Society," quoted in *Neue Zeit* (East Berlin, January 3, 1981).

64. *Frankfurter Allgemeine* (October 11, 1980), p. 5; and Reuter (November 10, 1980).

65. *Der Spiegel* (May 4, 1981), p. 62; and *Frankfurter Allgemeine* (August 21, 1981), p. 3. See also *Frankfurter Allgemeine* (August 18, 1981), p. 4.

66. *Keston News Service* No. 113 (January 16, 1981), pp. 11–12.

67. DPA (April 28, 1981), trans. in FBIS, *Daily Report* (Eastern Europe), April 29, 1981, p. E1.

68. Klemens Richter, "Zu einer Standortbestimmung der katholischen Kirche in der DDR," in *Deutschland Archiv,* Vol. 15, No. 8 (August 1982), p. 800.

69. Quoted in Klemens Richter, "Katholische Kirche in der DDR und Friedensbewegung," in *Deutschland Archiv,* Vol. 15, No. 7 (July 1982), p. 685. See also *Die Welt* (August 24, 1982); and *Neue Zürcher Zeitung* (September 8, 1982), p. 4.

70. Richter, "Katholische Kirche," p. 687.

71. DPA (January 3, 1983), trans. in FBIS, *Daily Report* (Eastern Europe), January 5, 1983, p. E3; and *Los Angeles Times* (January 5, 1983), p. 5.

72. *Preporod* (Sarajevo, October 15–31, 1979).

73. Romania/Situation Report, *Radio Free Europe Research* (September 23, 1981), pp. 10–11.

74. *Buletin de Informatie Pentru Romani in Exil* (Paris, December 1, 1981), p. 10, trans. in JPRS, *East Europe Report* No. 79864 (January 15, 1982), p. 51. See also "The 'Lord's Army' Movement in the Romanian Orthodox Church," in *Religion in Communist Lands,* Vol. 8, No. 4 (Winter 1980), pp. 314–317.

75. *Christian Science Monitor* (October 13, 1983), p. 13.

76. "Eastern Europe: Toward a 'Religious Revival'?" *Radio Free Europe Research* (May 23, 1984), p. 36.

77. Trevor Breeson, *Discretion and Valour: Religious Conditions in Russia and Eastern Europe,* rev. ed. (Philadelphia: Fortress Press, 1982), p. 285.

78. Diethild Treffert, "Ungarn: Einigkeit—Das Schlüsselproblem der Kirche," in *Herder Korrespondenz,* Vol. 35, No. 3 (March 1981), p. 154; Emmerich András, "Offene Konflikte in Ungarns Kirche," in *Herder Korrespondenz,* Vol. 36, No. 4 (April 1982), p. 170; and AKSA (April 2, 1982).

79. Steven Polgar, "The Third Issue of 'Beszelo' Appears in Hungary," *Radio Free Europe Research* (November 16, 1982), p. 8.

80. *Kirche im Osten,* Vol. 25 (1982), p. 142.

81. Quoted in Christopher Cviić, "Hungarian Balance Sheet," in *The Tablet* (July 31, 1982), p. 760.

82. *Keston News Service* No. 248 (April 17, 1986), p. 15.

83. Ibid. No. 246 (March 20, 1986), p. 5.

84. Bulányi's words, in ibid. No. 250 (May 15, 1986), p. 10.

85. *Foreign Report* (March 24, 1983), p. 5.

86. *HIS Press Service* (Vienna), No. 18 (November 1980), pp. 8–9.

87. Dennis J. Dunn, "Religious Renaissance in the USSR," in *Journal of Church and State,* Vol. 19, No. 1 (Winter 1977), pp. 23–24, 31; see also "Religious Revival Among Soviet Youth," in *Religion in Communist Dominated Areas,* Vol. 12, Nos. 10–12 (October–December 1973), p. 180.

88. David Kowalewski, "Protest for Religious Rights in the USSR: Characteristics and Consequences," in *Russian Review,* Vol. 39, No. 4 (October 1980), pp. 427, 429; and Vasyl Markus, "Religion and Nationality: The Uniates of the Ukraine," in Bociurkiw and Strong (eds.), *Religion and Atheism in the USSR and Eastern Europe,* p. 113.

89. *Izvestiia* (October 9, 1981), p. 3.

90. "Notes on Church-State Affairs," in *Journal of Church and State,* Vol. 23, No. 1 (Winter 1981), p. 172.

91. DPA (July 9, 1981); and *Frankfurter Allgemeine* (July 18, 1981), p. 4.

92. *Frankfurter Allgemeine* (August 3, 1981), p. 2.

93. Ibid. (August 25, 1981); and *Die Presse* (August 28, 1981).

94. *Keston News Service* No. 159 (October 7, 1982), p. 6.

95. *Polymya* (1981), No. 3, pp. 138–167, as summarized in Oxana Antić, "How the Pope is Faring in the Soviet Media," *Radio Liberty Research* (October 19, 1981), p. 4.

96. Alex Alexiev, *Dissent and Nationalism in the Soviet Baltic* (Santa Monica, Calif.: Rand Corp., September 1983), p. 26.

97. *Soviet Analyst,* Vol. 7, No. 24 (December 7, 1978), p. 5; *Kirche im Osten,*

Vol. 25 (1982), p. 134; and *Los Angeles Times* (March 3, 1979), p. 26.

98. *Soviet Analyst*, Vol. 7, No. 24 (December 7, 1978), p. 5; *Los Angeles Times* (August 22, 1981), Part I-A, p. 3; KNA (November 3, 1981); and Baltic Area/ Situation Report, *Radio Free Europe Research* (July 26, 1985), p. 38. For a thorough discussion of Lithuania's Catholic opposition in the 1970s, see V. Stanley Vardys, "Lithuania's Catholic Movement Reappraised," in *Survey*, Vol. 25, No. 3 (Summer 1980).

99. *Keston News Service* No. 111 (December 12, 1980), p. 7. This complaint is scarcely new. See, for instance, I. A. Matsyavičius, "Katolitsizm i sovremennaya ideologicheskaya bor'ba," in *Voprosy filosofii*, No. 8 (August 1976), pp. 158, 162.

100. See *Chronicle of the Lithuanian Catholic Church*, No. 47 (March 19, 1981).

101. Baltic Area/Situation Report, *Radio Free Europe Research* (March 4, 1986), p. 27.

102. As summarized in AKSA (July 9, 1982).

103. *Sovetskaya kultura* (January 21, 1985), as cited in Baltic Area/Situation Report, *Radio Free Europe Research* (March 4, 1986), p. 31.

104. Baltic Area/Situation Report, *Radio Free Europe Research* (March 4, 1986), p. 27.

105. *Frankfurter Allgemeine* (August 3, 1981), p. 2; *Keston News Service* No. 160 (October 21, 1982), p. 6; and *Los Angeles Times* (August 22, 1981), Part I-A, p. 3.

106. Otto Luchterhandt, "Kirche und Gesellschaft in der Sowjetunion," in *Osteuropa*, Vol. 30, No. 1 (January 1980), p. 46. For a recent report, see *Frankfurter Allgemeine* (November 23, 1985), p. 3.

107. Figures are given in *Catholic Herald* (March 28, 1980); and Iwan Hvat, "Die ukrainische katholische Kirche des byzantinischen Ritus," in *Kirche in Not*, Vol. 23 (1975), p. 113. See also *Frankfurter Allgemeine* (December 22, 1980), p. 3; and "La persecuzione religiosa in Ucraina (A cura della Commissione per i diritti dell'uomo del Congresso mondiale dei liberi ucraini)," in *Russia Cristiana*, Vol. 3, No. 2 (March-April 1978).

108. For fuller discussions of the suppression of the Uniate Church in Ukraine, see Markus, "Religion and Nationality: The Uniates of the Ukraine," pp. 104–107; Walter Dushnyck, "Religious Situation in Ukraine," in *Religion in Communist Dominated Areas*, Vol. 16, Nos. 4–6 (1977), pp. 75–76; and Denis Dirscherl, "The Soviet Destruction of the Greek Catholic Church," in *Journal of Church and State*, Vol. 12, No. 3 (Autumn 1970), pp. 421–439.

109. *Washington Post* (March 28, 1970), p. D8.

110. Reuter (February 13, 1983); and Roman Solchanyk, "Ukrainian Catholic Activist Iosyp Terelya Sentenced," *Radio Liberty Research* (September 3, 1985), pp. 1–2; and *Washington Post* (February 8, 1987) p. 1.

111. Roman Solchanyk, "Special Issue of *The Chronicle of the Catholic Church in the Ukraine* Reaches the West," *Radio Liberty Research* (September 18, 1985), p. 1.

112. *Washington Post* (October 6, 1977), p. A22. See also Dennis J. Dunn, *Detente and Papal-Communist Relations, 1962–1978* (Boulder, Colo.: Westview Press, 1979).

113. *News World* (October 5, 1977), summarized in *Ukrainian Quarterly*, Vol. 34, No. 2 (Summer 1978), p. 201.

114. Documentation, *Ukrainian Quarterly*, Vol. 36, No. 2 (Summer 1980), pp. 195, 220.

115. Ibid., Vol. 36, No. 4 (Winter 1980), p. 443; see also Vol. 36, No. 3 (Autumn 1980), p. 314.

116. Ibid., Vol. 35, No. 4 (Winter 1979), p. 413.

117. Ibid., Vol. 36, No. 3 (Autumn 1980), p. 330.

118. I. I. Migovich, "The Uniate-Nationalist Alliance in the Service of Imperialism," in *Kommunist Ukrainy*, No. 5 (May 1981), trans. in JPRS, *USSR Report* No. 78438 (July 2, 1981), p. 35. On the other hand, the pope firmly turned down Slipyj's requests that a "Ukrainian patriarchate" be formed and that the Vatican reexamine the premises of its dialogue with the Russian Orthodox Church. See Hansjakob Stehle, "The *Ostopolitik* of the Vatican and the Polish Pope," in *Religion in Communist Lands*, Vol. 8, No. 1 (Spring 1980), p. 18.

119. *Radyans'ka Ukrayina* (June 28, 1981), p. 3, trans. in JPRS, *USSR Report* No. 79071 (September 25, 1981), p. 54.

120. Ibid. (March 26, 1981), p. 4, trans. in JPRS, *USSR Report* No. 78786 (August 19, 1981), p. 38.

121. Ivan Hvat, "The Ukrainian Catholic Church, the Vatican and the Soviet Union during the Pontificate of Pope John Paul II," in *Religion in Communist Lands*, Vol. 11, No. 3 (Winter 1983), p. 275–277; and Alex Alexiev, "The Kremlin and the Vatican," in *Orbis*, Vol. 27, No. 3 (Fall 1983), p. 559.

122. Documentation, *Ukrainian Quarterly*, Vol. 37, No. 1 (Spring 1981), p. 109.

123. See Andrew Fedynsky, "Stirrings in the Soviet Ukraine," in *Washington Quarterly*, Vol. 4, No. 4 (Autumn 1981), pp. 121–122.

124. *Radyans'ka Ukrayina* (March 24 and 28, 1981), as cited in Antić, "How the Pope is Faring," p. 4.

125. These letters are reprinted, in translation, in *Ukrainian Quarterly*, Vol. 37 No. 3 (Autumn 1981), pp. 303–306.

126. Article by J. Aničas, in *Nauka i religiya* (June 1980), trans. in JPRS, *USSR Report* No. 76263 (August 20, 1980), p. 68.

127. *Radyans'ka Ukrayina* (March 26, 1981), p. 4, trans. in JPRS, *USSR Report* No. 78786 (August 19, 1981), p. 42.

128. Vladas Nyunka, "The Vatican's Eastern Policy," in *Kommunist* (August 1982), trans. in JPRS, *USSR Report* No. 82206 (November 9, 1982), p. 8.

129. V. Mahin, "Religiya v ideynom arsenale antikommunizma," in *Politicheskoe samoobrazovanie*, No. 12 (December 1982), p. 117.

130. Claire Sterling, *A Time of the Assassins* (New York: Holt, 1983), p. 116.

131. The Kremlin's involvement in the plot to kill the pontiff has been exhaustively documented by Paul Henze and Claire Sterling and need not be recapitulated here. See Paul B. Henze, *The Plot to Kill the Pope* (New York: Scribner, 1983); Paul B. Henze, "Misinformation and Disinformation: The Plot to Kill the Pope," in *Survey*, Vol. 27, Nos. 118–119 (Autumn-Winter 1983); and Sterling, *A Time of the Assassins*. See also *Corriere della Sera* (September 30, 1983), p. 7, (May 3, 1984), p. 5, (May 4, 1984), p. 9, (January 20, 1985), p. 1, (June 2, 1985), p. 5, and (June 13, 1985), p. 4; and *New York Times* (June 10, 1984), pp. 11, 20, and (May 28, 1985), pp. 1, 6.

132. "News in Brief," in *Religion in Communist Lands*, Vol. 9, Nos. 3–4 (Autumn 1981), p. 157.

133. *Neue Zürcher Zeitung* (January 5, 1982), p. 2.

134. *Los Angeles Times* (September 18, 1982), p. 16; Radio Warsaw (October 10, 1982), trans. in FBIS, *Daily Report* (Eastern Europe), October 12, 1982, p. G31.

135. *Frankfurter Allgemeine* (February 17, 1982), p. 6, and (February 18, 1982), pp. 1–2.

136. *Keston News Service* Nos. 161–162 (November 18, 1982), p. 2.
137. Ibid. No. 203 (July 5, 1984), p. 4.
138. *Los Angeles Times* (June 17, 1983), p. 14.
139. *Christian Science Monitor* (June 20, 1983), p. 4.
140. Karl Hartmann, "Politische Bilanz des zweiten Papstbesuches in Polen," in *Osteuropa*, Vol. 33, Nos. 11–12 (November-December 1983), pp. 894, 896.
141. Quoted in *Los Angeles Times* (June 17, 1983), pp. 1, 14.

9. PROTESTANTS AND CATHOLICS AFTER POPIELUSZKO

1. Trevor Beeson, *Discretion and Valour: Religious Conditions in Russia and Eastern Europe,* rev. ed. (Philadelphia: Fortress Press, 1982), pp. 247, 252–253.
2. Quoted in Vilmos Vajta, "The Hungarian Lutheran Church and the 'Theology of Diaconia,'" in *Religion in Communist Lands,* Vol. 12, No. 2 (Summer 1984), p. 136.
3. See Dionisie Ghermani, "Zwangsatheisierung in Rumänien," in *Kirche in Not,* Vol. 28 (1980); and Dionisie Ghermani, "Religionsbekämpfung in Rumänien," in *Wissenschaftlicher Dienst Südosteuropa,* Vol. 29, No. 1/2 (January–February 1980).
4. Dionisie Ghermani, "The Orthodox Church Press under Balkan Communism," in *Religion in Communist Dominated Areas,* Vol. 23 (1984), Nos. 10–12.
5. Earl A. Pope, "The Orthodox Church in Romania," in *Ostkirchliche Studien,* Vol. 31, No. 4 (December 1982), pp. 301, 307.
6. In 1982, for example, when Pope John Paul II appealed to the Bucharest regime to reconsider this matter, Orthodox Patriarch Justin quickly sent a telegram to Romanian President Ceauşescu expressing his "indignation" at the thought that the Uniate Church might be relegalized. See Dionisie Ghermani, "Die Unierte Kirche Rumaniens zu Beginn der Achtziger Jahre," in *Information und Berichte, Digest des Ostens* (1982), No. 7, pp. 7–9.
7. *Keston News Service* No. 249 (May 1, 1986), p. 9.
8. *Era Socialista* (Bucharest), No. 7 (April 10, 1984), trans. in Joint Publications Research Service (JRPS), *East Europe Report* No. EPS–84-063 (May 17, 1984), p. 40.
9. Joseph Ton, "Persecution of the Neo-Protestants in Romania," paper presented at the RCDA Conference on Religion in the Balkans, Marymount College, Arlington, Va., May 21–23, 1986, p. 2.
10. *Christian Science Monitor* (October 13, 1983), p. 13.
11. *Keston News Service* No. 213 (November 22, 1984), p. 6, No. 221 (March 21, 1985), p. 3, No. 229 (July 11, 1985), p. 5, and No. 230 (July 25, 1985), p. 2.
12. Ibid. No. 237 (October 31, 1985), p. 2.
13. Ibid. No. 191 (January 26, 1984), p. 8, No. 208 (September 13, 1984), p. 4, and No. 213 (November 22, 1984), p. 6.
14. Ibid., No. 208 (September 13, 1984), p. 3.
15. See ibid. No. 220 (March 7, 1985), p. 3; and No. 236 (October 17, 1985), p. 3.
16. Alexander Havadtoy, "The Hungarian Reformed Church in Rumania," paper presented at the RCDA Conference on Religion in the Balkans, Marymount College, Arlington, Va., May 21–23, 1986, pp. 1, 3–5.
17. Janice Broun, "The Latin-Rite Roman Catholic Church in Romania," in *Religion in Communist Lands,* Vol. 12, No. 2 (Summer 1984), pp. 173–174.

18. Vladimir Socor, "Changes in the Situation of the Roman Catholic Church in Romania?" *Radio Free Europe Research* (December 27, 1983), p. 2.

19. See Pedro Ramet, "The Czechoslovak Church under Pressure," in *The World Today,* Vol. 38, No. 9 (September 1982). More recent arrests occurred in December 1984 and involved two Franciscan priests and a nun. See *The Times* (London, December 3, 1984), p. 6.

20. The official figures are 30 percent of those over age fifteen in the Czech lands, 51 percent in Slovakia, and 36 percent in Czechoslovakia as a whole. See *Keston News Service* No. 194 (March 8, 1984), p. 6.

21. Quoted in Czechoslovakia/Situation Report, *Radio Free Europe Research* (February 13, 1985), p. 8.

22. *Pravda* (Bratislava, November 20, 1984), trans. in JPRS, *East Europe Report* No. EPS–84–156 (December 21, 1984), p. 15.

23. Interview with Frantiśek Cardinal Tomašek, in *Il Sabato* (June 14, 1985), trans. into German in *Pro fratribus: Stimmen der Schweigenden* No. 3 (September 1985).

24. *The Economist* (April 12, 1986), p. 54.

25. *Die Presse* (Vienna, June 1–2, 1983), trans. in *Religion in Communist Dominated Areas,* Vol. 22 (1983), Nos. 4–6, p. 87.

26. Vatican City International Service, in Slovak (December 12, 1984), trans. in JPRS, *East Europe Report* No. EPS–85–009 (January 17, 1985), p. 15.

27. *Keston News Service* No. 250 (May 15, 1986), p. 11.

28. Ibid. No. 191 (January 26, 1984), p. 8, and No. 218 (February 7, 1985), p. 11. See also *Frankfurter Allgemeine* (December 10, 1985), p. 7.

29. Czechoslovakia/Situation Report, *Radio Free Europe Research* (September 7, 1984), p. 17.

30. *Katoličke Noviný* (Bratislava, August 12, 1984), quoted in ibid., p. 18.

31. *Katoličke Noviný* (June 24, 1984), as cited in ibid., p. 19.

32. *Keston News Service* No. 208 (September 13, 1984), pp. 8–9.

33. See ibid. No. 234 (September 19, 1985), p. 5.

34. Ibid. No. 238 (November 14, 1985), p. 8.

35. For details, see ibid. No. 240 (December 12, 1985), pp. 7–8, and No. 249 (May 1, 1986), p. 12.

36. Bishop József Cserháti, in interview with *Kritika* (September 21, 1983), as quoted in Robert J. Patkai, "Analysis or Slander?" in *Religion in Communist Lands,* Vol. 12, No. 2 (Summer 1984), p. 147.

37. Hungary/Situation Report, *Radio Free Europe Research* (October 11, 1984), p. 6; and *Keston News Service* No. 214 (December 6, 1984), p. 7.

38. Hungary/Situation Report, *Radio Free Europe Research* (April 28, 1986), pp. 18–19; and *Keston News Service* No. 244 (February 20, 1986), p. 9.

39. Vajta, "The Hungarian Lutheran Church," p. 139.

40. Quoted in J. V. Eibner, "Zoltan Káldy: A New Way for the Church in Socialism?" in *Religion in Communist Lands,* Vol. 13, No. 1 (Spring 1985), p. 37.

41. See chapter 4.

42. Quoted in Eibner, "Zoltan Káldy," p. 41.

43. For a report of a proregime priests' "peace" rally, see Radio Budapest (May 23, 1985), trans. in Foreign Broadcast Information Service (FBIS), *Daily Report* (Eastern Europe), May 24, 1985, p. F8.

44. *Keston News Service* No. 227 (June 13, 1985), p. 6.

45. By one estimate, 2,000 to 4,000. See *Keston News Service* No. 207 (August 30, 1984), p. 6.

46. *Keston News Service* No. 255 (July 24, 1986), p. 14; and George Cushing, "Protestantism in Hungary," in *Religion in Communist Lands,* Vol. 10, No. 2 (Autumn 1982), p. 130.

47. Discussed in the previous chapter and in Janusz Bugajski, "Poland's Anti-Clergy Campaign," in *The Washington Quarterly,* Vol. 8, No. 4 (Fall 1985).

48. *Corriere della Sera* (Milan, August 3, 1984), p. 1; *Profil* (Vienna, October 1, 1984), p. 30; and *Frankfurter Allgemeine* (December 27, 1984), p. 3.

49. Quoted in Grazyna Sikorska, " 'To Kneel Only before God': Father Jerzy Popieluskzo," in *Religion in Communist Lands,* Vol. 12, No. 2 (Summer 1984), p. 152.

50. Jerzy Popieluszko, "Solidarity is Concern for One's Family Home" (Sermon of August 31, 1983), trans. in *Religion in Communist Dominated Areas,* Vol. 22 (1983) Nos. 10–12, pp. 149, 150.

51. Sermon of August 1983, quoted in Sikorska, "To Kneel," p. 153.

52. *Corriere della Sera* (October 29, 1985), p. 11.

53. *Tu i Teraz* (1984), No. 38, quoted in *Keston News Service* No. 209 (September 27, 1984), p. 7.

54. *Christian Science Monitor* (December 28, 1984), p. 1, and (January 10, 1985), p. 8; and *The Times* (London, January 5, 1985), p. 6, and (January 9, 1985), p. 4. Also Poland/Situation Report, *Radio Free Europe Research* (February 19, 1985), p. 4.

55. *The Times* (January 10, 1985), p. 6.

56. Quoted in Poland/Situation Report, *Radio Free Europe Research* (February 5, 1985), p. 10.

57. Ibid., p. 11; also see p. 6. For more on the Popieluszko affair, see Siegfried Lammich, "Der Popieluszko-Prozess," and articles trans. in "Der Tod des Priesters," all in *Osteuropa,* Vol. 35, No. 6 (June 1985). See also Leopold Labedz, "A Polish Murder Trial," in *Encounter* (May 1985), p. 32.

58. Poland/Situation Report, *Radio Free Europe Research* (February 5, 1985), p. 11, and (February 19, 1985), p. 7.

59. AFP (Paris, April 9, 1985), trans. in FBIS, *Daily Report* (Eastern Europe), April 10, 1985, p. G4; *Frankfurter Allgemeine* (April 11, 1985), p. 1, and (April 13, 1985), p. 4; and *New York Times* (December 5, 1985), p. 7.

60. *Keston News Service* No. 213 (November 22, 1984), p. 5 and No. 214 (December 6, 1984), p. 8; and *New York Times* (December 2, 1984), p. 5.

61. Bugajski, "Poland's Anti-Clergy," p. 163.

62. *Keston News Service* No. 168 (February 24, 1983), p. 5.

63. *Glas koncila* (Zagreb, March 17, 1985), p. 1.

64. Quoted in *Keston News Service* No. 208 (September 13, 1984), p. 9.

65. *The Times* (April 9, 1986), p. 11.

66. *New York Times* (May 26, 1986), p. 4.

67. *Polityka* (Warsaw, April 27, 1985), p. 7, trans. in JPRS, *East Europe Report* No. EPS–85-062 (May 31, 1985), p. 24.

68. AP (March 14, 1986); and *Deutsche Tagespost/Katholische Zeitung für Deutschland* (Würzburg, March 18, 1986).

69. *Rzeczywistosc* (Warsaw, February 2, 1986), p. 2, trans. in FBIS, *Daily Report* (Eastern Europe), February 28, 1986, p. G6.

70. Long-time member of "Znak" and author of *Katholische Gruppierungen in Polen: Pax und Znak, 1945–1976,* trans. from Polish by Wolfgang Grycz (Munich and Mainz: Kaiser and Grunewald, 1978).

71. *Niedziela* (March 4, 1984), excerpted in *Polityka* (March 31, 1984), p. 2, trans. in JPRS, *East Europe Report* No. EPS–84–051 (April 20, 1984), p. 140.

72. *Christian Science Monitor* (July 2, 1985), p. 13.

73. *Gosc Niedzielny* (Katowice, February 12, 1984), pp. 1, 5, trans. in JPRS, *East Europe Report* No. EPS–84–051 (April 20, 1984), p. 131; and *Keston News Service* No. 236 (October 17, 1985), p. 11.

74. *New York Times* (October 20, 1985), p. 3; and *Frankfurter Allgemeine* (October 21, 1985), p. 1.

75. Vienna ORF Teletext in German (August 20, 1985), trans. in FBIS, *Daily Report* (Eastern Europe), August 21, 1985, p. G6.

76. Vienna ORF Teletext in German (August 26, 1985), trans. in FBIS, *Daily Report* (Eastern Europe), August 27, 1985, p. G1.

77. *The Times* (March 21, 1986).

78. *Keston News Service* No. 222 (April 4, 1985), p. 5.

79. Ibid. No. 233 (September 5, 1985), p. 13.

80. *Gazeta Wspolczesna* (Bialystok, March 1, 1985), p. 3, trans. in FBIS, *Daily Report* (Eastern Europe), April 8, 1985, p. G3.

81. *Keston News Service* No. 235 (October 3, 1985), pp. 2–3.

82. E.g., *Frankfurter Allgemeine* (February 5, 1985), p. 3.

83. Quoted in *Neues Deutschland* (September 24, 1984), trans. in FBIS, *Daily Report* (Eastern Europe), September 26, 1984, p. E3.

84. DPA (Hamburg, September 22, 1984), trans. in FBIS, *Daily Report* (Eastern Europe), September 25, 1984, p. E14; *Süddeutsche Zeitung* (Munich, April 5–6, 1986), p. 2; and *Frankfurter Allgemeine* (April 7, 1986), p. 5.

85. *Informationen* (Bonn, January 27, 1984), p. 9, trans. in JPRS, *East Europe Report* No. EPS–84–032 (March 5, 1984), pp. 13–14; *Frankfurter Allgemeine* (February 1, 1984), p. 4; and *Frankfurter Rundschau* (March 22, 1986), p. 2.

86. Reinhard Henkys, "Kirche in der Deutschen Demokratischen Republik," in Paul Lendvai (ed.), *Religionsfreiheit und Menschenrechte* (Graz: Verlag Styria, 1983), p. 176.

10. PITFALLS IN THE STUDY OF CHURCH-STATE RELATIONS

1. See Arend Lijphart, "Comparative Politics and the Comparative Method," in *American Political Science Review,* Vol. 65, No. 3 (September 1971).

2. I have found this methodology useful in another context; see Pedro Ramet, "The Miracle at Medjugorje—A Functionalist Perspective," in *South Slav Journal,* Vol. 8, Nos. 1–2 (Spring-Summer 1985).

3. See Paul Mojzes, *Christian-Marxist Dialogue in Eastern Europe* (Minneapolis: Augsburg, 1981).

4. See Robert F. Goeckel, "The Luther Anniversary in East Germany," in *World Politics,* Vol. 37, No. 1 (October 1984).

5. David Hackett Fischer, *Historians' Fallacies* (New York: Harper, 1970), p. 4.

6. Timothy Ware, *The Orthodox Church,* rev. ed. (Harmondsworth: Penguin, 1980), p. 87 (my emphasis).

7. See David Mason, "The Polish Party in Crisis, 1980–1982," in *Slavic Review,* Vol. 43, No. 1 (Spring 1984).

11. CONCLUSION: TOWARD A THEORY OF CHURCH-STATE INTERACTION UNDER EUROPEAN COMMUNISM

1. A recent treatment of this topic is Nikola Dugandžija, *Religija i nacija* (Zagreb: Političke teme, 1983).

2. Quoted in Josef Közi-Horvath, "Katholische Kirche in Ungarn," in *Kirche in Not,* Vol. 29 (1981), p. 143. See also "Die Katholische Kirche in Ungarn," in *Kirche in Not,* Vol. 27 (1979); and Pál I. Fónyad, "Aus dem ungarischen Protestantismus," in *Kirche im Osten,* Vol. 24 (1981), pp. 134–138.

3. Bohdan R. Bociurkiw, "Institutional Religion and Nationality in the Soviet Union," in S. Enders Wimbush (ed.), *Soviet Nationalities in Strategic Perspective* (London: Croon & Helm, 1985), pp. 181, 197.

4. Drawn by Archie Brown in Introduction, Archie Brown and Jack Gray (eds.), *Political Culture and Political Change in Communist States* (New York: Holmes & Meier, 1977), pp. 7–8.

5. See Angela A. Aidala, "Social Change, Gender Roles, and New Religious Movements," in *Sociological Analysis,* Vol. 46, No. 3 (Fall 1985).

6. See Dennis J. Dunn, *The Catholic Church and the Soviet Government, 1939–1949* (Boulder, Colo.: East European Monographs, 1977), pp. 117–128, 143–170.

7. Bogdan Szajkowski, *Next to God . . . Poland: Politics and Religion in Contemporary Poland* (New York: St. Martin's, 1983), p. 55.

8. Bohdan R. Bociurkiw, "The Shaping of Soviet Religious Policy," in *Problems of Communism,* Vol. 22, No. 3 (May–June 1973), p. 41.

9. Otto Luchterhandt, *Die Gegenwartslage der Evangelischen Kirche in der DDR* (Tübingen: J. C. B. Mohr, 1982), pp. 14–18.

10. Discussed in chapter 5.

11. See Vladimir V. Kusin, "Husak's Czechoslovakia and Economic Stagnation," in *Problems of Communism,* Vol. 31, No. 3 (May–June 1982), esp. pp. 25–28.

12. *New York Times* (May 15, 1985), p. 6. See also *Politika* (Belgrade, February 3, 1985), p. 2.

13. For a Polish example, See *Gazeta Wspolclesna* (Bialystok, March 1, 1985), p. 3, trans. in Foreign Broadcast Information Service, *Daily Report* (Eastern Europe), April 8, 1985, p. G2.

14. Theo van der Voort, untitled, undated report, in Keston College archives, p. 11, as quoted in Jane Ellis, *The Russian Orthodox Church: A Contemporary History* (Bloomington: Indiana University Press, 1986), p. 113.

15. Romania/Situation Report, *Radio Free Europe Research* (August 13, 1985), p. 33.

Selected Bibliography

This bibliography is not a list of sources used in the research for this book, but rather a short listing of English-language materials for further reading. Foreign-language sources may be found by consulting the footnotes.

GENERAL

Beeson, Trevor. *Discretion and Valour: Religious Conditions in Russia and Eastern Europe*. Rev. ed. Philadelphia: Fortress Press, 1982.

Bociurkiw, Bohdan R., and John W. Strong, eds. *Religious and Atheism in the USSR and Eastern Europe*. London: Macmillan, 1975.

Dunn, Dennis J. *Detente and Papal-Communist Relations, 1962–1978*. Boulder, Colo.: Westview Press, 1979.

Greinacher, Norbert, and Virgil Elizondo, eds. *Churches in Socialist Societies of Eastern Europe*. New York: Seabury-Concilium, 1982.

Mojzes, Paul. *Christian-Marxist Dialogue in Eastern Europe*. Minneapolis: Augsburg, 1981.

Ramet, Pedro, ed. *Eastern Christianity and Politics in the Twentieth Century*. Durham, N.C.: Duke University Press, forthcoming.

———, ed. *Religion and Nationalism in Soviet and East European Politics*. Durham, N.C.: Duke University Press, 1984.

Tobias, Robert. *Communist-Christian Encounter in East Europe*. Indianapolis: School of Religion Press, 1956.

US Library of Congress. *The Church under Communism*. Washington D.C.: Government Printing Office, 1965.

Weingartner, Erich, ed. *Church within Socialism*. Rome: IDOC, 1976.

ALBANIA

Kolsti, John. "Albanianism: From the Humanists to Hoxha." In George Klein and Milan J. Reban, eds., *The Politics of Ethnicity in Eastern Europe*. Boulder, Colo.: East European Monographs, 1981.

Sinishta, Gjon. *The Fulfilled Promise: A Documentary Account of Religious Persecution in Albania*. Santa Clara: No publisher listed, 1976.

———. "Grave Violations of Religious Rights in Albania." *Occasional Papers on Religion in Eastern Europe* (July 1983).

Tönnes, Bernhard. "Religious Persecution in Albania." *Religion in Communist Lands* (Winter 1982).

BULGARIA

Broun, Janice. "Catholics in Bulgaria." *Religion in Communist Lands* (Winter 1983).
Churches and Religions in the People's Republic of Bulgaria. Sofia: Sofia Synodal Publishing House, 1975.
Johansen, Alf. "The Bulgarian Orthodox Church." *Occasional Papers on Religion in Eastern Europe* (December 1981).
Raikin, Spas T. "The Communists and the Bulgarian Orthodox Church, 1944–48: The Rise and Fall of Exarch Stefan." *Religion in Communist Lands* (Winter 1984).

CZECHOSLOVAKIA

Hlinka, Anton. *Freedom Denied: Czechoslovakia after Helsinki.* Seewis: Stefanus Verlag, 1977.
Nemec, Ludvik. *Church and State in Czechoslovakia.* New York: Vantage Press, 1955.
Ramet, Pedro. "The Czechoslovak Church under Pressure." *The World Today* (September 1982).
Tomsky, Alexander. "*Modus Moriendi* of the Catholic Church in Czechoslovakia." *Religion in Communist Lands* (Spring 1982).

GERMAN DEMOCRATIC REPUBLIC

Bowers, Stephen R. "Private Institutions in Service to the State: The German Democratic Republic's Church in Socialism." *East European Quarterly* (March 1982).
Glass, George. "Church-State Relations in East Germany." *East Central Europe,* Vol. 6, Part 2 (1979).
Goeckel, Robert F. "The Luther Anniversary in East Germany." *World Politics* (October 1984).
Sandford, John. *The Sword and the Ploughshare.* London: Merlin Press, 1983.

HUNGARY

András, Emmerich, and Julius Morel, eds. *Church in Transition: Hungary's Catholic Church from 1945 to 1982.* Vienna: Hungarian Institute for Sociology of Religion, 1983.
———. *Hungarian Catholicism: A Handbook.* Vienna: Hungarian Institute for Sociology of Religion, 1983.
Cushing, George. "Protestantism in Hungary." *Religion in Communist Lands* (Autumn 1982).
Laszlo, Leslie. "Religion in a Communist Consumer Society: The Case of Kádár's Hungary." *Occational Papers on Religion in Eastern Europe* (September 1981).

POLAND

Keim, Paul. "Polish Protestants: Ecumenism in a Dual Diaspora." *Religion in Communist Lands* (Winter 1983).
Poman-Srzednicki, Maciej. *Religious Change in Contemporary Poland: Secu-*

larization and Politics. London: Routledge & Kegan Paul, 1982.
Szajkowski, Bogdan. *Next to God . . . Poland: Politics and Religion in Contemporary Poland*. New York: St. Martin's Press, 1983.
Wyszynski, Stefan Cardinal. *A Freedom Within* [Prison Notes], trans. Barbara Krzywicki-Herburt and Rev. Walter J. Ziemba. New York: Harcourt Brace Jovanovich, 1983.

ROMANIA

Broun, Janice. "The Latin-Rite Roman Catholic Church of Romania." *Religion in Communist Lands* (Summer 1984).
Pope, Earl. "The Orthodox Church in Romania." *Ostkirchliche Studien* (December 1982).
Scarfe, Alan. "A Call for Truth: An Appraisal of Romanian Baptist Church-State Relationships." *Journal of Church and State* (Autumn 1979).
Slg, Sr. Eileen Mary. "Orthodox Monasticism in Romania Today." *Religion in Communist Lands* (Spring 1980).

YUGOSLAVIA

Alexander, Stella. *Church and State in Yugoslavia since 1945*. Cambridge: Cambridge University Press, 1979.
Laurentin, Rene, and Ljudevit Rupcic. *Is the Virgin Mary Appearing at Medjugorje?* Washington, D.C.: Fowler Wright, 1985.
Pattee, Richard. *The Case of Cardinal Aloysius Stepinac*. Milwaukee: Bruce Publishing Co., 1953.
Samardžić, Radovan. *Religious Communities in Yugoslavia*. Belgrade: Jugoslovenski pregled, 1981.

SOVIET UNION

Bennigsen, Alexandre, and Marie Broxup. *The Islamic Threat to the Soviet State*. New York: St. Martin's Press, 1983.
Bociurkiw, Bohdan R. "Religion and Nationalism in the Contemporary Ukraine." In George W. Simmonds, ed., *Nationalism in the USSR and Eastern Europe*. Detroit: University of Detroit Press, 1977.
Chichlo, Boris. "The Cult of the Bear and Soviet Ideology in Siberia." *Religion in Communist Lands* (Summer 1985).
Dunn, Dennis J. *The Catholic Church and the Soviet Government, 1939–1949*. Boulder, Colo.: East European Monographs, 1977.
———, ed. *Religion and Modernization in the Soviet Union*. Boulder, Colo.: Westview Press, 1977.
Ellis, Jane. *The Russian Orthodox Church: A Contemporary History*. Bloomington: Indiana University Press, 1986.
Lang, David M. "Religion and Nationalism—A Case Study: The Caucasus." *Survey* (January 1968).
Oganessyan, Edward. "The Armenian Church in the USSR." *Religion in Communist Lands* (Winter 1979).
Pospielovsky, Dimitry. *The Russian Orthodox Church under the Soviet Regime, 1917–1982*. Crestwood, N.Y.: St. Vladimir's Seminary Press, 1984, 2 vols.

Powell, David E. *Antireligious Propaganda in the Soviet Union*. Cambridge, Mass.: MIT Press, 1975.

Rakowska-Harmstone, Teresa. "Religion and Nationalism in Soviet Central Asia." In Raymond G. Gastil, ed., *Freedom in the World*. Westport, Conn.: Greenwood Press, 1981.

Rywkin, Michael. *Moscow's Muslim Challenge*. Armonk, N.Y.: M. E. Sharpe, 1982.

Sapiets, Marite. "One Hundred Years of Adventism in Russia and the Soviet Union." *Religion in Communist Lands* (Winter 1984).

———. "The Situation of the Roman Catholic Church in Belorussia." *Religion in Communist Lands* (Autumn 1982).

Simon, Gerhard. *Church, State and Opposition in the USSR*. Berkeley: University of California Press, 1974.

Vardys, V. Stanley. *The Catholic Church, Dissent and Nationality in Soviet Lithuania*. Boulder, Colo.: East European Monographs, 1978.

Index